The Scientific Study of
DREAMS

The Scientific Study of
DREAMS

Neural Networks, Cognitive Development, and Content Analysis

G. William Domhoff

AMERICAN PSYCHOLOGICAL ASSOCIATION

WASHINGTON, DC

First Printing, November 2002
Second Printing, July 2003

Published by
American Psychological Association
750 First Street, NE
Washington, DC 20002
www.apa.org

To order
APA Order Department
P.O. Box 92984
Washington, DC 20090-2984
Tel: (800) 374-2721
Direct: (202) 336-5510
Fax: (202) 336-5502
TDD/TTY: (202) 336-6123
Online: www.apa.org/books/
Email: order@apa.org

In the U.K., Europe, Africa, and the Middle East, copies may be ordered from
American Psychological Association
3 Henrietta Street
Covent Garden, London
WC2E 8LU England

Typeset in Goudy by World Composition Services, Inc., Sterling, VA

Printer: Port City Press, Baltimore, MD
Cover Designer: Berg Design, Albany, NY
Technical/Production Editor: Kristen R. Sullivan

The opinions and statements published are the responsibility of the authors, and such opinions and statements do not necessarily represent the policies of the American Psychological Association.

Library of Congress Cataloging-in-Publication Data
Domhoff, G. William
   The scientific study of dreams : neural networks, cognitive development, and content analysis / by G. William Domhoff.—1st ed.
      p. cm.
   Includes bibliographical references and index.
   ISBN 1-55798-935-4 (alk. paper)
   1. Dreams. 2. Dreams—Physiological aspects. 3. Dream interpretation. I. Title.
BF1091 .D66 2002
154.6′3—dc21

2002026114

British Library Cataloguing-in-Publication Data
A CIP record is available from the British Library.

Printed in the United States of America

With thanks to the greatest Dream Team of them all:
Adam Schneider, Sarah Dunn, Melissa Bowen, Heidi Block,
Thomas Van Rompay, and Ryan Harvey.

CONTENTS

ACKNOWLEDGMENTS

Thanks to David Foulkes for two careful readings of the entire manuscript; to Adam Schneider for his superlative work in creating the tables and figures in the book; to Teenie Matlock and Raymond Gibbs, Jr., for their help in developing the ideas about figurative thinking in dreams; to Sarah Dunn, Heidi Block, and Melissa Bowen for their many helpful analyses of the dream series that is discussed in chapter 5; to Thomas Van Rompay for the analyses of the dream series discussed in chapter 4; and to Ryan Harvey for his contributions to the analysis of the Barb Sanders dream series in chapter 5.

A special thanks to Robert Stickgold and Richard Zweigenhaft for their many useful comments on parts of chapters 1 and 6; to Linda J. Mealey and Nicholas S. Thompson for comments and suggestions that greatly improved the discussion of the accuracy of dream reports in chapter 2; to Kelly Buckley for his suggestions on chapters 5 and 6; and to Raymond Gibbs, Jr., for his reassurances on the discussion of cognitive theory in chapter 1. I also want to thank Mark Solms for answering many questions about the neural network for dreaming and Lawrence Wichlinski for background information on the role of neurochemicals in dreaming.

The Scientific Study of
DREAMS

INTRODUCTION:
THE NEUROCOGNITIVE
APPROACH TO DREAMS

Building on established descriptive findings in three separate areas of dream research, this book attempts to show that it is now possible to take the study of dreaming and dreams to a higher level that can rightly be called scientific. For reasons that become apparent throughout the book, it has not been easy for inquiries into dreams to escape from anecdotal clinical theories, on the one side, and neurophysiological reductionism, on the other. It is only since the 1990s that new neuropsychological and neuroimaging findings can be combined with replications concerning the lack of dreaming in young children and the consistency of adult dream content to suggest the new neurocognitive synthesis that is presented here.

In addition to proposing a neurocognitive model of dreaming, the book provides a methodological foundation for testing some aspects of the model and includes new findings on dream content that demonstrate the possibilities of those methods. The model is an open-ended and tentative one; it is meant as a starting point for future research. The work upon which it builds has come to maturity and a possible integration at an ideal moment, because advances in neuroscience, content analysis, cognitive linguistics, statistics, and computer software make it possible to test the new model.

The timing may be right for consideration of a new model because the empirical findings from systematic studies do not support any of the best known clinical theories. This point has been made in several reviews of the accumulating research evidence (Domhoff, 1999a; Fisher & Greenberg, 1996; Foulkes, 1996a, 1999). However, the full case against all of these theories is brought together for the first time in chapter 6 of this book. This critique is placed at the end of the book so that much of the empirical evidence on which is it based can be presented first.

This approach also differs from the neuropsychological model called activation–synthesis theory, which starts at the level of single-cell firings in the brain stems of lesioned cats and moves to speculations about how the brain stem may have direct effects on dream content (Hobson, 1988; Hobson & McCarley, 1977; Hobson, Pace-Schott, & Stickgold, 2000b). By way of contrast, the neurocognitive model suggested in this book begins at the phenomenological level with the subjective experience of dreaming and with waking dream reports, then proceeds to a neuropsychological level. The similarities and differences between the two models are explored throughout the book and in chapter 6.

The model presented in this book starts with findings from neuropsychological assessments of people with brain lesions who report changes in their patterns of dreaming (Solms, 1997). These neuropsychological findings are corroborated and expanded by neuroimaging studies of rapid eye movement (REM) sleep, the stage of sleep during which dreaming most vividly occurs (Braun et al., 1997, 1998; Heiss, Pawlik, Herholz, Wagner, & Wienhard, 1985; Maquet et al., 1996; Nofzinger, Mintun, Wiseman, Kupfer, & Moore, 1997). This work allows the model to explain the origins of dreaming and to glimpse the outlines of the neural network that underlies this form of cognition.

Next, the model adds findings on children who were observed over many hundreds of nights in the sleep laboratory (Foulkes, 1982, 1999; Foulkes, Hollifield, Sullivan, Bradley, & Terry, 1990). This work allows the model to explain how dreaming develops in terms of the cognitive processes that make it possible. This work combines with the findings on the neural network to make the model truly neurocognitive.

Finally, the model explains the nature of dream content by incorporating insights drawn from quantitative investigations of many thousands of dream reports using a rigorous system of content analysis (Domhoff, 1996; Hall & Van de Castle, 1966). This coding system rests at the nominal level of measurement, uses percentages and rates to correct for differences in the length of dream reports, and has high reliability. It is one of the few coding systems that has been used extensively by investigators other than those who created the system, including researchers from Japan, India, Switzerland, and the Netherlands, and it has proven useful with dreams collected by anthropologists in small traditional societies as well (Domhoff, 1996).

The results from these three empirical areas of dream research make it possible to state the following generalizations that lead to a neurocognitive model and many testable hypotheses:

- Dreaming occurs when a relatively specific neural network— located primarily in the limbic, paralimbic, and associational areas of the forebrain—is activated in the absence of external input coupled with a letting go of control by the self. If defects occur in this network, dreaming can be lost temporarily or permanently, or it can be impaired in some way, such as through the loss of visual dream imagery.

- Dreaming is a cognitive achievement that develops gradually over the first 8 or 9 years of life.
- The "output" of the conceptual systems in the neural network for dream generation, called *dream content* and available to scientists through written or transcribed *dream reports*, is drawn from many of the same schemata and memory systems as waking thought and is generally continuous with waking conceptions; this content includes a great deal of previously unrealized repetition in characters, social interactions, misfortunes, negative emotions, and themes.

These generalizations lead to several hypotheses concerning the links between the neuropsychological, developmental, and content analysis findings:

- Because specific neural defects can lead to the loss or impairment of dreaming and because dreaming develops gradually in children, adultlike dreaming may depend on the maturation of the neural network for dreaming. For example, the complete loss of dreaming in adults due to injuries in or near either parieto-temporal-occipital junction, along with the finding that increased dream reporting in young children correlates with visuo-spatial skills, together suggest that the ability to dream in children may depend in part upon the development of the neural network for spatial construction, which is centered in this region.
- The importance of limbic structures in dreaming and the repetitive nature of dream content suggest that the "emotional brain" mapped out by LeDoux (1996) may be one basis for the repetitive nature of much dream content, including the nightmarish dreams accompanying posttraumatic stress disorder and temporal-lobe epileptic seizures.
- The fact that dreams can be made more vivid and frightening by drugs affecting the dopaminergic and cholinergic systems suggests that the relationship between the neural network for dreaming and dream content can be studied by determining the influence of various drugs on specific aspects of dream content.
- Because defects in the neural network for dreaming can lead to changes in dream content, the general relationship between this network and specific aspects of dream content can be

studied by examining the dream reports of patients in a wide variety of disease states.

- The many established parallels between waking cognition and dreaming raise the possibility that some dreams may make use of the system of figurative thinking, which cognitive scientists have shown to be pervasive in waking thought (Fauconnier, 1997; Gibbs, 1994; Lakoff, 1987).

Although the model explains the neural and cognitive bases for dreaming and shows that dream content is psychologically meaningful in that it is coherent, relates to other psychological variables, and is generally continuous with waking conceptions and concerns, it does not claim any purpose or function for dreams. On the basis of current evidence, it is more likely that dreams are an accidental by-product of two great evolutionary adaptations, sleep and consciousness (Antrobus, 1993; Flanagan, 1995; Foulkes, 1993). This point is discussed in detail in chapter 6 as part of the critique of traditional dream theories.

However, the fact that dreams sometimes dramatize emotional preoccupations, or contain parallels with the figurative dimensions of waking thought, may explain why many societies have invented uses for dreams, usually in conjunction with religious ceremonies or medicinal practices. These possible uses are not discussed in this book because the focus here is exclusively on understanding the process of dreaming and the nature of dream content. It therefore does not present the many anthropological studies of beliefs about dreams in different cultures (Tedlock, 1991). The rich literature on the Western use of dreams in religion (Bulkeley, 2001) and artistic creativity (Barrett, 2001) is not discussed. Nor is the literature on dreams and psychotherapy considered, although systematic studies of a cognitive–experiential approach to the use of dreams in therapy shows that talking about them is rated as helpful by clients (Hill, 1996; Hill et al., 2001). Thus, the book is strictly concerned with the development of a neurocognitive model of dreams.

Chapter 1 presents the main findings on which the new model is based along with several examples of how the three different types of findings can be related to each other. The chapter also discusses the methodology on which the developmental findings are based in greater detail than otherwise would be necessary, because parts of that methodology have been inadequately characterized in some sources. Chapter 2 explores the methods that can be used to link dream content to the neural network for dreaming, on the one hand, and to waking personal concerns, on the other. It argues that good methods for the systematic study of dream content do exist, even though most of the literature on dreams is weak as a result of the use of unreliable and unvalidated coding systems, poorly collected samples, small sample sizes, and inadequate statistical procedures.

Chapter 3 turns to a detailed presentation of the updated version of the coding system developed by Calvin S. Hall and Robert Van de Castle, which is now equipped with new statistical procedures as well as a spreadsheet for calculating p values and effect sizes. The chapter suggests that the system can yield the kind of detailed findings that would be necessary to test aspects of the neurocognitive model. Chapter 4 introduces a new resource for studying dream content, DreamBank.net (http://www.dreambank.net), an Internet archive of more than 11,000 dream reports for use in a wide range of studies. The chapter explains the capabilities of the search program and statistical procedures available on the site. Several small studies are presented as examples of how the site can be used to develop the neurocognitive model, including the possibility that it can be used to study figurative thinking in dreams.

Chapter 5 argues that the understanding of dream meaning can be advanced through detailed analyses of long dream journals, and it presents a methodology for doing such studies in conjunction with the Hall–Van de Castle coding system and the search program on DreamBank.net. It presents the basic findings from a dream journal containing 3,116 dream reports written down over a 20-year period to demonstrate the power of this approach, and to show the considerable regularity and psychological coherence that is present in a significant portion of dream life. To elaborate on the neurocognitive model, the chapter suggests that future studies need to be conducted with participants who have experienced various types of neurological injuries or developmental irregularities.

As noted, chapter 6 contains a detailed discussion of the main dream theories of the 20th century. It begins with a focus on the many claims made by Freud and Jung and shows that the empirical literature does not support any of their specific hypotheses. Similarly, it demonstrates the failings of the original version of activation–synthesis theory while noting that the recent version of the theory has taken steps in a neurocognitive direction in the light of new findings. However, activation–synthesis theory still lacks a fully developed cognitive dimension and has little or nothing to say about dream content. The chapter also includes an analysis of the difficulties that face all problem-solving theories of dreaming. In effect, then, chapter 6 clears the way for the new research directions presented throughout the book.

In writing this book, I have attempted to be as eclectic and encompassing as possible in incorporating ideas, methods, and findings from many different sources. I do, however, state the weaknesses of other explanatory systems quite frankly, because of their amazing persistence despite the absence of systematic empirical evidence for their main claims about the construction and meaning of dreams. It is time for the study of dreams to be incorporated into cognitive science in general and cognitive psychology in particular if understanding is to advance in this field, which has been slow to develop any new thinking until the past 10 years.

Thanks to the new methods and findings that emerged in the 1990s, the difficulty in advancing the scientific study of dreaming and dreams no longer lies in the planning and execution of solid studies. Instead, two new problems confront researchers. The first is to loosen the hold of dubious traditional theories on young researchers who develop an interest in dreams. The second is to encourage established cognitive psychologists and neuropsychologists to allow their students to incorporate dreams into scientific psychology's research agenda. I hope that this book contributes to the resolution of these two problems.

1

TOWARD A NEUROCOGNITIVE
MODEL OF DREAMS

The neurocognitive model of dreaming and dreams proposed in this chapter has three basic components. First, the *neurophysiological substrate* underlies and activates the process of dreaming. Second, the *conceptual system* of schemata and scripts generates the process of dreaming. Third, *dream content* results from this cognitive process. This chapter discusses each of these components and suggests some of the specific ways in which they may relate to each other.

THE NEURAL NETWORK FOR DREAMING

Research in neuropsychology and neuroimaging converged in the late 1990s to suggest the broad outlines of a neural network for dreaming that is very different from what had been imagined in the past. Some disparities exist between the lesion and imaging results, and a few disagreements can be found among the imaging studies, all of which use positron emission tomography (PET) scan technology, but the findings are strikingly consistent and provide the starting point for more detailed studies. However, it would be extremely premature to overspecify the network at a time when new discoveries are being made each year and so much remains to be learned (Antrobus, 2000a; Morrison & Sanford, 2000).

The neural substrate for dreaming provides the necessary level of activation needed for dreaming and, perhaps, constrains the types of thinking that are possible. It seems to be responsible for determining the degree of vividness and intensity experienced in dreaming, and it may account for other formal features of dreaming, such as its realistic and self-participatory nature, its general lack of self-reflectiveness, and its occasional incongruities of form. However, the neural substrate cannot account for the narrative nature of dreaming or the substance of dream content, which are products of the conceptual systems discussed later in this chapter.

9

Researchers with varied theoretical perspectives have four major areas of agreement about the contours of the neural network. First, the mechanisms that generate rapid eye movement (REM) sleep "support our most vivid and elaborate dreaming" (Foulkes, 1999, p. 6). Second, forebrain controls of the REM generator are located in the tegmental region in the middle of the pons. Third, a complex forebrain network is necessary for dreaming. Fourth, this forebrain network plays the major role in shaping dream content (Hobson et al., 2000b; Solms, 2000). Based on these agreements, this book concentrates on the development of a neurocognitive model of dreams that can encompass the whole range of dream content and relate that content to waking conceptions and concerns.

Theorists also disagree on some points. For example, there are varying opinions concerning the mixture of neurochemicals that modulate the brain during REM sleep (Gottesmann, 2000; Hobson et al., 2000b; Perry & Piggott, 2000). Differences also exist as to whether the neural network for dreaming always includes the area in the pons that is necessary for REM (Foulkes, 1999; Hobson et al., 2000b; Solms, 2000). These and various other unresolved issues related to the neural substrate for dreaming are discussed in chapter 6 as part of the critique of activation–synthesis theory.

The neuropsychological and neuroimaging results are interchangeable in some ways, but the neuropsychological studies provide the best starting point because they always include a crucial psychological component, the presence or absence of the subjective sense of dreaming. The neuroimaging studies, in contrast, are a mapping of sleep stages, although one research group did collect dream reports from several REM awakenings as well as one non-REM (NREM) awakening (Maquet, 2000, p. 224). Dreaming is highly correlated with REM, but sleep stages are an imperfect indicator of dreaming because at least some degree of dreaming occurs in NREM (Foulkes, 1966, 1985; Hobson, Pace-Schott, & Stickgold, 2000a). To connect neuroimaging work more closely to the process of dreaming, there is a need for studies of NREM periods from which dreams are reported and of REM periods in which no dreams are recalled upon awakening (Maquet, 2000, p. 224). It would be especially useful to have studies of the light stage of NREM (Stage II NREM) after the first four REM periods because many dreams seem to occur at this time (Antrobus, Kondo, & Reinsel, 1995; Cicogna, Natale, Occhionero, & Bosinelli, 1998).

The primary source of neuropsychological information on dreaming is a study by Solms (1997) in which 361 consecutive patients with neurological problems were asked in great detail between 1985 and 1989 about any changes they had noticed in the frequency and nature of their dreaming since their injury or illness. Solms then integrated the results with the findings from 73 published studies in the neurological literature that mention deficits and excesses in dreaming. Twenty-nine of the 361 patients turned out to be free of any brain lesions. They were used as a control group because they had been faced with the possibility of brain injuries, admitted to the hospital, and subjected to the same routines and tests as the patients who did suffer lesions.

The responses from the remaining patients concerning changes in their dreaming were correlated with the findings from their neurological tests and brain scans. Solms then focused on the patients with focal brain lesions so that causal inferences about specific regions of the brain could be made. These analyses led to the conclusion that two different types of dreaming "deficits" can occur—loss of visual dreaming and complete loss (i.e., cessation) of dreaming. Two types of dreaming "excesses" occur—the intrusion of dreaming into waking thought and increased nightmare frequency. It is noteworthy that all four types of changes in dreaming correlate with waking cognitive defects. In addition, they relate to relatively specific brain sites. The result is the general outline of a neural network for dreaming that can be linked at many points to waking cognition, on the one side, and to the results of neuroimaging studies, on the other (Solms, 1997, 2000). Figure 1.1 presents an overview of this network.

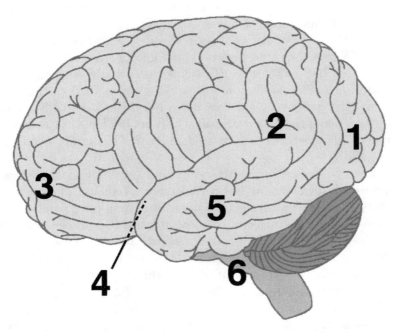

Figure 1.1. Parts of the brain that relate to dreaming, as determined by lesion studies. Injuries to these sites can cause defects in visual imagery in dreams (site 1), loss of dreaming (sites 2 and 3), excessive or intrusive dreaming (site 4), increased frequency of nightmares (site 5), and loss of REM sleep and possible loss of the activation necessary for dreaming (site 6).

The Solms study provides seven specific findings relating dreaming and neurological structures. First, 200 of the 332 patients with brain lesions reported no changes in dreaming. This is highly useful information because it reveals the parts of the brain that are not necessary for dreaming. Instead of the diffuse cortical activity suggested by EEG recordings using scalp electrodes, the neural network for dreaming is surprisingly localized and does not include vast areas of the brain that are essential to waking cognition—the dorsolateral prefrontal cortex, the sensorimotor cortex, and the primary visual cortex. For example, lesions in the dorsolateral prefrontal cortex that cause waking deficits of self-monitoring and decision making have no effect on dreaming. These findings are supported and supplemented by a neuro-imaging study revealing that all of these areas, along with the opercular cortex and posterior cingulate cortex, are as inactive during REM as they are during NREM (Braun et al., 1997).

Second, Solms found changes in dreaming due to injuries in the medial occipito-temporal region of the visual association cortex in two patients. One patient lost all visual imagery in dreams for a short time, and the other was able to see static dream images from time to time. Both had highly specific lesion sites and deficits in waking mental imagery. These findings correspond with 13 cases that go back to the 1880s in the neurological literature, including cases of losses of facial imagery or color vision in dreaming. They also parallel findings in sleep laboratory studies by Foulkes and his colleagues. The case with no visual imagery in dreams is similar to Kerr, Foulkes, and Jurkovic's (1978) laboratory study of a patient with damage in her visual association cortex. This patient had neither waking mental imagery nor any visual imagery in her dreams. As to Solms's case with static dream imagery, it is described by him (1997, p. 105) as "strikingly reminiscent" of a second patient studied in the laboratory by Kerr and Foulkes (1981).

These findings are of theoretical interest because they show that the neural network for dreaming has considerable specificity. They are also of interest because the visual impairments in dreaming have parallel waking deficits, a finding that suggests that the network has close relationships with at least some aspects of waking mental imagery. Once again, the neuroimaging findings are consistent with the neuropsychological findings, because the visual association cortex—and the auditory association cortex as well—are reactivated during REM (Braun et al., 1998).

Third, Solms found 47 patients with either unilateral or bilateral injuries in or near the region of the parieto-temporal-occipital junction who reported complete loss of dreaming and showed a decline in waking visuospatial abilities. This discovery led to the hypothesis that the cortical network for spatial representation, which is centered in the inferior parietal lobes and important in the creation of waking mental imagery, is essential for dreaming. Solms also reports there is even some evidence that the left parietal region "contributes symbolic (quasispatial) mechanisms to the dream process whereas the right parietal region contributes concrete spatial mechanisms," but he also stresses that this claim needs further investigation (1997, p. 271). These results, which are supported by many individual cases in the literature, are also consistent with neuroimaging findings that show reactivation of the right inferior parietal lobe, an area thought to be important in spatial cognition (Maquet, 2000; Maquet et al., 1996). As shown later in the chapter, these findings also may provide a crucial link to developmental studies of dreaming.

Any claim by a person that dreaming has been lost raises the possibility that it may be memory for the dream that has failed. Evidence that such people actually have ceased to dream comes first from the fact that those who reported loss of dreaming were no more likely to have memory disorders than those who reported that they continued to dream (Solms, 1997, pp. 160–161). Second, in two laboratory studies of people with neurological deficits, awakenings from REM did not produce any dream recall in most participants. In the first study, nine leucotomized people with schizophrenia who claimed that they no longer dreamed were awakened from all REM periods during two nights in the laboratory and compared with a control sample of hospitalized patients with schizophrenia who had not been leucotomized (Jus et al., 1973). Out of 66 awakenings, only two produced dream reports, and they were both from the same person; in contrast, half or more of the awakenings with the control group led to dream reports. In the second study, only 3 of 12 patients who reported that they had not dreamed over the course of a 10-day observation period could recall a dream from REM awakenings. In comparison, 7 patients with neurological deficits who said they continued to dream demonstrated 75% dream recall after REM awakenings (Murri, Massetani, Siciliano, & Arena, 1985). It therefore seems safe to conclude that claims concerning the loss of dreaming are credible.

Fourth, Solms found that patients with bifrontal lesions in the white matter inferior to the frontal horns of the lateral ventricles in the ventromesial region also reported loss of dreaming. This area provides a crucial link between the basal forebrain and limbic structures on one side and many parts of the frontal cortex. The evidence for the importance of this area is based on only nine cases, but the finding is strengthened by the results from studies of leucotomized people with schizophrenia that were previously overlooked in the dream research literature. The studies reported the loss of dreaming in 70% to 90% of the hundreds of people with schizophrenia who were leucotomized between 1940 and 1975 as a way to control their symptoms (Frank, 1946, 1950; Solms, 1997, 2000). Moreover, as just noted, the absence of dreaming in people who have been leucotomized has been confirmed with awakenings in the laboratory during REM (Jus et al., 1973).

Once again highlighting the parallels between waking cognition and dreaming, most of the people in those studies were lacking in initiative, curiosity, and fantasy in waking life. These findings also fit with the neuroimaging studies, which show that the basal forebrain and limbic region are highly active during REM (Braun et al., 1997; Maquet, 2000; Nofzinger et al., 1997).

Fifth, 10 of Solms's patients reported an increased frequency and vividness of dreaming, often accompanied by the intrusion of dreaming into waking life. They also said that their dreams now seemed more realistic. The most frequently involved areas were the medial prefrontal cortex, the anterior cingulate cortex, and the basal forebrain. Some of the patients said that they felt like they were always dreaming or that their thoughts quickly turned into pictures or realistic events, a finding that suggested to Solms (1997, pp. 198–199), following an idea presented by Luria (1973), that they had lost the "selectivity of mental processes." Observations by members of the hospital staff support the idea that the patients were suffering from a confusion between dreaming and waking thought. Whitty and Lewin (1957) reported several similar cases. Damasio, Graff-Radford, Eslinger, Damasio, and Kassell (1985) described their patients with similar lesions as suffering from "waking dreams" (p. 269). It is also noteworthy that the medial prefrontal cortex is involved in processes of arousal and attention in waking life and that injuries to this area can lead to confabulation and compulsive fabrication (Braun et al., 1997; Hobson et al., 2000b, p. 808).

Neuroimaging studies reveal that the medial prefrontal cortex, anterior cingulate cortex, and basal forebrain are reactivated during REM (Braun et al., 1997; Maquet et al., 1996; Nofzinger et al., 1997). Adding a new dimension to the picture, Nofzinger et al. (1999, 2001) discovered that people with depression have much weaker reactivation of the medial prefrontal cortex, anterior cingulate cortex, and right anterior insula in REM than normal participants do. It is as though their neural network for dreaming has shrunk to a small core area. Because evidence indicates that people with depression may dream less than their nondepressed counterparts (Armitage, Rochlen, Fitch, Trivedi, & Rush, 1995) and that the few dreams they do have are bland (Barrett & Loeffler, 1992; Kramer & Roth, 1973), this finding demonstrates the potential of using atypical cases to learn more about the relationship between dream content and the functioning of the neural substrate for dreaming.

Sixth, Solms found that injuries to the temporal lobe caused increased nightmares of a repetitive nature for nine patients, five of whom had symptoms of epilepsy. In keeping with this discovery, there are many instances in the literature of epileptics reporting nightmares, which are often caused by temporal-lobe seizures during NREM. These patients sometimes suffer from daytime hallucinations as well (see Solms, 2000, p. 847, for a summary and references). Then, too, studies using stereotaxic electrodes to locate the sites causing seizures show that the "dreamy state" sometimes experienced as part of the diagnostic process is related to the temporal-limbic region. In one such study, the amygdala, anterior hippocampus, and temporal cortex were involved in every spontaneous occurrence of this state during the procedure (Bancaud, Brunet-Bourgin, Chauvel, & Halgren, 1994). Thus, the possibility arises that the seizures may be activating the neural substrate for dreaming (Hobson et al., 2000a, p. 1031; Solms, 1997, p. 243). In addition, the neuroimaging results are consistent with the inclusion of the temporal lobe in the neural network for dreaming. They show that the occipital-temporal region is reactivated during REM, along with nearby limbic areas (Braun et al., 1997; Maquet, 2000).

Seventh, and finally, Solms had 53 patients with brain stem lesions who were able to state whether they continued to dream. Forty-three "reported a preservation of the subjective experience of dreaming" (Solms, 1997, p. 154). Solms concluded that the results showed that REM is not necessary for dreaming. However, his findings are not fully convincing on this issue because it is difficult to eliminate REM, even with experimental lesions in animals (Hobson, Stickgold, & Pace-Schott, 1998). Because Solms's patients were not tested in the sleep laboratory for the absence of REM, it is therefore not certain that the relevant areas of the brain stem were affected. Furthermore, it may be that "any lesion capable of destroying the pontine REM sleep generator mechanism would have to be so extensive as to eliminate consciousness altogether" (Hobson et al., 1998, p. R10). Still, some reports describe people who lost REM and remained sentient (Gironell, Calzada, Sagales, & Barraquer-Bordas, 1995; Lavie, 1984, 1990); unfortunately, they were not awakened to see whether they could report dreams, but their positive case histories show that future studies of the presence or absence of dreaming in people without REM may be possible.

As expected on the basis of earlier lesion studies with cats (Hobson, McCarley, & Wyzinski, 1975; McCarley & Hobson, 1975), the neuroimaging studies found that the pontine tegmentum is far more active in REM than NREM; one study suggested that it is even more active in REM than in waking (Braun et al., 1997). This reactivation seems to extend to the thalamus through cholinergic pathways, and then to the basal ganglia, basal forebrain, and limbic and paralimbic regions.

These findings, while far more specific than anything that could have been imagined in the early 1990s, nonetheless leave open many questions about the exact contours of the dream network; the studies have methodological differences, and the participants had individual differences (Hobson et al., 2000b; Maquet, 2000). They also lead to inevitable speculation about the functioning of the network. Braun et al. (1997) stressed that the activation levels during REM are comparable to those in waking but without the involvement of the frontal areas so important to waking cognition: "REM sleep may constitute a state of generalized brain activity with the specific exclusion of executive systems that normally participate in the highest order analysis and integration of neural information" (p. 1190). Braun et al. also emphasized the functional connections among the pons, basal forebrain, limbic structures, and medial prefrontal cortex during REM.

According to Maquet (2000, p. 222), the amygdala may be the central structure in the modulation of cortical activity in REM, as evidenced by the fact that it is tightly connected to the anterior cingulate cortex and the inferior parietal lobule, which are reactivated in REM, but has few connections to the dorsolateral prefrontal cortex and parietal lobes, which are relatively inactive throughout sleep. Meanwhile, Nofzinger et al. (1997, 2001) highlighted the importance of the anterior cingulate cortex, which plays a role in attentional states, performance monitoring, and error detection in waking thought.

Solms (2000) stated that the neuroimaging findings are generally consistent with his neuropsychological findings, but he doubted that the REM generator is a necessary part of the neural substrate for dreaming. Instead, he argued that dreaming is generated by the dopaminergic system, which has its origins in dopaminergic cells in the ventral tegmentum, just above the pons, and then fans out to the amygdala, anterior cingulate gyrus, and frontal cortex. He agreed that the cholinergic pathways originating in the pons are the most frequent instigators of the necessary level of forebrain activation, but he asserted that dreaming occurs "only if and when the initial activation stage engages the dopaminergic circuits of the ventromesial forebrain" (Solms, 2000, p. 849). Activation–synthesis theorists, on the other hand, see the neuroimaging results as strong support for their emphasis on the brain stem generator; at the same time, they welcome the insights into the forebrain network provided by both the neuroimaging and neuropsychological findings (Hobson et al., 2000a, 2000b).

These slightly different perspectives share the idea that the association cortices, paralimbic structures, and limbic structures may operate as a closed loop to generate the process of dreaming. This loop is the starting point for the neurocognitive model proposed in this book. On the one hand, this subsystem is cut off from the primary sensory cortices that provide information about the external world and, on the other, from the prefrontal cortices that integrate incoming sensory information with memory and emotion in the process of decision making (cf. Braun et al., 1998, p. 94). This model implies that an unconstrained and freewheeling conceptual system can operate when sufficient activation occurs. Its relative isolation may account for the "single-mindedness" of dreams (i.e., the lack of parallel thoughts and reflective awareness; Rechtschaffen, 1978, 1997). At the same time, as evidence presented throughout this book shows, the neural network for dreaming contains enough cognitive processing areas, such as the medial frontal cortex, anterior cingulate cortex and, perhaps, the orbital-frontal cortex, to produce coherent dramatizations that often portray the dreamer's conceptions and concerns in waking life (Foulkes, 1985, pp. 209–213; Hall, 1953b). This emphasis on conceptions and concerns, which is based on inferences from detailed studies of dream content, provides the cognitive dimension that is lacking in activation–synthesis theory.

Although the basic outlines of the neural network for dreaming seem clear, it is equally certain that much remains to be learned about its functioning. In addition to further neuroimaging studies using fMRI and transcranial magnetic stimulation as well as PET scans, this process could be greatly aided by clinical neuropsychologists who familiarize themselves with the new model and then look for people with either pure lesions in relevant areas or complaints about changes in their dreaming. Such studies could be especially helpful with people who previously kept a dream journal and are willing and able to report dreams as their lesions heal.

For now, what seems certain is that progress toward an increasingly detailed mapping of the neural network for dreaming is inevitable: Neuropsychology is making rapid strides, and neuroimaging studies are becoming increasingly sophisticated and common. Because of the potential of transcranial magnetic procedures, it might even be possible to shape dream content by stimulating different regions within the neural network for dreaming (Mazziotta, Toga, & Frackowiak, 2000; Stewart, Ellison, Walsh, & Cowey, 2001). The stage is therefore set for a consideration of how this network might be integrated with other areas of dream research to build a neurocognitive model. For example, the forebrain portion of the neural substrate for dreaming seems to be a good starting point for understanding the occasional occurrence of an awareness of dreaming during a dream.

THE QUESTION OF "LUCID DREAMING"

The phenomenon of becoming aware of a dream while it is ongoing enjoyed a flurry of attention and speculation in the 1980s under the morally toned label of *lucid dreaming*— implying a superior or elite status for "lucid dreamers"—and efforts were made to link it to meditation and other altered states of consciousness (Gackenbach & Bosveld, 1989; LaBerge, 1985). Although often remarked upon in books on dreams in the prelaboratory era, lucid dreaming could not be studied systematically until it was shown in the laboratory that it occurs during REM (LaBerge, Nagel, Dement, & Zarcone, 1981). Although too few people have been studied in the laboratory to establish the frequency of lucid dreaming, laboratory and nonlaboratory studies suggest that the degree of self-awareness and sense of conscious control can vary greatly from person to person and even within any given lucid dream (Barrett, 1992). However, as Foulkes (1990b) noted, much more laboratory work needs to be done concerning "the conditions under which certain kinds of generic and autobiographical knowledge prove to be accessible during dreaming in the service of an ongoing comprehension and evaluation of dream events" (p. 121).

If dreaming is the form that consciousness takes during sleep (Foulkes, 1999), and if changes in the neural network for dreaming underlie different dreaming states, then lucid dreaming may be the product of a dream state in which the higher order neural patterns that give human beings "core consciousness" and an "autobiographical self" are more active than usual (Damasio, 1999). This speculation is consistent with Rechtschaffen's (1997) use of the confabulations caused by frontal-lobe injuries to argue that the loss of reflective awareness in dreams is the result of the lack of frontal-lobe activity. It also fits with the finding that the high levels of alpha activity during REM are related to lucid dream reports (Ogilvie, 1982; Tyson, Ogilvie, & Hunt, 1984) and with the knowledge that self-awareness during REM is associated with phasic (i.e., intermittent) activation within the REM period (Bradley, Hollifield, & Foulkes, 1992). The content of lucid dreams also has a more realistic nature, which would be expected from this line of reasoning (Gackenbach, 1988).

Then, too, it is noteworthy that dream reports in an exploratory PET scan study of 12 male participants showed a greater sense of control when the medial frontal cortex was more active, and a greater sense of things being out of control when the amygdala was most active (Shapiro et al., 1995). Some nonlaboratory evidence suggests that the neural network for dreaming includes more frontal cortex activity during lucid dreaming than during nonlucid dreaming: Lucid dreams seem to occur most frequently in the home setting after an early morning awakening—between 5:00 a.m. and 6:30 a.m.—that is followed by imagery rehearsal and a conscious attempt to be aware of dreaming upon falling back to sleep (LaBerge, 1985). Thus, the new question of interest is the state of the neural network for dreaming during the experience of lucid dreaming and how that state relates to indicators of REM and Stage II NREM (Hobson et al., 2000a, p. 1020; Hobson et al., 2000b, p. 837).

THE DEVELOPMENT OF DREAMING COGNITION

The serendipitous discovery of REM sleep in 1953, especially the finding that the four or five REM periods of the night occupy 20% to 25% of adult sleep time and lead to dream reports from 80% to 90% of awakenings in normal adults, triggered an enormous advance in the understanding of both sleep and dreaming (Dement & Kleitman, 1957a, 1957b; Foulkes,

1966; Kamiya, 1961). Those studies demonstrated that dreaming is far more ubiquitous in both REM and NREM than any previous dream theorist ever imagined, a finding that has major implications, discussed in chapter 6, for traditional clinical and functional theories of dreaming. They also revealed that dreaming has many important parallels with waking cognition.

In addition, laboratory dream studies show that dreaming cannot be triggered by external stimuli and that it is difficult to influence dream content with either presleep stimuli, such as fear-arousing or exciting movies, or with concurrent stimuli administered during REM, such as a spray of water, sounds, or the names of significant people in the dreamers' lives (Foulkes, 1985, 1996a; Rechtschaffen, 1978). For example, in a large study comparing the influence of neutral and affect-arousing presleep films on the REM dreams of 24 adult participants, only 5% of 179 awakenings showed any sign of incorporation (Foulkes & Rechtschaffen, 1964); similar results were obtained in a study of boys between ages 7 and 11 (Foulkes, Pivik, Steadman, Spear, & Symonds, 1967). In the most frequently cited study of the influence of external stimuli applied during REM, the sound of a bell was only incorporated in 20 of the 204 instigations with 12 participants (Dement & Wolpert, 1958b). Somatosensory stimuli from sprays of water, electrical pulses to the hand, and pressure from a blood pressure cuff seem to have the highest rate of incorporation, at around 40% (Sauvageau, Nielsen, & Montplaisir, 1998, p. 132). However, the criteria for incorporation were loose in most of these studies, and the researchers sometimes included what were assumed to be metaphoric expressions of the stimulus (Arkin & Antrobus, 1991).

Overall, Foulkes's judgment seems to be the best starting point for developing a neurocognitive model of dreaming:

> Probably the most general conclusion to be reached from a wide variety of disparate stimuli employed and analyses undertaken is that dreams are relatively autonomous, or "isolated," mental phenomena, in that they are not readily susceptible to either induction or modification by immediate presleep manipulation, at least those within the realm of possibility in ethical human experimentation. (1996a, p. 614)

However, on the rare occasions when stimuli are incorporated, "the speed and ingenious fit of the incorporation into the meaning and imagery context of the ongoing dream" are often "remarkable," suggesting the high cognitive level of the dreaming brain (Antrobus, 2000b, p. 474).

Laboratory studies further show that the content of dream reports, whether from REM or NREM awakenings, is in large measure a coherent and reasonable simulation of the real world. This conclusion joins with the neuropsychological findings on people with brain lesions in suggesting that a greater parallel exists between waking thought and dreaming than is assumed by either clinical or activation–synthesis theorists (Cavallero &

Foulkes, 1993; Foulkes, 1985; Meier, 1993; Snyder, 1970; Strauch & Meier, 1996). Some of the laboratory findings on dream content are discussed in detail in chapter 2.

In addition, findings from three laboratory studies suggest that waking thought can have dreamlike qualities when participants are relaxing in a darkened room. In the first two of these studies, awake participants monitored by EEG gave dreamlike responses to 15% to 20% of the requests for reports of what was going through their minds (Foulkes & Fleisher, 1975; Foulkes & Scott, 1973). In another laboratory study, judges who compared REM reports with thought reports from awake participants reclining in a darkened room rated the waking reports as more dreamlike (Reinsel, Antrobus, & Wollman, 1992; Reinsel, Wollman, & Antrobus, 1986). Furthermore, a field study of waking consciousness—which used pagers to contact participants—discovered that 9% of the 1,425 thought samples had "more than a trace" of dreamlike thought and another 16% had a "trace" of such thought (Klinger & Cox, 1987/1988). Taken together, these studies lead to the idea that dreaming may not always be a function of sleep, thereby providing another possible link between waking cognition and dreaming. Instead, at least some forms of dreaming simply may require a high level of brain activation in combination with a reduction in external stimulation and a decrease in self-control (Antrobus, 1991; Foulkes, 1999; Llinas & Pare, 1991).

Within the context of this general evidence for the overlap of waking cognition and dreaming, two large-scale studies of dreaming in children—one longitudinal, one cross-sectional—provide systematic evidence that offers a developmental dimension to a neurocognitive model of dreams (Foulkes, 1982, 1999; Foulkes et al., 1990). The longitudinal study began with seven boys and seven girls ages 3 to 4 and took place over a 5-year span; the study also included eight girls and eight boys ages 9 to 10 to account for the years between ages 9 and 15. Remarkably, all 14 children in the younger group participated in all 5 years of the study. Twelve of the 16 children in the older group completed the study; the other 4 moved out of town.

To check on the possibility that participation in the study improved dream recall and accounted for any increases in the frequency and narrative complexity of dream reports, six boys ages 11 to 13 were added to the older group in the third year and seven girls ages 7 to 9 were added to the younger group in the fifth year. The new participants generally did not differ on any dream measures from the original participants. In total, 26 children between ages 3 and 15 participated for 5 full years, 34 participated for at least 3 years, and 43 participated for at least 1 complete year. Normative dream data for each group were collected during the first, third, and fifth years of the study, when children slept in the laboratory for nine nights each. They responded to three awakenings per night from either REM or NREM, for a total of 2,711 awakenings. All the awakenings were carried out by Foulkes to ensure experimenter consistency. During the second and fourth years, the children participated in a variety of methodological studies, the most important of which compared dreams collected after a night of uninterrupted sleep in the laboratory with dreams collected in the morning at home by parents.

In addition to gathering information on the frequency of dream recall and the content of the dream reports, other members of the project team administered a wide range of personality and cognitive tests and obtained information about school performance. Observations of the social skills and play patterns of the youngest group were made at a 2-week nursery school during the first three summers of the study. A total of 657 nondream variables were correlated with the dream data because "it would have constituted criminal neglect to have collected so many dream data and not to have searched far and wide for waking variables related to them" (Foulkes, 1999, p. 49).

The cross-sectional study focused on children ages 5 to 8 to see whether the most interesting results of the longitudinal study could be replicated. It included 20 children at each age who were within 1 month of their birthdays, so a total of 80 children spent three nights in the sleep laboratory. They were each awakened 10 times, and all 800 awakenings, as in the longitudinal study, were carried out by Foulkes. The children took several cognitive tests measuring visuospatial, verbal, descriptive, and memory abilities that had correlated with dream recall or length of dream reports in the first study. The children also took three interview-based tests that claimed to measure aspects of the development of self-awareness. In neither study did Foulkes know the results of the daytime tests until he had collected all the dream data.

There are several replicated results from these two studies that are important for a neurocognitive model of dreams. None of the findings on rate of recall, report length, or narrative complexity showed any gender differences. First, and most unexpected, the median rate of dream recall was only 20% to 30% from REM awakenings until ages 9 to 11, when the median recall rate of 79% from REM awakenings approached adult levels. Recall from NREM awakenings went from 6% at ages 5 to 7 to 39% at ages 11 to 13. For both REM and NREM awakenings, recall came first from awakenings late in the night, then from awakenings in the middle of the night, and finally from awakenings early in the sleep period.

Second, until ages 13 to 15, the children's dream reports had different content from what is reported by adults. For children under age 5, the REM reports consisted primarily of static and bland images in which they saw an animal or were thinking about eating or sleeping. The dreams of children ages 5 to 8 showed a sequence of events in which characters moved about and interacted, but the dream narratives were not well developed. The dreamer did not appear regularly as an active participant in her or his dreams until around age 8. Compared with the dream reports of adults, those of the young children were notable for their low levels of aggressions, misfortunes, and negative emotions (Domhoff, 1996; Foulkes, 1982, 1999). Gender differences in dream content did begin to appear in late childhood (Domhoff, 1996; Foulkes, 1982) but were more prevalent by adolescence (Trupin, 1976). The findings on children ages 9 to 15 have been replicated and extended in a major longitudinal project by Strauch (1996; Strauch & Lederbogen, 1999) that was based on 12 boys and 12 girls studied at 2-year intervals in the sleep laboratory and at home.

The results on both recall and content are of great theoretical importance because they suggest that young children do not dream in the fashion assumed by all previous theorists on the basis of anecdotal and clinical accounts. Instead, they reveal dreaming to be a cognitive achievement that develops gradually in the same way in which most other cognitive abilities develop in children. The frequency and cognitive structure of children's dreams is not adultlike until ages 9 to 11, and the dream reports are not adultlike in length or content until ages 11 to 13. The content generally differs from what was expected on the basis of anecdotal accounts and nonlaboratory studies.

Foulkes's findings on the waking correlates of dreaming and dream content in children provide further surprises because verbal and linguistic skills did not play a role in dream recall or report length until dreaming is fully developed, and none of the personality measures correlated with dream content until preadolescence. The one good and consistent predictor of the frequency of dream reporting in children ages 5 to 9 in both studies was visuospatial skills, as best measured by the Block Design test of the Wechsler Intelligence Scale for Children (WISC) and the Embedded Figures Test. This finding leads to the hypothesis that visual imagination may develop gradually and be a necessary cognitive prerequisite for dreaming.

There has been no rush to draw out the implications of these findings, perhaps because they do not agree with common sense: Everyone has anecdotal examples of dreams from young children, and children seem to understand the concept of dreaming. In addition, as many as half of college students in two different samples claimed to remember a dream from childhood, although it may be significant that the average estimated age for such dreams is 6.5 years, compared with the usual 3.5 years for their earliest memory (Domhoff, 1993a). Skeptics therefore argue that the low rates of recall in young children may be the result of waking cognitive factors rather than a lack of dreaming.

For example, Hunt (1989) thinks the problem may be an inability to distinguish the "embedded" experience of a dream from similar subjective states; others say that children simply may lack the linguistic skills to translate the nonverbal experience of dreaming into the narrative report necessary to show evidence of dreaming (Hobson et al., 2000b; Weinstein, Schwartz, & Arkin, 1991). Foulkes found these alternative explanations unlikely because none of the several linguistic, descriptive, memory, or storytelling tests administered to the children correlated with rates of recall. Such explanations are also contradicted by the fact that both REM and NREM reports are first given late in the sleep period; it does not seem likely that either discriminatory or narrative skills would be unavailable earlier in the night once they had developed.

The idea that young children do not dream well until their visuospatial skills are developed is supported by Foulkes' unanticipated findings with two of the boys ages 11 to 13 who were added to the study during its third year. Both boys had average memory and verbal skills and were adequate students in school, but they both scored low on visuospatial skills. Neither boy reported many dreams during REM awakenings, far below the average for all other children in their age group. Because neither boy lacked the linguistic skills claimed by critics to be the reason why young children do not report dreams when awakened in the laboratory, it seems more likely that they were not dreaming (Foulkes, 1982, pp. 180–181, 225–226).

Findings on the presence or absence of visual imagery in people who lose their sight through disease or accident before or after ages 5 to 7 also support Foulkes's argument. As is well known, those who become blind after this critical period "continue to be able while awake to conjure up mental images of persons, objects, and events, and they continue to dream in imagery" (Foulkes, 1999, p. 15). This point includes visual dream images of people they met after they became blind, which supports the generally accepted idea that they have a system of imagery independent of perceptual capabilities. On the other hand, people who become blind before ages 5 to 7 do not have waking visual imagery or visual dreams.

The likelihood that preschool children do not dream often or well may have implications for an unexpected finding in studies of how children come to understand imagination, pretense, and dreams. Several studies suggest that by age 3, children understand mental states and readily distinguish between the real and the imaginary. However, preschool children do less well on questions inquiring about dreams: "Whereas 3- and 4-year-olds are reported to have a sensitive understanding of the origins of imagination, early work on dreams suggests that children of this same age are quite confused about their origins" (Woolley, 1995, p. 195). Some 3-year-olds also "appeared to conceive of dreams as shared fantasies, claiming that dream content is shared between sleeping individuals" (Woolley, 1995, p. 189).

These differences are often explained by noting that pretense and imagination are deliberate mental activities that are facilitated by toys and interactions with adults. Woolley (1995, p. 195) speculates that "dream origins are simply more difficult for children," perhaps because dreams are not willful mental states. If Foulkes's findings are used as a starting point, however, this failure of understanding may be due to a lack of personal experience with dreams. In fact, many of the explanations for dreams offered by preschool children—that they are shared fantasies, that they come from God, or that they are produced by the people who appear in them—seem to reflect what they are told by their parents along with what they deduce from storybooks. This alternative hypothesis suggests the need for new research on the way in which children's "theory of mind" interacts with what they learn about dreams from their culture to produce possibly fabricated reports when they sense an expectation or pressure to describe a dream (Ceci, Bruck, & Battin, 2000).

Once children have the ability to dream, their linguistic and descriptive skills begin to correlate with the length and narrative complexity of their dream reports. Still, it is not until ages 11 to 13 that dream content shows any relationship to personality dimensions. For example, the more individualistic and assertive children portray themselves as more active in their dreams. Children with more violence in their waking fantasies have more aggressive interactions in their dreams, and those who display the most hostility before going to bed in the laboratory more often dream of themselves as angry. These findings on the continuity of dream content with waking thought support findings in earlier studies of children in the laboratory (Foulkes, 1967; Foulkes, Larson, Swanson, & Rardin, 1969; Foulkes et al., 1967) and suggest that dreams can reflect personal concerns and emotional preoccupations once there is an adequate level of cognitive development. As shown in Domhoff (1996) and evidence presented throughout this book, this finding is all that remains of the large claims by Freud and Jung (see chapter 6, this volume).

Foulkes's findings raise the possibility that the development of dreaming may be based on the maturation of the neural network for dreaming discussed in the previous section. This hypothesis is the first and most crucial one in an effort to create a neurocognitive model of dreams. The idea is suggested most strongly by the parallel between the dependence of dreaming in children on visuospatial skills, which are based primarily in the parietal lobes (Robertson, 1998), and the loss of dreaming in adults with injuries to either parietal lobe. The hypothesis is also suggested by the static nature of preschool children's dreams, which may relate to the absence of movement imagery in the dreams of adults with lesions in specific areas of the visual association cortex.

More generally, if the low levels of dreaming in children and the differences in their dream reports from the dream reports of normative adult samples are treated as though they are "deficits," then the search could be made for possible causal "defects" in the neural network necessary for dreaming. Welsh, Pennington, and Groisser (1993) followed this strategy in studying the development of frontal-lobe executive functions in children; the researchers used neuropsychological tests in conjunction with standard developmental tests. The search could be widened to include neuroimaging studies of the developing brain as well as myelination studies (Chugani, 1999; Paus et al., 1999; Rivkin, 2000; Thatcher, 1996). Indeed, because myelination of the inferior parietal lobules is not functionally complete until ages 5 to 7, dreaming may not be fully developed until after that age period (Janowsky & Carper, 1996; Mark Solms, Department of Neurology and Psychology, University of Cape Town, personal communication, June 14, 1999). The fruitfulness of this approach is also seen in studies showing that the presence or absence of visual imagery in blind adults depends on whether they lost their sight before or after ages 5 to 7 (Hurovitz, Dunn, Domhoff, & Fiss, 1999).

The integration of the neural network for dreaming with Foulkes's developmental findings would provide a solid basis for a model that is genuinely neurocognitive instead of simply neuropsychological, in the sense that doing so could relate a neural system to the development of dreaming. However, it is necessary to include what is known about the nature of dream content before the cognitive dimension of dreams can be folded into modern-day cognitive theory and then incorporated into a neurocognitive model of dreams.

THE NATURE OF DREAM CONTENT

Although there are several systems of content analysis that have made one or more contributions to the understanding of dream content (Foulkes & Shepherd, 1971; Gottschalk & Gleser, 1969; Winget & Kramer, 1979), the largest and most systematic body of findings on what people dream about comes from a comprehensive set of descriptive empirical categories developed by Hall (1951) and then finalized with the help of Van de Castle (Hall & Van de Castle, 1966). Four general findings with this Hall–Van de Castle system must be encompassed by a neurocognitive model.

First, several different studies revealed that the dream lives of college men and women in the United States remained the same throughout the second half of the 20th century despite major cultural changes (Domhoff, 1996; Dudley & Swank, 1990; Hall, Domhoff, Blick, & Weesner, 1982; Hall & Van de Castle, 1966; Tonay, 1990/1991). These findings also provide a normative basis for many other studies, as explained in chapter 3. Second, little or no change in dream content occurs once adulthood is reached. That is, older dreamers do not differ from college students, except perhaps for a decline in physical aggressions and negative emotions (Cote, Lortie-Lussier, Roy, & DeKoninck, 1996; Hall & Domhoff, 1963b, 1964; Howe & Blick, 1983; Inge Strauch, Department of Psychology, University of Zurich, personal communication, January 24, 2000; Zepelin, 1980), nor does dream content change much in longitudinal studies of dream journals provided by adults, a claim that holds true for periods as long as four or five decades and for people keeping journals into their 70s (Domhoff, 1996; Hall & Nordby, 1972; Lortie-Lussier, Cote, & Vachon, 2000; Smith & Hall, 1964).

The third relevant result with the Hall–Van de Castle system is that there is a stable pattern of cross-cultural similarities and differences in dream content. Most of the research on which this conclusion is based, much of it unpublished work by Hall, is summarized in Domhoff (1996, chapter 6). No significant additions to this literature have been made since the volume was published. Everywhere in the world, for example, women and men have the same differences in the percentage of gendered characters who are men or women. Women dream equally of men and women, but 67% of the gendered characters in men's dreams are other men (Hall, 1984). The same gender differences are found in short stories by male and female authors (Hall & Domhoff, 1963a) and in stories told by preschool children (Domhoff, 1996, p. 89). The low percentage of men in the dreams of Japanese women seemed to be the major exception to this generalization (Yamanaka, Morita, & Matsumoto, 1982), but a later study of several different samples revealed the same percentages as elsewhere (Nishigawa, Brubaker, & Domhoff, 2001).

For both men and women cross-culturally, dreams usually contain more aggression than friendliness, more misfortune than good fortune, and more negative emotions than positive emotions. In addition to these similarities, there are also a few differences that make sense on the basis of cultural differences. For instance, people in small, traditional societies have a higher percentage of animal characters in their dreams than people from large, industrial societies. Moreover, there are large variations from society to society in the percentage of all aggressive interactions that are physical in nature, although men in most societies have a higher percentage of physical aggression in their dreams than women do (Domhoff, 1996; Gregor, 1981; O'Nell & O'Nell, 1977).

Finally, studies of dream journals have demonstrated wide individual differences on a variety of Hall–Van de Castle content indicators, which are explained in chapter 3. Those differences generally relate to the waking concerns or past emotional preoccupations of the dreamers. Thus, a continuity exists between most aspects of dream content and waking thought (Bell & Hall, 1971; Domhoff, 1996; Hall & Lind, 1970; Hall & Nordby, 1972). This finding leads to the hypothesis of a *continuity principle*, which is compatible with Foulkes's (1967, 1982, 1999) findings in laboratory studies with both children and adults.

The continuity principle is best demonstrated by blind analyses of dream journals, in which nothing is known about the dreamer until he or she later answers questions developed on the basis of the content analysis. In particular, blind analyses lead to accurate portrayals of the dreamers' conceptions and concerns regarding the important people in their lives. This emphasis on questions developed from the results of content analyses follows from three conclusions that are based on earlier attempts to find correlations between dream content and standard personality measures. First, the findings with projective techniques are meager and inconsistent (Domhoff, 1996; Hall, 1956), a situation that may be a function of the inadequacies of those instruments (Lilienfeld, Wood, & Garb, 2000). Second, the results with structured personality tests, although usually consistent with the continuity principle, did not lead to new insights, so such tests were seldom used after the early 1970s (Domhoff, 1996). Third, past research shows that dreams most directly reveal concerns, interests, and worries, rather than personality traits, suggesting that an open-ended neurocognitive approach may be most useful at this juncture (Domhoff, 1996, chapter 8; Hall, 1953c; Hall & Nordby, 1972). Chapter 5 explains how studies using questions that are based on a dream series are conducted.

Several of the discoveries with the Hall–Van de Castle system, especially the consistency of adult dream content over time, lead to the idea that a *repetition principle* operates in the dream process at least some of the time (Domhoff, 1993b, 1996). The tendency to repeat has gone unnoticed by those who study one dream at a time with clinical study participants, use samples of individual dream reports from groups of people, or hold to Jung's (1974) theory that a dream series shows a pattern of symbolic change toward greater personal integration. The relative absence of the repeated themes in dreams collected over several weeks from participants in laboratory studies suggests that the pervasiveness of repetitive dreaming may be overestimated by selective dream recall in everyday dream journals (David Foulkes, personal communication, March 25, 2001). Thus, the fact of repetition is solidly established, but its relative frequency remains to be determined.

The idea of a repetition principle in dreams not only describes the consistency over years and decades in characters, social interactions, activities, and settings in the longitudinal studies using the Hall–Van de Castle system but also encompasses three other repetitive aspects of dream life that must be comprehended within a neurocognitive model of dreaming. First, the extensive clinical literature on the repetitive nightmares of people suffering from posttraumatic stress disorder fits well with the idea of a repetition principle (Hartmann, 1984, 1998; Kramer, 2000b; Kramer,

Schoen, & Kinney, 1987). This literature shows that such dreams are more frequent and persistent than was realized until systematic studies began in the aftermath of the Vietnam War (Barrett, 1996).

Second, the repetition principle can encompass the recurrent dreams that 50% to 80% of people claim to have had at one time or another in their lives. Such dreams often start in late childhood or early adolescence, sometimes last for a lifetime, and are usually highly negative in content and emotionally upsetting (Cartwright & Romanek, 1978; Domhoff, 1996; Zadra, 1996). Third, the idea of a repetition principle can incorporate the repeated themes found in most series of 20 or more dreams (Hall, 1947, 1953c). In other words, it is not just Hall–Van de Castle indicators that are consistent over many years, but also general themes, such as being lost, preparing meals, or being late for an examination. In a study of 649 dreams over a 50-year period, for example, just six themes accounted for at least part of the content in 71% of the dream reports (Domhoff, 1993b).

The concept of a repetition principle suggests several potential links between dream content and the neural substrate for dreaming, particularly dreams' possible relationship to the vigilance–fear system that seems to be centered in the amygdala (LeDoux, 1996; Whalen, 1998). The best examples of this point, of course, are the repetitive nightmares of posttraumatic stress disorder. These nightmares sometimes happen in Stage II of NREM (Van der Kolk, Blitz, Burr, Sherry, & Hartmann, 1984) and seem to have parallels with the nightmares people with epilepsy suffer as a result of seizures in NREM (Solms, 1997, 2000). In addition, as noted in the discussion of the neural network for dreaming, the dreamy states sometimes experienced by epileptics are usually related to the temporal-limbic region (Bancaud et al., 1994). Thus, future neuroimaging work on both posttraumatic stress disorder and epilepsy may hold promise for links between the repetition principle and the neural network for dreaming.

However, there need not be an exclusive focus on people with brain injuries. The consistency of emotionally painful themes and of heightened scores on Hall–Van de Castle indicators in the dreams of many people without diagnoses of brain injury or other medical conditions suggests that their dream life is often "stuck" in the past in a way that fits with the persistence of negative memories stored in the vigilance–fear system (Domhoff, 1996; see chapter 5). Both dreams and the vigilance–fear system seem to provide a neurocognitive record of traumas, upsets, and tensions over a lifetime. Moreover, both may persist even when the person is emotionally recovered and unhampered by the past during waking life. This possibility suggests that dreams may not always be symptomatic of present-day problems, contrary to what all clinical theories assume.

Systematic studies showing the effects of different drugs on dream content, when conducted in conjunction with neuroimaging studies, might help pinpoint relationships between repetitive dream content and specific components of the dream-generation network. The promise of such studies is seen in the fact that both the anticholinergic beladonna alkaloids (Ketchum, Sidell, Crowell, Aghajanian, & Hayes, 1973; Wichlinski, 2000) and dopamine (Hartmann, Russ, Oldfield, Falke, & Skoff, 1980; Solms, 2000) intensify the dream experience. People with epilepsy or Parkinson's disease might be candidates for such content studies because it already is known that the medications that eliminate epileptic seizures also reduce or eliminate nightmares and that L-dopa potentiates the dream experience for people with Parkinson's disease (Hartmann, 1984; Perry, Walker, Grace, & Perry, 1999; Solms, 1997).

Although early studies concerning the effect of drugs on dream content led to few clear results for a variety of reasons (Roth, Kramer, & Salis, 1979), the potential for pretest–posttest studies of individual cases is shown in the large positive changes in the dream content of a 21-year-old woman after she began taking sertraline (Zoloft), a selective serotonin reuptake inhibitor, to cope with anxiety attacks (Kirschner, 1999). The positive changes included increased friendly interactions and fewer aggressive interactions and negative emotions. It is also of interest that she showed a decline in "elements from the past," which might be an indication that the repetition principle was having less influence on her dreams.

Dream content and the neural network for dreaming also might be linked by investigations that correlate specific neurological defects with atypical scores on the Hall–Van de Castle indicators. People who have suffered damage to the amygdala might be ideal candidates for future defect studies because they have lost their capacity for fear in waking life and express predominantly positive emotions (Adolphs & Damasio, 1998; Damasio, 1999; Pace-Schott, 2000). It therefore could be hypothesized on the basis of the continuity principle that the proportion of negative emotions in their dreams would be far lower than the 80% figure that several different studies have found (Hall et al., 1982; Hall & Van de Castle, 1966; Roussy, Raymond, & De Koninck, 2000; Tonay, 1990/1991).

The potential for such studies is demonstrated in older reports cited by Solms (1997) that show a decline in "narrative complexity" in the dream reports of people with specific neurological defects through injuries or operations. It is also seen in a study showing that 17 men with chronic brain syndrome had more family members, less aggression, and less emotional content in the 31 dreams they reported than does the Hall–Van de Castle normative sample that is described in chapter 3 (Kramer, Roth, & Trinder, 1975). This pattern of findings suggests that their dreams were bland, a characterization that fits with the waking personalities of people with that condition (Torda, 1969). It might even be that there is a different profile on Hall–Van de Castle indicators for each type of defect, a possibility that was demonstrated in a sample of 104 dream reports from 20 men with schizophrenia (Domhoff, 1999b, p. 127)

It also could be useful to look for changes in dream content as the process of dreaming returns in people who have injuries to one or the other parietal lobe. It might be that content is simple and banal at first, reflecting only a partial recovery. Then, too, this approach could be used to test the idea that the left parietal lobe is more involved in symbolic (i.e., quasispatial) constructions and the right parietal lobe in concrete, spatial constructions (Solms, 1997, p. 271).

DREAM CONTENT AND WAKING COGNITION

Findings from the study of dream content suggest links not only with the neural network for dreaming but also with waking cognition. In particular, the continuity principle provides the same kind of strong connection between dreaming and waking cognition that has been demonstrated by the neuropsychological and developmental evidence presented earlier in this chapter. This continuity leads to the hypothesis that both dreaming and waking cognition deal with the same psychological issues to a large extent. This hypothesis provides the basis for linking a neurocognitive model of dreams with what is known about waking cognition.

However, as the evidence concerning the repetition principle in the previous section indicates, the continuity principle does not operate entirely according to current personal interests and concerns. Dream content is also continuous in varying degrees for different people with past waking concerns. Discrepancies between current waking concerns and current dream content, such as dreaming about painful events that are no longer thought about in waking life, could be used to see how the continuity and repetition principles interact with each other to shape dream content.

The starting point for adding a cognitive dimension to the model is the notion of a *conceptual system*, or system of schemata and scripts, which is the organizational basis for all human knowledge and beliefs. Most of this system is thought to be unconscious, in the sense that it is outside conscious awareness, but people can become conscious of the system as well. The conceptual system consists of both experientially based and figurative concepts, both of which are processed and understood equally fast and well according to experimental studies (Gibbs, 1994, 1999). The conceptual system builds on three types of experiential categories—*basic level, spatial relations,* and *sensorimotor*—which in turn are based on bodily sensations and interactions with the world (Lakoff & Johnson, 1999).

Basic-level categories arise through the interaction of inherited neural structures with patterns of stimuli from the environment. They reflect distinctions among types of animals, such as cows, horses, and goats; types of social interactions, such as friendly and aggressive interactions; and types of actions, such as walking and running. Basic-level categories are most directly distinguished from other categories in that a single mental image can represent an entire category, such as a "dog," "cat," "boat," or "car" (Murphy & Lassaline, 1997). In addition to the large number of basic-level categories, there are also spatial-relations categories that are experiential in nature, such as "up," "down," "in front of," and "in back of." Comparative linguistic studies show that "there is a relatively small collection of primitive image schemas [sic] that structure systems of spatial relations in the world's languages" (Lakoff & Johnson, 1999, p. 35). Finally, sensorimotor categories are based on direct experience of such varied qualities as temperature, motion, and touch.

Dreams are thought of as highly "symbolic" in many different cultures, including Western civilization, but the findings from content analysis suggest that dreams may consist primarily of constructions arising from experiential categories. Based on his reading of thousands of dreams collected from children, teenagers, and adults in the sleep laboratory, Foulkes (1985) concluded that most dreams are simulations of real-world experiences. Young adult dreamers are often shopping, playing sports, visiting with their friends, arguing with their parents, worrying about the faithfulness of their lovers, or feeling tempted to be unfaithful themselves. The content of young children's dreams is usually even more realistic.

Although the Hall–Van de Castle coding system is accurately described as empirical and descriptive, it is noteworthy that most of its coding categories are basic-level categories. This point holds true for all the social interaction, activity, and emotions categories and for most of the character categories. This coding system therefore makes good theoretical sense to the degree that dreams are constructed from experiential categories. Perhaps this focus on basic-level categories also explains why the system can be learned and used with high intercoder reliability by new researchers in many different countries.

The theory of cognitive functioning sketched out in the previous paragraphs provides a basis for adding a cognitive dimension to the neurocognitive model because the theory fits well with earlier work on dream content by Hall (1953b), Foulkes (1985), Antrobus (1978, 1991), Fiss (1986), and other dream researchers who approach the topic from a cognitive perspective. The model begins with the proposition that dreaming is what the mature brain does when (a) the neural network for dreaming outlined earlier in the chapter is at an adequate level of activation, (b) external stimuli are occluded, and (c) the self has been relinquished (Foulkes, 1999). This view accounts for dreaming at sleep onset, in REM sleep, and at times of sufficient activation during NREM (Antrobus, 2000b; Antrobus et al., 1995; Vogel,

1991). It also explains why dreaming sometimes occurs in awake participants who are resting quietly in a darkened sleep laboratory, where EEG recordings verify that the participants are in fact awake (Foulkes & Fleisher, 1975; Foulkes & Scott, 1973).

Once instigated, dreaming draws on memory schemata, general knowledge, and episodic memories to produce reasonable simulations of the real world (Antrobus, 1991; Foulkes, 1985, 1999), with due allowance for an occasional highly unusual or extremely memorable dream (Bulkeley, 1999; Hunt, 1989; Knudson & Minier, 1999; Kuiken & Sikora, 1993). Generally speaking, these simulations express the dreamer's "conceptions," which also are the basis for action in the waking world from the standpoint of cognitive theory. In particular, dreams express several key aspects of people's conceptual systems, especially conceptions of the self, family, and friends (Hall, 1953b).

The emphasis in the theory is on conceptions of "self" and "others" because studies of adult dream content show that dreams reflect relatively little about a person's attitudes toward current events and politics (Hall, 1951). Similarly, Foulkes (1982, 1999) found that children between ages 5 and 15 dreamed little of their two most time-consuming daytime activities: going to school and watching television. Instead, they dreamed about recreational activities. An emphasis on the highly personal nature of dreams may explain why the dreams of college students in the United States have not changed over the past 50 years; the culture has changed, but personal concerns probably remain stable. This emphasis also may explain why dreams are more similar than they are different around the world. As anthropologist Thomas Gregor (1981) suggested at the conclusion of his detailed study of 385 dream reports from men and women in a small native group deep in the Amazon jungle, "it may be possible to show that the dream experience is less variant than other aspects of culture" (p. 389).

Starting with the idea that dreams usually express highly personal conceptions, it is possible to build a complex picture of a dreamer's conceptual system because people usually have more than one conception of themselves and the important people in their lives. Moreover, these conceptions of self and others can be contradictory as well as numerous. Some of the apparent contradictions may disappear, however. For example, closer analysis may show that a parent is seen as supportive in some contexts, such as when facing exams or problems at work, but restrictive in others, such as when the dreamer wants to engage in sexual activities (Hall, 1947). It is possible that conceptual maps of the dreaming mind that are based on findings from content analyses could be expressed in network terms (e.g., Markman, 1999; Osgood, 1959).

In addition, it is possible that the use of conceptions is more diffuse during dreaming because the cognitive system is unconstrained by the requirements of the waking world (Foulkes, 1985). This hypothesis might help account for the repetitive nature of dream content related to significant people and interests. It is as though the "updated" versions of key concepts are no more likely to be used than the older ones.

This neurocognitive model also contains a way to assess the weight to be given to the conceptions expressed in dreams: by determining the relative frequency of their occurrence. Because findings with the Hall–Van de Castle system show that frequency reveals the intensity of a concern or interest, it can be said that dreams reveal both conceptions and concerns, and therefore have at least some degree of psychological meaning. This point further integrates the Hall–Van de Castle coding system with a neurocognitive model because not only do its categories relate to basic-level concepts, but its frequencies relate to conscious concerns.

Even though dreams seem to be based to a large extent on experiential-level categories, the emphasis in a neurocognitive model on the close parallels between waking thought and dreaming raises the possibility that some of the unusual and not immediately understandable features of dreams may be the product of figurative thinking—conceptual metaphors, metonymies, ironies, and conceptual blends (Fauconnier, 1997; Gibbs, 1994; Lakoff & Johnson, 1999). Figurative concepts are sometimes thought of as mere embellishments of speech that are not necessary for thinking, but following a wide range of experimental studies summarized by Gibbs (1994), many of which were carried out by him and his students, many cognitive scientists now see figurative concepts as an important part of people's conceptual system. The system of conceptual metaphors is learned anew by each person as a result of repeated experiences within the course of childhood development.

Lakoff and Johnson (1999) estimated that perhaps hundreds of "primary" conceptual metaphors "map" well-understood experiential categories (i.e., the *source domain*) to more complex or abstract matters of human concern (i.e., the *target domain*). For example, basic experiences like warmth and motion are used to understand more difficult concepts like "friendship" ("they have a warm relationship") and "time" (time often "goes by slowly," but sometimes "time flies by"). Just as in waking thought, figurative thinking may be used in dreams when it expresses a conception better and more succinctly than an experiential concept does (Hall, 1953a; Lakoff, 1997). This idea also provides a plausible explanation for why many different metaphoric expressions in dreams seem to exist for one "referent": Each metaphor provides a slightly different conception of the referent object.

One avenue into the possibility of a link between waking figurative thought and dream content might be found in typical dreams, such as flying under one's own power or finding oneself inappropriately dressed in public. A content analysis of 983 dream reports in 2-week journals kept by 126 students in a college course demonstrates that flying dreams accounted for only 0.5% of the total; the figures for other typical dreams—such as teeth falling out, falling in space, or finding money—are even lower (Domhoff, 1996, p. 198). However, several survey studies have suggested that at least a significant minority of respondents have had one or more of such dreams (Griffith, Miyago, & Tago, 1958; Nielsen, Zadra, Germain, & Montplaisir, 1999; Ward, Beck, & Rascoe, 1961). These infrequent dreams may be examples of "primary" metaphors, which are based on repeated correlations between two dimensions of experience that are common in childhood development. For example, tasting something sweet (a physiological process) and then experiencing pleasure (an emotion) lead to the metaphor that "pleasure is tasty" (Grady, 1999).

Consider dreams of flying under one's own power, which were reported by a little more than half of college students in two surveys and said by them to be generally positive in tone (Domhoff, 1996). Searching for a metaphor related to flying, the possibility arises that these dreams may be instances of the primary metaphor "happiness is up," as found in such expressions as "high as a kite," "walking on air," and "floating on cloud nine." This speculation could explain why people sometimes become apprehensive about falling during their positive flying dreams, just as people worry that they may "crash" or "have the air let out of their balloon" when they are too elated in waking life.

Similarly, it may be that dreams of appearing inappropriately dressed in public, which are reportedly experienced by 40% to 50% of college students, usually beginning in their midteens, and sometimes more than once, are instances of the conceptual metaphor "embarrassment is exposure" (Domhoff, 1996, p. 203). This metaphor is expressed through such well-known phrases as "caught red-handed," "caught with egg on your face," and "caught with your pants down" (Holland & Kipnis, 1994). It might be evidence for this conjecture that when college students are asked to write down the dream in which they experienced the greatest feeling of embarrassment, they most often spontaneously report one in which they are inadequately attired in a public place (Domhoff, 1996).

These two hypothetical examples aside, the few attempts to undertake systematic studies of metaphor in dreams suggest that most dreams do not seem to relate obviously to primary metaphors (Hall, 1953a). Rather, most dreams are like dramas or plays in which the dreamer acts out various scenarios that revolve around a few basic personal themes (Greenberg & Pearlman, 1993; Hall, 1947). Dreams seem to be instances of the "thematic" point on the repetition dimension, that is, specific episodes or examples relating to general emotional preoccupations, usually negative in nature. They appear to take the form of proverbs or parables, which can be understood only by extracting "generic" information from specific stories (Lakoff, 1993b; Lakoff & Turner, 1989).

These complex dreams may rely on "resemblance" metaphors, which depend on the perception of the common aspects in two representational schemata (Grady, 1999), or on conceptual blends, which often start with basic conceptual metaphors and then are elaborated into highly novel thoughts (Grady, Oakley, & Coulson, 1999). Hall (1953a) showed that blind analyses of a series of dreams can lead to plausible and potentially verifiable inferences when figurative forms of thought related to a major concern are used several times in the dream series. To take his best example, a young woman who provided a series of dreams had an especially striking one in which she is searching for her wedding gown because she and her husband are to be married again on their first wedding anniversary. However, she is disappointed when she found the gown: It is dirty and torn. With tears in her eyes, she puts the gown under her arm and goes to the church, only to have her husband ask why she has brought the gown. She reported that in the dream she is "confused and bewildered and felt strange and alone" (Hall, 1953a, p. 179).

Looking at the dream from a figurative point of view, Hall hypothesized that the state of the dress might express her conception of her marriage. In today's terms, the dream may be a conceptual blend that is based on a metonymy. To test this hypothesis, Hall looked to see if other dreams in the series might suggest that the marriage was in difficulty and found several: (a) the stone from her engagement ring is missing; (b) her husband has tuberculosis; (c) one of her women friends is going through a divorce; and (d) a friend who is about to be married receives a lot of useless bric-a-brac for wedding presents. If the Hall–Van de Castle system had been available when this analysis was made, the case could have been improved by comparing the dreamer's aggressions-per-character ratio with her husband to the same ratio with other men. If it had been higher with her husband than with other men, and if the dreamer had had a lower rate of friendly interactions as well, then the metaphoric hypothesis would have been supported by means of a nonmetaphoric content analysis.

Two later chapters in this volume provide methods that might aid in the search for figurative meaning in dream content. Chapter 4 suggests new ways to conduct empirical studies on metaphors in dreams through the use of sophisticated software to search for phrases and strings of words in large numbers of online dream reports. Chapter 5 presents findings with this method as one part of a study of 3,116 dreams from one person over a 20-year period. Because some of the findings presented there contradict the continuity principle, it may be that those findings involve dream elements that are figurative in nature. For example, the series contains instances of the dreamer riding horses or shooting guns well, but contrary to expectations, she does not ride or shoot in waking life and is fearful of both horses and guns.

The possibility that some dreams may be based on figurative thinking provides a way for a neurocognitive model to incorporate the interesting idea that past experiences are sometimes used as personal metaphors to express current conflicts that have similar emotions and feelings at their core (Kramer et al., 1987). This idea comes from a study of Vietnam veterans who had recovered from their posttraumatic stress disorder but returned to the Veterans Administration for help when war-related themes began to appear in their dreams in the face of new life stressors, such as marital conflict, conflicts with children, or work-related tensions. In effect, the new war-related dreams may have been conceptual blends that combined past experiences with aspects of the stressful situations the veterans were enduring. The resemblance is in the similarity of the feelings in both the war and the new situation. "It's a war zone out there," they might be thinking in relation to their current problems.

If dreaming is in part figurative, especially with regard to primary metaphors, resemblance metaphors, metonymies, and conceptual blends, then a neurocognitive model could advance in parallel with new understandings in cognitive linguistics. However, it still would be necessary to do the same kinds of thematic and Hall–Van de Castle content analyses to understand any given series of dreams, because many resemblance metaphors and most conceptual blends are likely to be unique to the dreamer. In addition, to the degree that dreams are like proverbs and parables, it remains necessary to study many dreams in searching for the "generic" or underlying pattern.

For now, it needs to be stressed that there is little or no systematic evidence that dreams make use of the vast system of figurative thought available to most people in waking life through a combination of developmental experiences and cultural heritage. Of all the possible connections among the three areas of dream research suggested in this chapter, the idea that studies of dream content may provide bridges to waking figurative thought is by far the most speculative. It is also an issue that divides dream theorists. For example, both Foulkes (1999, p. 110) and Hobson et al. (2000b), who disagree on many issues, are together in doubting that unusual constructions in dreams are meaningful. For Foulkes, dreams reveal the limited nature of the cognitive abilities possessed by the sleeping brain; for Hobson et al., dreams are often reflections of the unique neuromodulation of the neural network for dreaming, a form of delirium during sleep.

Even if it turns out that dreams make little or no use of figurative thought, a cognitive theory is useful in explaining why dreams hold great fascination for many people in many different cultures: Dreams seem to have parallels with waking figurative thought. The parallels with the metaphoric dimensions of waking thought may be why some societies have used dreams in their cultural practices and rituals. In that sense, dreams have "emergent" uses that have been developed in the course of history and passed on through culture. This view also explains the use of dreams in psychotherapy: Dream interpreters use metaphoric interpretations that are plausible to the client. It may be that dreams simply provide a platform from which the client and therapist, through a process of negotiation about metaphoric meanings, can develop a new narrative about the client's life. For the foreseeable future, then, metaphoric interpretations are the fool's gold of dream theories. With their glitter of seeming insight and the accompanying feelings of enrichment and closure, metaphoric interpretations deceive interpreters and dreamers alike.

The neurocognitive model described in this volume also can incorporate the unexpected finding that nightmares often can be eliminated by having people write out and visually rehearse a new ending of their own choosing for the dream (Krakow, Kellner, Pathak, & Lambert, 1995). This process may be an instance of the cognitive distancing that many people achieve by writing about personal feelings and events (Pennebaker & Graybeal, 2001; Pennebaker & Keough, 1999; Pennebaker & Seagal, 1999).

In closing this discussion of dreaming and cognition, it is worth mentioning that a new neurocognitive model might turn out to be useful in understanding the development of consciousness. Foulkes (1990a, 1999) offered this fresh idea in light of his cross-sectional study of children ages 5 to 8. If it is assumed that dreaming is the form that consciousness takes during sleep, then the origins of consciousness can be explored by conducting detailed studies of the development of the ability to dream. As one part of this general idea, Foulkes further suggested that the ability to include oneself in a dream, which is not fully developed until around age 8, may be an index of when a child has a full sense of self. He reached this conclusion after finding that three waking tests designed to assess the development of the "self" concept did not correlate with each other and did not predict the inclusion of the dreamer as a character in his or her dream reports (Foulkes, 1999, p. 95).

CONCLUSION

Other possible links may exist among the three areas of dream research discussed in this chapter. However, enough has been said to demonstrate that there is a large body of established empirical findings upon which to base a new model. Moreover, the research tools, such as the rapid advances in neuroimaging and neurochemistry, are now available to do the many studies that would be necessary to test and develop the model. As noted earlier, the growing number of neuropsychologists in clinical settings may be an important resource for developing this model, because they could easily screen for changes in dreaming as they examine people with lesions in relevant areas of the brain.

The advent of personal computers and the constant improvements in software are also important because they have made content analysis somewhat less labor intensive and far more accurate than it was in the past. These advances include a spreadsheet that calculates all the Hall–Van de Castle content indicators (Schneider & Domhoff, 1995) and is discussed in chapter 3. In addition, a new search program allows users to find single words, strings of words, or phrases in the more than 11,000 dream reports available on DreamBank.net (Schneider & Domhoff, 1999). This search program may prove especially useful for conducting the metaphoric studies that are necessary to determine the degree to which there are limits to the meaning in dreams. The use of DreamBank.net for new approaches to content analysis is demonstrated in chapter 4.

2

METHODOLOGICAL ISSUES IN
THE STUDY OF DREAM CONTENT

This chapter examines the major methodological issues that arise in the kind of scientific studies of dream content that would be necessary for the full elaboration of the neurocognitive model presented in chapter 1. Those issues include the degree to which dream reports actually reflect the dreaming experience, the usefulness of various methods of collecting dream reports, the representativeness of the people who provide dreams, the value of several different methods of dream analysis, and problems having to do with statistics and sample size. This chapter suggests that although many dream studies have used inadequate methods of dream collection and data analysis, sound methods exist for collecting representative samples of dream reports as well as analyzing dream content. These conclusions provide the basis for a detailed presentation of the Hall–Van de Castle coding system in chapter 3, and for the kinds of studies presented in chapters 4 and 5 that could be used in developing the model.

The study of dreams is a unique topic for psychological investigation for several reasons. First, as shown through the experimental studies discussed in chapter 1, it has not been possible to shape dreams to any appreciable extent by the application of external stimuli or the use of verbal instructions, a situation that makes the experimental method less useful than it usually is. Second, dreams cannot be observed by anyone but the dreamer while they are happening, so the observational methods so important to some realms of scientific endeavor are completely irrelevant. Third, dreams cannot be reported by dreamers while they are dreaming; it is therefore difficult to use the methods for studying subjective experiences under waking conditions, except after immediate awakenings (Fiss, 1983, 1991).

For all of these reasons, the dream experience is usually available to investigators only as a verbal or written report of a waking memory. The fleeting rare exceptions are mentioned in the next section. Thus, the study of dream content is generally two steps removed from the process of dreaming. This point inevitably raises questions concerning the degree to which dream reports faithfully represent the process of dreaming. Skeptics therefore sometimes claim that the dreams that are recalled are bound to be those that are particularly salient, a criticism that implies that samples are selective and unrepresentative. However, despite all these potential problems, evidence has indicated that dream reports provide a sound basis for understanding both the formal structure and content of dreaming, as discussed in the next section.

THE ACCURACY AND REPRESENTATIVENESS OF DREAM REPORTS

One of the most curious and least understood facts about dreams is how few of them are recalled in everyday life compared with the recall rate of 80% to 90% for normative samples of young adults when awakened in the sleep laboratory. The rival neurophysiological and cognitive explanations for this lack of recall are discussed briefly in chapter 6. For purposes of this chapter, however, there is a more immediate and tractable question: Are the few dreams that people recall a representative sample of their dream life?

Because of the inaccessibility of dreaming to outside observers, any argument for the accuracy of dream reports must begin with evidence that a phenomenon exists (i.e., dreaming) that the dream report describes. It then has to demonstrate that at least some dream reports—that is, those collected in sleep laboratories from night awakenings—are accurate reflections of dreaming. Next, it needs to show that the dream reports that seem most questionable—those written down at home or collected with a standard form in a group setting—are enough like laboratory reports to be regarded as useful.

The fact of dreaming would seem to be well established by findings in sleep laboratories since the early 1950s, but skeptics can note that even after all of those studies, the self-report evidence is consistent with the possibility that dreaming happens during the process of awakening or of telling the dream. Eye movements and a unique brain wave pattern are not the same thing as dreaming. Ultimately, no definitive way may establish the fact of dreaming beyond the ubiquity of this subjective experience, but two unusual phenomena go a good part of the way in dealing with this issue: sleep talking and REM sleep-behavior disorder. Careful studies of a large number of sleep-talking episodes show that those that happen in REM are consistent with what the dreamer reports after an immediate awakening (Arkin, 1981). This finding provides objective evidence corroborating what the sleep talker then reports. More dramatically, the actions that occur during episodes of REM sleep-behavior disorder are often found to fit the actions that patients report when they are awakened (Mahowald & Schenck, 2000). These rare exceptions to the inaccessibility of dreaming to third-person observation provide independent evidence that dream reports can be accurate, at least when the reports occur shortly after the dream experience.

Even if the fact of dreaming is granted, it remains the case that self-report data are notoriously unreliable on everything from voting to church attendance to eating habits. They are often based on impression management and cultural stereotypes. It is therefore important to show that dream reports are not typical self-report data. People do not feel responsible for their dreams, so they have no reason to withhold information or distort their reports (Foulkes, 1979; Hall & Van de Castle, 1966). They tend to experience dreams as something that happens to them, not as something for which they are personally responsible. Many people are therefore willing to volunteer their dreams if asked. The willingness of people to report accurately is increased when their reports are anonymous, as they are for most of the group studies cited in this book. In addition, people have no reason to distort dreams written in a personal dream journal not originally meant for later researchers.

The atypical nature of dream reports when compared to other types of self-reports is demonstrated empirically by comparing them with what people claim they dream about in response to questionnaires, where they provide culturally stereotypic distortions. Four different samples of college students were asked about the frequency with which they dreamed about aggressive, friendly, and sexual interactions; they then wrote down five dreams over a 2-week period. In response to the questionnaire, they claimed that they dream most frequently of friendly interactions, then sexual interactions, followed by aggressive interactions. The actual order in the dreams they later turned in to the investigators and in all other carefully analyzed samples was (1) aggressive interactions, (2) friendly interactions, and (3) sexual interactions (Bernstein & Belicki, 1995). Thus, the rank-order correlation between expressed opinions and a content analysis of social interactions is negative. These findings show that self-reports on dream content are worthless at best and often misleading. Even more important, they suggest that a descriptive report of a dream experience is not a typical form of self-report information: The dream experience is so direct, immediate, and compelling that a report on it is not likely to be distorted by filtering it through cultural beliefs. This point is especially strong for awakenings in the sleep laboratory while the person is in the process of dreaming.

As noted briefly in chapter 1, several different studies of dream content in the laboratory provide a consistent picture of dream content as being more mundane and coherent than standard cultural stereotypes, although dreams have some unusual aspects as well (Cavallero & Foulkes, 1993; Foulkes, 1985; Meier, 1993; Snyder, 1970; Strauch & Meier, 1996). Other laboratory studies show that dream content does not differ from early to late REM periods (Dement & Wolpert, 1958a; Domhoff & Kamiya, 1964b;

Foulkes, 1966; Hall, 1966b; Strauch & Meier, 1996; Trosman, Rechtschaffen, Offenkrantz, & Wolpert, 1960), even though REM periods become longer and more intense throughout the night (Antrobus et al., 1995). One study of five participants did find one difference among the many comparisons it made between early and later REM periods: a greater number of references to the past in later REM periods (Verdone, 1965). However, that finding was not replicated in a larger study with 11 participants over a greater number of nights (Hall, 1966b). The findings on the consistency of dream content throughout the night are important because they show that any bias toward late-night dreams in a sample of dream reports does not produce a biased sample of dream content.

Studies in the laboratory comparing dreams reported after nighttime awakenings with those that are still remembered in the morning provide a way of assessing the saliency issue in dream samples. Such studies are not a complete simulation of dream recall at home because a "priming" has occurred as a result of the night reports, but they provide a close approximation (Baekland & Lasky, 1968; Meier, Ruef, Zeigler, & Hall, 1968; Strauch, 1969; Trinder & Kramer, 1971). These studies first show that much dream recall comes from dreams late in a sleep period, as has also been found in studies of participants asked to keep dream diaries at home or leave reports on a telephone answering machine (Belicki, 1987; Domhoff, 1969). This finding is important because it shows that recency, not saliency, is the most important factor in dream recall. Moreover, these studies also demonstrate that the duration of a dream, as indexed by the length of the report given at the night awakening, is an important predictor of morning dream recall. Finally, these studies provide evidence that the emotional intensity of the dream content also can affect recall.

In the most sustained of these studies, Meier et al. (1968) compared the night and morning recall of a man who was awakened at the end of every REM period for 45 nights. Of the 138 dreams he reported when awakened, he recalled 88 in the morning. Dreams from the last 105 minutes of the sleep period were recalled 83% of the time in the morning, compared with 63%, 55%, and 54% for the three preceding 105-minute periods. Long dream reports were recalled 87% of the time, compared with 48% recall for short reports. Dream reports judged as more emotionally intense by the dreamer and an independent rater were recalled 83% of the time, compared with 56% for those judged less intense. An analysis of the interactions among these three variables found that recency can compensate for both shortness of reports and low intensity and that length can compensate for low intensity. These results strongly suggest that recency and duration lead to many everyday dream reports that are not unusually high in saliency. Because it already has been shown that dream content does not change throughout the night, it therefore follows that recency and duration are providing a more representative sample of dreams than an exclusive emphasis on saliency would suggest.

The findings presented in the previous paragraphs establish that dream reports collected in the sleep laboratory provide a reasonably representative sample of dream life. Within this context, studies that directly compare dreams reported after laboratory awakenings with dreams written down at home by the same participants provide a good basis for judging the representativeness of everyday dream recall. Although one early study claimed there were some differences between what came to be called "lab" and "home" dreams (Domhoff & Kamiya, 1964a), primarily on indicators of aggression, five later studies introducing controls for methods of reporting and other confounds suggested no important differences (Foulkes, 1979; Heynick & deJong, 1985; Strauch & Meier, 1996; Weisz & Foulkes, 1970; Zepelin, 1972).

The most comprehensive comparison of dream content inside and outside the sleep laboratory was carried out by Hall (1966a) as one part of a study concerning the many potential problems that might affect the accuracy and representativeness of dream reports. The results from this study are worth recounting in detail because they make the best possible case that everyday dream recall can provide a good sample of dream life. The study was conducted in a large house in a quiet residential neighborhood, where the 11 young adult male participants between ages 19 and 25 could have their own sleeping quarters for a month and report dreams in the least threatening atmosphere possible, thereby minimizing any inhibitory effects from the usual laboratory setting in a science or medical building. A total of 414 planned awakenings took place.

Because the aim of the study was to determine the conditions that led to the most representative sample of dream reports, seven adjustment nights were provided before the formal collection of reports began. The time it took the participants to fall asleep was noted. In a carefully balanced design, only one awakening occurred on some nights, and multiple awakenings occurred on others. Dreams were collected by means of tape-recorded reports from the first four REM periods of the night under both the single-awakening and the multiple-awakening schedules. Participants were asked after each awakening to estimate how long they had been dreaming. They also were asked to rate the clarity of their recall, the vividness of the dream, the emotional intensity of the dream, and whether the dream took place in the past or present. Unplanned "spontaneous" awakenings were noted, and any dream reports from them were transcribed for comparison with dream reports from scheduled awakenings. Finally, participants wrote down any dreams they remembered at home for a 2-week period. Some wrote their dream reports before their stay in the laboratory, some before and during their stay, and some during and after their stay. The goal was to have at least 15 dreams written down at home by each person, but one participant wrote down only 11 and another did not write down any.

Participants had little difficulty adjusting to the laboratory situation. Beginning with the first night that the EEG machine was turned on, which was the third adjustment night, it took them no longer to fall asleep than it did on later nights (Hall, 1966b, p. 38). Then, too, the small percentage of dream reports that included allusions to the experimental situation (7.2% to 13.5%) did not vary from the fourth adjustment night, when they were first awakened to report a dream, to the end of their laboratory visits (Hall, 1966b, p. 32). This range is much lower and narrower than the 20% to 30% reported in previous studies (Dement, Kahn, & Roffwarg, 1965; Domhoff & Kamiya, 1964a; Whitman, Pierce, Maas, & Baldridge, 1962). Contrary to expectations, which were based on a study by Dement and Kleitman (1957b) that reported that five participants could correctly distinguish between awakenings after 5 or 15 minutes of REM dreaming, no correlation was found between the amount of REM time before an awakening and participants' estimates of how long they had been dreaming (Hall, 1966b, pp. 10–11, 38–39).

The most important result from the comparisons of dream reports collected in different ways within the laboratory was their general similarity, whether from single or multiple awakenings, or early or late REM periods, on the several Hall–Van de Castle categories that were used. Moreover, the results for the rating scales responded to by the dreamers at the time of awakening were similar in showing no differences, except that participants reported better recall and greater clarity for each successive awakening on nights when there were multiple awakenings, a finding that could be the result of a practice effect. In addition, the 57 dream reports from participants who had spontaneous awakenings did not differ from those collected on their single-awakening nights (Hall, 1966b, pp. 25–26). These results replicate and extend studies showing that it is possible to collect a representative sample of a person's dream life in the sleep laboratory.

Several differences were found between laboratory and home dream reports on 26 comparisons for each participant using the nonparametric Wilcoxon matched pairs, signed-rank test. Most of the statistically significant differences concerned the larger number of aggressions and misfortunes in home dream reports. At the same time, home and laboratory dreams had few differences in types of characters and no differences in the percentage of dreams with at least one "bizarre" (i.e., unusual) element. The finding on bizarre elements does not support a finding of more such elements in laboratory dream reports in the study by Domhoff and Kamiya (1964a). A later study by Hunt, Ogilvie, Belicki, Belicki, and Atalick (1982) also reported no differences in bizarreness between home and laboratory dream reports.

The nature of the differences between dream reports under the two conditions was summarized by findings with what Hall termed the *dramatic intensity index*, which he calculated by adding together all aggressions, friendly interactions, sexual activities, successes, failures, good fortunes, and misfortunes. This index showed consistent differences between reports written at home and laboratory dreams collected through either single or multiple awakenings for both early and late REM periods (Hall, 1966b). This finding provides support for the claim that there is a saliency bias in home dream samples. However, a reanalysis of the original codings revealed that most of the variance in this index was provided by aggressive elements and that the overall picture is very different when effect sizes are considered (Domhoff & Schneider, 1999).

The reanalysis of the Hall and Van de Castle data was based on eight young men who provided at least 15 home dreams and at least 34 laboratory dreams. When more than 15 home dream reports were provided, the first 15 were used. When more than 34 laboratory dream reports were available, reports from adjustment nights and spontaneous awakenings were eliminated first, and then an equal number of single-awakening and multiple-awakening reports were removed from the sample if additional reports had to be discarded. The result was a group sample of 120 dream reports written down at home and 272 dream reports transcribed from tape-recorded reports in the laboratory.

Three of the four statistically significant differences found in the reanalysis involved aggression. The home dream reports contained a higher percentage of dreams with at least one incident of aggression; a higher rate of aggressions per character; and a higher percentage of aggressions that were physical in nature, as defined by destruction of personal property, chases, physical attacks, and murders. On the basis of an effect-size statistic explained in chapter 3, the effect sizes were small even when the differences were statistically significant, except in the case of the physical aggression percentage, which showed a large difference. Because the number of dreams involved in this analysis is large, especially compared with most published dream studies, it is likely that the findings on effect size are accurate.

The higher frequency of aggression in home dream reports supports the concern that there is some selective recall in everyday dream reports. Even here, however, it is noteworthy that 44% of the dreams did not contain any form of aggression, whether physical or nonphysical, and 72% were without any physical aggression. These findings are fairly similar to those obtained with a normative sample of young men (see chapter 3), in which 53% of the reports had no form of aggression and 74% had no physical aggression. Moreover, only 10% of the home and laboratory reports in the Hall study had a bizarre element, which is lower than what might be expected if only atypical content is recalled. If dream reports have a strong bias for atypical elements, then it also might be predicted that a large number of sexual dreams would be reported, but only 9% of the home reports in the Hall study contained so much as a sensual hug or kiss, compared with 5% of the laboratory reports. A reference to sexual intercourse occurred in only 2.5% of the home reports and 0.7% of the laboratory reports; the former number is not that different from the figure of 3.4% in the Hall–Van de Castle male normative sample described in chapter 3.

The fact that the most consistent differences between laboratory and home dream reports relate to aggression fits with findings on the variability of aggression in conjunction with several other factors. First, the difference in aggression between the early teens and young adulthood is the largest difference between the two age groups (Avila-White, Schneider, & Domhoff, 1999). Second, a decline in aggression may occur in old age (Hall & Domhoff, 1963b; Zepelin, 1980), although some results from longitudinal studies make this cross-sectional finding less certain (Domhoff, 1996, chapter 7). Third, large variations exist from culture to culture in aggression (Domhoff, 1996, chapter 6). Fourth, large individual and gender differences have been found on some measures of aggression in dreams (Domhoff, 1996, chapter 8; Hall & Domhoff, 1963b; Paolino, 1964). In short, these findings suggest that variations in aggression could be valuable in developing a neurocognitive model because aggression might be especially sensitive to drug effects or lesions in one or another part of the neural network for dreaming.

In light of the several different arguments and laboratory studies presented in this section, it seems safe to conclude that the dreams people recall in the laboratory and at home are, in fact, a reasonably representative sample of dream life. If reports obtained immediately after awakenings in the sleep laboratory are taken as an excellent starting point for assessing the adequacy of home dream reports, then the saliency claim is limited to the tendency for greater aggression in home dream reports.

METHODS FOR COLLECTING DREAM REPORTS

The arguments and evidence presented in the previous section do not mean that all methods for collecting dreams are equally useful. Strengths and weaknesses are connected with each of the five main methods. Three are generally quite useful: awakenings in the sleep laboratory; anonymous written reports collected in group settings; and personal dream journals kept over the space of months, years, or decades. The remaining two—dream diaries kept at home for a week or two at the request of investigators and dreams collected in the psychotherapy relationship—have serious weaknesses.

Sleep Laboratory Awakenings

Sleep laboratories are the best source of dream reports because they provide the opportunity for collecting large representative samples of people's dreams under controlled conditions (Foulkes, 1966, 1985). Awakenings during REM or from Stage II NREM late in the sleep period maximize the probability of recall and make it possible to collect as many as four or five dreams in a single night (Antrobus et al., 1995; Fosse, Stickgold, & Hobson, 2001; Foulkes, 1979). However, there are some problems with this method. The main problem is that it is a costly and time-consuming process. Laboratories are expensive to equip and staff, and participants have to be paid. The sleep laboratory has been especially difficult to use in the United States since the 1970s because of the decline in outside funding for dream research (Foulkes, 1996a).

Even though several dreams can be collected each night, it still can take many months to obtain 10 or more dreams from each of a dozen participants. In addition, frequent awakenings can be taxing for participants, who often resist full awakenings and complete reporting. Moreover, staying up most of the night several times a week can be onerous for investigators.

Most Recent Dream Method

The most objective and structured context for the efficient and inexpensive collection of dream reports outside the sleep laboratory is a group setting in which reports can be written on a standardized form by anonymous participants, who reveal only basic background information such as age and gender. Pioneered by Hartmann, Elkin, and Garg (1991), the "most recent dream" method provides a way to collect dreams from people in classrooms and waiting rooms in many different regions or countries in the space of 15 to 20 minutes for adults and 20 to 30 minutes for teenagers and preadolescent children (Avila-White et al., 1999; Domhoff, 1996).

The main drawback of this method is that the available time does not usually permit collection of any personality or cognitive measures on the people providing the reports. In studying children, serious problems remain with determining the age at which researchers can be confident in the authenticity of the dream reports. When the frequencies for "creatures," video game characters, and physical aggressions in these reports are compared with findings from laboratory reports from children of the same age, there is reason to believe that young children up to at least age 10 are using their waking imaginations to provide a report that fits cultural stereotypes about the nature of dreams. This problem may be especially great with boys. At this point, the method cannot be recommended for use with children below the sixth grade (Saline, 1999).

The standardized Hall–Van de Castle form on which the most recent dreams are collected begins by simply asking the respondents to "write down the most recent dream" they can remember, "whether it was last night, last week, or last month" (Domhoff, 1996, p. 67). To reinforce the emphasis on the last dream recalled and to make it possible to eliminate dreams from months or years in the past if the researchers so desire, participants are also asked to write down the date on which they think the dream occurred. The instructions then explain what the report should include, using language developed by Hall (1951, 1953c) for collecting dreams from college students.

The usefulness of the method with adequate sample sizes has been demonstrated most directly by comparing the results from Avila-White, Schneider, and Domhoff's (1999) most recent dream study of 12- to 13-year-old girls and boys with the findings for the same age group in two longitudinal studies in the sleep laboratory (Foulkes, 1982; Strauch & Lederbogen, 1999). Where direct comparisons were possible, there were many similarities. The method also receives support because most recent dream samples collected from college students match the findings from a large-scale normative study discussed in the next chapter (Domhoff, 1996).

Personal Dream Journals

Dream journals, which are called "dream series" in the research literature, are an underused source of dream reports, even though they are a form of "personal document" long recognized in psychology as having the potential to provide insights into personality and cognitive styles (Allport, 1942; Baldwin, 1942; Smith, 2000). Nonreactive archival sources, such as dream journals, have the advantage of not being influenced by the purposes of the investigators who analyze them. Generalizations that are based on nonreactive archival data are considered most impressive when they derive from a diversity of archives likely to have different types of possible bias (Webb, Campbell, Schwartz, Sechrest, & Grove, 1981). As summarized in chapter 1, dream journals kept for different reasons lead to the finding of great consistency in dream content over time

For all their potential usefulness, however, dream journals are not without their drawbacks. Even after showing initial willingness, some people may not want to provide all of their dreams for scientific scrutiny. Journals may have unexpected gaps or omissions. Care must be taken to ensure that they are authentic. Journals from dream popularizers who have made enthusiastic claims about their dreams probably should be avoided, as should dream journals posted on the Internet by individuals. Thus, personal dream journals are best used selectively.

In future studies using dream journals, it might be worthwhile to collect a laboratory sample of dreams from the person as well or to collect dreams at home through systematic awakenings using a sleep monitoring device called "the Nightcap," which is a small portable unit that detects eyelid and head movements using separate movement sensors. The sensors can be attached to a headband or taped directly to the forehead. Signals are sent to a small, portable bedside unit weighing less than 5 pounds. The information it stores can be sent to a personal computer and used to perform awakenings in REM or NREM with high levels of accuracy (Ajilore, Stickgold, Rittenhouse, & Hobson, 1995; Stickgold, Pace-Schott, & Hobson, 1994).

The use of dream series for the study of dreams was introduced into the clinical research tradition by Wilhelm Stekel (1911) and Havelock Ellis (Ellis, 1928). The most influential early analysis of a dream series was published in 1935 by Jung to demonstrate the search for personal integration and wholeness in 74 dreams from a natural scientist suffering from depression and drinking problems. This dream diarist was subsequently revealed to be Wolfgang Pauli, one of the most brilliant physicists of the 20th century and the winner of a Nobel Prize in 1946 (Lindorff, 1995; Zabriskie, 1995). Some of these dreams are available in books on Pauli (Meier, 1992; von Meyenn, 1993); many others are in Pauli's unedited correspondence with Marie-Louise von Franz, which is stored in the Pauli Archives at the ETH-Bibliothek in Zurich, Switzerland. A Hall–Van de Castle content analysis of this unique series might be worthwhile once it is possible to assemble all the pieces in one place.

Jung's original analysis of the Pauli series was expanded in 1944 to include 400 dreams (Jung, 1974; Lindorff, 1995). Although the primary emphasis is on how symbols for psychological wholeness relate to religious themes and the practice of alchemy in the Middle Ages, a footnote at the end contains the results of a quantitative analysis in which the 400 dreams are divided into eight groups of 50. It claims that the occurrence of the "mandala motif" (i.e., the symbolic expression of the search for wholeness) increases from a range of 2 to 9 per 50 dreams in the first four sets to 11 to 17 in the second four sets (Jung, 1974, p. 296).

Dream series kept for personal, artistic, or intellectual reasons have been the basis of the most systematic studies. For example, Smith and Hall (1964) used a journal kept on and off for 50 years for personal interest to show that the dreamer did not dream more of the past when she was in her 70s than she did when she was under 40. Her journal also showed a consistency over many decades in several themes that are spelled out later in this chapter. The dreams are now available on http://www.DreamBank.net under the pseudonym "Dorothea."

Chapters 4 and 5 provide new evidence for the potential of this source of useful data when it is combined with rigorous methods of content analysis.

Brief Dream Diaries

The most frequently used method of collecting dreams outside the laboratory is to ask participants, usually high school or college students, to keep a dream diary for a period of 1 or 2 weeks or until they have written down a prescribed number of dreams. The method has the advantage of being easy and inexpensive. It has led to some useful collections of dream reports from gifted girls ages 8 to 13 (Latta, 1998), conscientious volunteer college students (Hall, 1947, 1953c; Tonay, 1990/1991), and blind men and women (Hurovitz et al., 1999), most of which are now available on DreamBank.net. It reaches its highest and most useful level when the diary is based on dreams collected during the night with the aid of the Nightcap for monitoring sleep at home (Fosse et al., 2001; Stickgold et al., 1994).

When used without the aid of the Nightcap, this method has many drawbacks and often leads to highly inadequate samples. First, it can take weeks or months to obtain even four dreams, as seen in a study of gender differences by Bursik (1998), in which it took 4 months to obtain four dreams from 40 men and 40 women in one of her undergraduate psychology classes, and in studies by Lortie-Lussier and co-workers, in which it usually took several weeks to obtain a minimum of two dreams from the adult women and men in their studies (Cote et al., 1996; Lortie-Lussier, Schwab, & de Koninck, 1985).

Second, a large minority of participants drop out or turn in only one or two dreams, leading to questions about the representativeness of those who do turn in dreams. For example, both Buckley (1970) and Howard (1978) reported difficulties in obtaining completed dream diaries from their teenage volunteers, especially from boys. In a study of teenagers' dreams, Winegar and Levin (1997) had only 182 initial volunteers out of the 550 students in the classrooms they visited. Then, only 115 of those 182 turned in at least two dreams of 35 words or more, which is a minimum report length. By contrast, dream reports collected from teenagers in laboratories and classrooms are usually between 100 and 300 words in length (Avila-White et al., 1999; Foulkes, 1982; Strauch & Lederbogen, 1999).

Samples often consist of different numbers of reports from each participant, a situation that raises questions about how to standardize the contribution of each participant to the total sample. Solutions to this problem that draw only one or two dreams from each dream diary unnecessarily waste data and lead to such small sample sizes that any differences that might exist cannot be detected. Finally, the demand characteristics of a dream-diary study can be extremely strong, especially when researchers have to prod unmotivated participants one or more times to write down their dreams. Such pressures increase the probability of hasty or confabulated reports. In a survey of several hundred students in a psychology class at the University of California, Berkeley, most of whom had chosen not to voluntarily keep a dream diary for 2 weeks, 43% said that they would be likely to make up dreams if required to turn in dream reports as part of a course assignment (Tonay, 1990/1991). This is one of several problems in a flawed study of gender differences in dreams by Bursik (1998), which is critiqued by Domhoff (1999b).

The Psychotherapy Setting

Work with clients by Freud, Jung, and their many co-workers was a major source of dream reports for the analysis of dreams in the first half of the 20th century. Such reports have the virtue of rich accompanying biographical and fantasy materials, and they can be analyzed in great detail as part of the person's psychotherapy. For all their usefulness in the past as a source of hypotheses concerning dream meaning, the nature of the thera- peutic relationship burdens them with serious drawbacks for systematic studies.

Because the primary focus of psychotherapy is on people and their problems, not on dreams, the actual report of the dream may be transformed in the process of discussing it or not written down in full detail by the therapist until after the session or later in the day. Moreover, the dreams reported by clients tend to focus on the issues in the forefront of the therapeutic relationship, as shown in a study comparing dreams reported during awakenings in a sleep laboratory and those told to the participants' psychotherapist (Whitman, Kramer, & Baldridge, 1963). As a result, the full range of the clients' dream life is not covered, leading to an unrepresentative sample. Then, too, the dreams analyzed in published case studies are not usually presented in full detail, meaning that later use of them is impossible without contacting the therapists, who are often concerned about protecting the privacy of their clients. Most damaging of all, the demand characteristics of a psychotherapy relationship are far greater than those of an experimental setting, a point that is elaborated later in this chapter in a discussion of free association as a method for analyzing dream content.

In summary, when the advantages and disadvantages of the various methods of obtaining dream reports are weighed, it seems that most recent dreams and dream journals provide the best currently available sources. The most recent dream method is more structured, standardized, and faster than the dream diary method, making it possible to obtain dreams from more members of a group than does the dream diary approach. The use of individual dream journals enables the study of a larger number of dreams than otherwise would be feasible. It also provides a more representative sample of a person's dream life than the dreams obtained from a person in psychotherapy.

THE REPRESENTATIVENESS OF DREAM RECALLERS

There are many people who do not recall even one dream a week and therefore are less likely to contribute dream reports, regardless of the method of collection. Is it then possible to generalize about dream content on the basis of those people who are able and willing to provide dream reports? For personality variables, the answer has been inadvertently provided by a large number of studies stretching over several decades. The studies attempted to find personality differences between those who recall dreams and those who do not, as determined by responses to a simple questionnaire or the total number of dreams entered into a 2-week dream diary.

The most important finding from the studies, which used a wide range of personality tests, is that no consistent differences exist between recallers and nonrecallers (Domhoff, 1996, chapter 3): On the personality dimensions that psychologists can measure, study participants who contributed dreams were similar to those who did not (Berrien, 1933; Cohen, 1979; Domhoff & Gerson, 1967; Farley, Schmuller, & Fischbach, 1971; Stickel, 1956; Tonay, 1993; Trinder & Kramer, 1971). Cohen (1979), who conducted several excellent studies on this question, provided a good summary of the literature when he concluded: "Correlations between dream recall frequency and specific personality measures have been weak, trivial, or inconsistent" (p. 161). Based on their own findings 21 years after Cohen wrote, along with a review of the more recent literature, Blagrove and Akehurst (2000) reached the same general conclusion.

On the other hand, cognitive variables seem to have a slightly greater correlation with dream recall than do personality variables (Cohen, 1979; Cory, Ormiston, Simmel, & Dainoff, 1975; Fitch & Armitage, 1989; Hartmann et al., 1991; Hiscock & Cohen, 1973; Martinelli, 1983). This is especially the case for visuospatial ability, which was investigated in adults who had little or no dream recall by Butler and Watson (1985) as a follow-up to the developmental findings by Foulkes (1982) discussed in chapter 1.

Physiological factors unrelated to personality or cognitive variables also seem to play a part in making some people less able to recall their dreams, as seen in a study showing that some low recallers have high waking thresholds and are difficult to arouse in a sleep laboratory (Zimmerman, 1970). Recall frequencies also vary with mood and stress levels (Armitage, 1992; Cohen, 1979). Still, none of the various factors mentioned up to this point seems as important as an interest in dreams (Cohen & Wolfe, 1973;

Strauch, 1969), a finding that does not correlate with personality variables (Tonay, 1993) and is supported by the fact that less variation in recall usually occurs among adult participants who are studied in sleep laboratories.

Generally speaking, then, there seems to be no one reason why some people do not recall dreams with any degree of regularity (Schredl & Montasser, 1996, 1997). Goodenough's (1991) assessment of this literature summarizes the issue well: "People apparently may be non-reporters for a variety of distinctly different reasons" (p. 157). It therefore follows that a representative sample of people is able to contribute to studies of dream content. That is, for purposes of group comparisons, dream recallers provide diverse and representative samples on personality and cognitive factors if an adequate sample is available. As demonstrated in chapter 3, "adequate sample size" means at least 125 dream reports per sample because many of the elements in dreams appear in half or less of all dream reports.

These findings have another implication as well: They suggest that for purposes of studying the relationship between dream content and waking cognition outside the laboratory, it might make sense to focus on people who are good dream recallers. This atypical strategy gains plausibility within the context of the many general findings on dream content that are presented in a previous study (Domhoff, 1996) and throughout this book. A research methodology for using unique participants with good recall skills is presented and demonstrated in chapter 5.

METHODS FOR ANALYZING DREAM CONTENT

Once dream reports have been collected, four methods may be used to analyze dream content. The methods range from the subjective to the objective, and vary in the number of dreams with which they may be used. As is the case with collecting dreams, each method of analysis has strengths and weaknesses. In the present stage of dream research, however, the relatively objective and quantitative methods seem to have the greatest potential for testing hypotheses originally developed on the basis of individualistic and subjective methods. In the order of their appearance in the dream literature, the methods are (a) free association, which led Freud (1900) to the conclusions on which he built his wish-fulfillment theory of dreams; (b) symbolic interpretation, which was one basis for Jung's (1963) break with Freud and the development of his own theory; (c) thematic analysis of dream journals, which involves a search for repeated topics, activities, or events; and (d) content analysis, which involves the construction of rating scales or nominal categories to study large numbers of dreams from either groups or individuals.

Free Association

The free-association method consists of instructing dreamers to say whatever comes into their minds about each element of the dream without any censoring of their thoughts. A chain of free associations can be long and can lead to seemingly unrelated topics. Once the free associations are obtained for all parts of the dream, they are organized to infer the underlying motives for the dream itself (the *latent content*, in Freud's terms). Although used primarily by Freudians, the method can be used by non-Freudians because it often reveals the day-to-day events incorporated into the dream and the emotional concerns of the dreamer (Cipolli & Poli, 1992).

The free association method for systematic research has major problems. Most generally, it is impossible to be sure within a psychotherapy setting whether the free associations actually explain the dream, because so much else is known about the dreamer that could be playing a role in constructing a "meaning" for the dream. Even more seriously—and despite claims by psychotherapists that they maintain a neutral and nonjudgmental stance—it is difficult to rule out an alternative analysis of dream interpretation developed by social psychologists and memory researchers. The basic idea is that therapists unknowingly shape their clients' associations through complex processes of suggestion, persuasion, and conversion.

The social psychology of the psychotherapy relationship begins with the client's desire for help and a great respect for the expertise of the therapist. In that context, a dream interpretation by the therapist that comes as a surprise or seems unlikely to the client leads him or her into a state of uncertainty and cognitive dissonance. Gradually, however, the client comes to agree with the therapist about the meaning of the dream through the tendency to obey authority figures and a desire to reduce cognitive dissonance (Loftus & Ketcham, 1994; Ofshe & Watters, 1994). This sequence of events is reinforced if details in later dream reports provide an occasion for resolving the cognitive dissonance. Because dreams are generally thought to be beyond the reach of suggestion, such confirmatory dreams can play a powerful role in a conversion process.

As a result of this sequence of events, the person takes on a new identity as "a client of a famous therapist" or as a member of "an exclusive school of thought." In effect, the person is "cured" by taking on a new identity that includes an in-group language for understanding the world, attendance at events with fellow converts, and even becoming a practitioner of the therapy. In other words, the explanation developed by social and cognitive psychologists for why dream analysis and hypnosis can lead to "recovered memories" and "believed-in imaginings" is applicable to the interpretation of dreams within the psychotherapy process (Ayella, 1998; de Rivera & Sarbin, 1998). Moreover, experimental evidence from simulated dream interpretations supports this interpretation of what can happen in psychotherapy. In those studies, a clinical psychologist convinced many participants that they had the experience of being lost before age 3 (Mazzoni & Loftus, 1998; Mazzoni, Loftus, Seitz, & Lynn, 1999). Until clinical theorists can answer the foregoing analysis and evidence by showing that suggestion is not operating in dream interpretation, the usefulness of free association as an objective method for understanding dreams in psychotherapy remains in question.

The usefulness of free association outside of psychotherapy also is in doubt. Foulkes's (1978) extensive effort to use the method as a research tool with dreams collected in the laboratory did not prove to be successful in creating a "grammar of dreams." Instead, Foulkes (1996a) later wrote that "extensive experience in association gathering" convinced him of the "inherent arbitrariness" of the method (p. 617). For example, a dreamer's free associations would fail to mention direct, real-life parallels to the dream that were known independently to the person collecting the free associations. Moreover, two studies published 35 years apart were unsuccessful in establishing the incremental validity of free associations in blind analyses of dream series containing 15 to 25 dreams. Both studies found that the analysts who had free associations along with the dream series made no more correct inferences than did those who only had the dream series (Popp, Luborsky, & Crits-Christoph, 1992; Reis, 1959). Thus, it seems unlikely that free associations can be considered a useful tool for systematic analyses of dream content outside the clinical situation. The method proved arbitrary in one study and superfluous in two others.

Metaphoric Analysis

"Symbolic" interpretations are used as a supplement to free associations in psychotherapy settings and in some studies of long-term dream journals. They are the essence of Jung's (1974) "amplification" method (see also Mattoon, 1978). This method differs from free association in that both the dreamer and the dream interpreter produce a wide range of images and associations directly related to the dream. They do so by returning to the dream after each new thought or image, rather than having one association lead to the next. In light of the work of Hall (1953a), Lakoff (1993a, 1997), and States (1987), it seems clear that these symbolic interpretations are now more appropriately thought of as metaphoric analyses.

In fact, it can be argued that the rival clinical schools of symbolic interpretation are particular applications of common metaphoric understandings to aspects of dreams, as the work of the neo-Freudian Erich Fromm (1949, 1951) demonstrates. Even the analyses made by phenomenological and existential theorists, such as Boss (1958, 1977) and Perls (Downing &

Marmorstein, 1973), who claim to reject symbolic interpretations, are actually metaphoric glosses of dreams, as can be seen by reading through their case examples.

There are several problems with metaphoric analyses, starting with a fact mentioned in chapter 1: No systematic evidence indicates whether dreams are metaphoric in nature. Even if some aspects of dream content are metaphoric, no guidelines exist as to which of many possible conceptual metaphors should be applied. Although Hall (1953a) argued that the repetition of elements in a dream series can lead to plausible evidence for applying one or another conceptual metaphor, and he provided some rough guidelines for identifying possible metaphors in dreams, metaphoric analysis as a rigorous and systematic approach remains undeveloped.

Thematic Analysis

The third method of dream analysis, the thematic method, shades off from metaphoric analysis. It involves reading through a dream series several times to see if certain settings, objects, or events appear several times. The various possibilities are seen as pieces of a puzzle that must fit together before any tentative analysis is taken more seriously. Sometimes the search for themes is made easier by the presence of one or more seemingly obvious or "barefaced" dreams, which Hall (1947) called *spotlight dreams*. Spotlight dreams often contain several key topics in the series in a direct fashion. Inferences that are based on spotlight dreams are then examined by going back through the dream series to see if less obvious dreams turn out to have a similar structure.

A study using this approach on 649 dreams over a 50-year period found that six themes appeared with the same frequency throughout the dream series (Hall & Nordby, 1972; Smith & Hall, 1964). The dreamer was thinking about, preparing, or eating food in 20% of her dreams; misplacing an object, usually her purse, in 17%; finding herself in a small or disorderly room in 10%; interacting with her mother in 10%; going to the bathroom in 8%; and being late or missing a bus or train in 6%. As mentioned in chapter 1, these six themes account for at least part of the content in 71% of the dreams.

Although it is a little easier for investigators to reach agreement on the presence of themes than it is on metaphors, considerable room for disagreement remains. The method also suffers because the findings tend to be unique to each dreamer, allowing little opportunity for generalizations across dreamers or groups of dreamers. Finally, thematic analyses tend to be general. They do not go far in providing detailed statements about dream content that can be tested on new dream samples or correlated with the effects of brain lesions or drugs.

Content Analysis

Dissatisfaction with the reliability and generalizability of free associative, symbolic, and thematic methods of studying dream content led to the use of the more objective and quantitative approach called *content analysis*. Content analysis is a general method that attempts to use carefully defined categories to extract meaning from a text, such as a newspaper article, transcribed conversation, short story, or dream report. One of the earliest proponents of content analysis stated that the "fundamental objective" of this method is to convert the "symbolic behavior" of people into "scientific data," by which he meant data that were (a) objective and reproducible; (b) susceptible to measurement and quantification; (c) significant for either pure or applied theory; and (d) generalizable (Cartwright, 1953, p. 466). Hall (1969a) defined content analysis as "the categorization of units of qualitative material in order to obtain frequencies which can be subjected to statistical operations and tests of significance" (p. 175). Thanks to the development of sophisticated software, content analysis now includes programs for aggregating words and phrases into "semantic networks" that do not rely on predetermined categories (Roberts, 1997).

The most difficult task in carrying out a content analysis is to develop categories that lead to reliable and valid findings. Unfortunately, there are no general rules for constructing such categories, nor has it been found that categories created for one type of text can be readily used with texts of another kind. For the most part, content categories have been developed through trial and error after full immersion in the type of text to be analyzed. They usually go through several versions before they are ready for regular use.

Two main issues are involved in developing content categories: determining the level of measurement and deciding whether to use empirical or theoretical categories. Concerning the level of measurement, the choice is basically between rating scales at the ordinal level, which imply the existence of degrees of difference that can be ranked, and discrete categories at the nominal level. "Activity level" and "emotional intensity" are examples of dimensions that have been used on rating scales for the study of dreams. Indoor and outdoor settings and male and female characters are examples of categories at a nominal level of measurement, where a simple tabulation of frequencies is made for each category.

Empirical categories are based on what appear to be natural dimensions, or clusterings that derive from human experience, without regard to any particular psychological theory. As noted in chapter 1, the categories are usually basic-level cognitive categories. "Characters," "social interactions," and "vividness" are examples of empirical categories that seem to fit with everyday understandings. *Theoretical* categories, on the other hand, bring together seemingly disparate and unconnected elements in dream reports on the basis of a careful rendering of a concept from a theory of interest to the investigator. "Anima," "castration anxiety," and "ego synthesis" are examples of theoretical scales developed for the study of dream reports from Jungian, Freudian, and Eriksonian theory, respectively (Hall, 1969a; Sheppard, 1969).

The rating–nominal and empirical–theoretical dichotomies lead to the possibility of four different types of scales, and in fact, all four types have been used in dream research, some more frequently than others. Generally speaking, most of the coding systems for the study of dreams have been empirical rating scales. A factor analysis of the codings of 100 REM dream reports with several different empirical scales suggests that these scales boil down to five basic dimensions: degree of vividness and distortion; degree of anxiety and hostility; degree of initiative and striving; level of activity; and amount of sexuality (Hauri, 1975). It also can be said that some types of scales have been more useful. In particular, empirical scales, whether at the nominal or ordinal level, have proven to be more useful than either type of theoretical scale. Theoretical scales are difficult to construct as a result of the fuzziness of most personality theories, and they are equally difficult to apply because of the ambiguity of many dream actions (Hall, 1969a). Domhoff (1996, p. 10) provides details on the failure of two scales developed to test Freudian ideas.

Rating Scales for Dream Content

Rating scales, as already noted, are based on the assumption that a characteristic can be ranked or weighed. All ratings scales in dream research have been at the ordinal level and have rested on the assumption that "more" or "less" is the most that can be judged in a dream report. Nevertheless, one group of theorists assigned widely different weights to the points along their psychoanalytic scales for ego functioning, a decision hard to justify in measurement terms (Sheppard, 1963, 1969). Ordinal scales have been used with great benefit in a wide variety of studies, the most important of which are the longitudinal and cross-sectional studies by Foulkes and his co-workers (1982; Foulkes et al., 1990). The scales used in their work made it possible to demonstrate the systematic changes in dream content from the preschool to teen years that are discussed in chapter 1.

Rating scales are most useful for characteristics of dream reports with degrees of intensity in waking life, such as activity level or emotionality, or without specific content, such as clarity of visual imagery or vividness. Sometimes useful ratings on these kinds of dimensions are made by the dreamers themselves. For example, Foulkes (1966) used ratings by both judges and participants on dramatic quality, degree of unpleasantness, and clarity in showing that few differences exist in the dream reports from the first three REM periods of the night. In a similar fashion, Howe and Blick (1983) had women rate their dream reports on several emotionality dimensions, finding that the older women gave more benign ratings to their dream emotions.

According to Cohen (1979), four dimensions of dream salience can be rated by participants in dream studies: emotionality, bizarreness, activity, and vividness. These dimensions are somewhat similar to the findings from Hauri's (1975) factor analysis of rating scales, which also pinpointed vividness and activity dimensions; Hauri's factor of anxiety–hostility may be similar to Cohen's emotionality dimension as well. Cohen's conclusion is supported in a study using many pairs of polar adjectives and 7-point Likert scales to establish correlations between levels of EEG activity and immediate ratings of dream experiences by laboratory participants (Takeuchi, Ogilvie, Ferrelli, Murphy, & Belicki, 2001). A factor analysis showed that the Dream Property Scale (Takeuchi et al., 2001) derived from these polar adjectives has the following four main factors:

1. Emotionality/evaluation, as indexed by pairings such as relaxed–tense and pleasant–unpleasant.
2. Rationality/bizarreness, as indexed by pairings such as familiar–unfamiliar and ordinary–strange.
3. Activity, as indexed by pairings such as alert–drowsy and dynamic–static.
4. Impression/vividness, as indexed by pairings such as clear–fuzzy and focused–unfocused.

It is noteworthy that two of the dimensions, Emotionality/evaluation and Activity, are similar to two of the three dimensions that have been found to be universal to virtually all kinds of ratings of affective meaning in many different language families across the world (Osgood, May, & Miron, 1975). The third universal dimension of affective meaning, potency, which is best indexed by the polar adjectives strong–weak, may have some overlaps with the Rationality/bizarreness dimension of the Dream Property Scale.

Despite these examples of useful applications, there are nonetheless serious drawbacks to rating scales when it comes to detailed studies of dream content. First, it is often difficult to establish reliability with some scales, especially when researchers from outside the original investigative team try to use them (Domhoff, 1996; Winget & Kramer, 1979). Partly for this reason, new investigators tend to create their own rating scales, leading to a situation in which many scales have not been fully tested for either reliability or validity. For example, in a study of the possible differences between the dreams of people who differ on the permeability of their personal boundaries, three of the new scales used in the study had to be excluded from the analysis because of low intercoder reliabilities (Hartmann, Rosen,

& Rand, 1998). This constant creation of new scales also means that results cannot be directly compared from study to study, making it difficult to build a solid and reliable research literature.

Second, much of the specific information in dream reports can be lost or unused with rating scales. A "bizzareness" scale, for instance, does not include the fact that in one set of dream reports the high degree of bizarreness may be due to metamorphoses, in another to impossible actions by specific dream characters, and in still another to implausible settings or objects. Similarly, the highest rating on a hostility scale may be the result of either a murder or a fatal illness, but the difference between the two may be as informative as the extremity of the situation.

Third, many rating scales rest on assumptions that are psychologically untenable when they are examined critically. For example, in a dependency rating scale created by Whitman, Pierce, Maas, and Baldridge (1961), a score of 6 is assigned if the person eats food and a score of 1 is assigned if the person seeks help from others. Because the ratings for each dream are added together to create the total score, this rating system implicitly assumes that "mentioning a ham sandwich shows six times as much dependency as accepting a helping hand from another" (Van de Castle, 1969, p. 193).

This type of psychologically untenable assumption is most prevalent in rating scales for aggressive actions. With most of these scales, murders receive the highest rating; injury and damage to personal possessions receive medium scores; and insults, rejections, and expressions of hostility receive low scores. The ratings for each dream are added together, and an average aggression score is calculated for each individual or group. Such a procedure implies that several angry thoughts or a few damaged possessions are psychologically equivalent to one murder, a weighting that seems indefensible once it is made explicit (Hall, 1969a, 1969b). A rating scale for levels of anger is reasonable, but a rating scale for aggressions that range from insults to murders is not. This problem is one of the major failings with the Gottschalk and Gleser (1969) scales, which were originally developed to study psychotherapy records and other forms of waking talk. Despite their use in several dream studies, the scales do not adapt well to the study of dream content. Domhoff (1996, pp. 30–37) presents critiques of several other inadequate rating scales.

Fourth, and finally, rating scales are usually not of much use in trying to relate the substance of dream content to waking conceptions, concerns, and interests. They are best used for relating features of dreaming to the neurophysiology of sleep. Thus, as useful as the Dream Property Scale is for relating perceived Emotionality/evaluation or Activity level to EEG variables, it cannot be used to study the meaning that might be found in dream reports.

Nominal Scales

Nominal scales do not suffer from the problems facing rating scales. Higher reliabilities can be obtained because discrete scales usually are more clearly defined and seldom require the subtle judgments that rating scales often do. No information is lost because numerous categories can be created and then aggregated, if necessary, later in the data analysis. Nominal categories do not contain the questionable psychological assumptions built into some rating scales. Nonetheless, nominal-level coding systems are not without their difficulties and drawbacks, which result in less use of them than might be expected.

First, it takes time to create carefully defined categories that can lead to high intercoder reliability, and there may be some gray areas even with well-defined categories. Second, the categories may not prove to be useful because they are not as likely to be created on the basis of intuitions about the data. Most important, a good coding system at the nominal level is far more labor intensive than rating systems. It takes many hours to learn a full set of nominal categories and then many more hours to apply them to a sample of dreams than is the case with most rating systems.

The Hall–Van de Castle coding system used in this book is atypical in the area of dream research in that its categories are nominal in nature. The system originally contained both empirical and theoretical categories, but the theoretical categories did not prove to have any more usefulness or validity than did the theoretical rating scales, and they have long since been abandoned (Domhoff, 1996). The original Hall–Van de Castle system consists of eight general categories, most of which are divided into two or more subcategories. The categories encompass the five dimensions found in rating scales by Hauri's (1975) factor analysis. As noted earlier, this system is discussed in detail in chapter 3.

DETERMINING A UNIT OF ANALYSIS

Whether rating scales or nominal categories are used, it is necessary to decide on the unit of analysis to be used in making standardized comparisons from dream sample to dream sample. First, and most crucially, wide individual differences exist in report length, and women's dreams often are found to be longer than those of men (Bursik, 1998; Hall & Van de Castle, 1966; Winegar & Levin, 1997). Varying lengths are a problem because longer reports are likely to have more of most things in them. Second, dream reports can vary from group to group or person to person in the frequency with which certain elements appear, even when report length is held constant. This difference in "density" seems to be especially the case for the frequency of characters, meaning that some dream reports are more likely to contain social interactions than others are. Once again, there is a gender difference: More characters exist in women's reports, an interesting finding in and of itself, but one that should be taken into account in analyzing social interactions (Hall, 1969a, 1969b).

The failure to correct for dream length is a problem with both rating scales and nominal categories. For instance, a frequently used theoretical rating scale for "primary process thinking" in dream content, which requires difficult judgments concerning differing degrees of distortion and improbability, correlates .60 with the length of the dream report (Auld, Goldenberg, & Weiss, 1968). When controls for dream length are included, the previously reported positive relationships between this scale and creativity measures disappear (Livingston & Levin, 1991; Wood & Domino, 1989). Similarly, correction for dream length eliminates seeming gender differences in several Hall–Van de Castle categories.

The failure to control for length is one of several methodological problems in a study by Kramer, Kinney, and Scharf (1983), which wrongly claimed that previous gender differences reversed or disappeared; in their sample, the men's dream reports were longer than those of the women (see Domhoff, 1996, pp. 79–82, for a full critique). In a study comparing dream reports from women who worked in the home with those from women and men who worked outside the home, the few differences cannot be regarded as solid findings because no correction was made for the fact that the dreams of the women who worked at home averaged 220 words, those of the women who worked outside the home 200 words, and those of the men only 180 words (Lortie-Lussier, Simond, Rinfret, & De Koninck, 1992).

Two main strategies have been used to correct for differing lengths of reports. First, the mean number of lines or words per dream report was used as the unit of analysis. However, that strategy does not deal with the differing "wordiness" of participants and leads to cumbersome findings such as "there were 2.3 human characters per every 10 lines (or 100 words) in the dream narratives." Worse, a control for length that relies on the number of words does not allow for complicated or unusual elements that might take more words to describe; consequently, dividing by the number of words could wash out real and important differences, especially in studies concerned with creativity or unusual features in dreams (Hunt, Ruzycki-Hunt, Pariak, & Belicki, 1993).

Second, investigators established minimum and maximum lengths for the reports to be analyzed, thereby making it possible to use the dream report as a whole as the unit of analysis. This approach was used by Hall and Van de Castle (1966) when they eliminated reports of fewer than 50 or more than 300 words in a normative study of dreams from college men and women (see chapter 3). This is, in fact, the only approach possible with rating scales because ratings are based on the dream as a whole. In effect, this limitation is another disadvantage of using rating scales to study dream content.

There is, however, a far better way to create sensible units of analysis with nominal categories, which is to convert categorical frequencies into percentages and ratios. This approach is now used with the Hall–Van de Castle system, as shown in chapter 3. For example, it is possible to make dreams from groups all over the world comparable with regard to their inclusion of animals by creating an "animal percent." The animal percent is simply the total number of animals in the dreams divided by the total number of all types of characters. As shown with systematic data in chapter 3, this approach is independent of report length or character density within broad limits; it effectively deals with both problems at the same time. In addition, findings presented as percentages and ratios are readily communicated and comprehended. People immediately understand if it is reported that the animal percent in dreams declines from the 30% to 40% range in childhood to 4% to 6% in adulthood and is higher in the small traditional societies studied by cultural anthropologists than it is in industrialized democracies (Domhoff, 1996; Van de Castle, 1983).

Percentage indicators also make it possible to resolve an important controversy over the way to compare REM and NREM reports. When lengths are held constant, the seeming differences between the two types of reports disappear (Antrobus, 1983; Foulkes & Schmidt, 1983). However, critics argue that no correction should be made because NREM mentation is, in fact, of briefer duration and more thoughtlike than REM mentation (Hobson et al., 2000b, p. 800; Hunt, 2000). Using 125 REM and 55 NREM reports collected by Foulkes and Rechtschaffen (1964), a reanalysis that was based on percentage indicators for activities in dreams was used as a test case. Although 87% of the REM reports and 89% of the NREM reports had at least one activity in them, the proportion of all activities that were cognitive activities was 20% in NREM reports, but only 11% in REM reports. Conversely, higher visual and verbal proportions occurred in REM than in NREM reports: 12% versus 6% for visual, 37% versus 22% for verbal (Domhoff & Schneider, 1999. p. 149). Thus, differences between REM and NREM reports persist when percentage indicators are used to control for length.

THE PROBLEMS OF STATISTICAL ANALYSIS

The nature of the data in most studies of dream content leads to difficult statistical problems that call into question published claims that are based on parametric tests like the t test and analysis of variance. First, statistics textbooks generally argue that it is risky to use parametric statistics with ordinal or nominal data because such statistics require that the points along any measurement scale reflect an underlying continuous distribution with at least equal intervals (e.g., Leach, 1979; Reynolds, 1984; Siegel & Castellan, 1988). It is not impossible to add, subtract, multiply, or divide the frequencies derived from nominal categories; it is just that such an analysis may be misleading or in error because assumptions are being violated. As Siegel and Castellan (1988) stressed:

> It should be obvious that a mean and standard deviation may be computed for any set of numbers. However, statistics computed from these numbers only "make sense" if the original assignment procedure imparted "arithmetical" interpretations to the assignments. This is a subtle and critical point. (p. 33)

Although evidence has indicated that using parametric statistics usually is not fatal if distributions are close to normal (Sawilowsky & Blair, 1992), it is certain that most ordinal and nominal data collected on people outside a laboratory setting are not normally distributed, a situation that violates one of the most important underlying assumptions for the application of parametric statistics (Micceri, 1989). Under these circumstances, which apply to most of the elements that appear in dream reports, nonparametric statistics have been shown to work much better, especially when sample sizes are uneven. Empirical studies show this approach to be true even with the larger sample sizes that are thought to favor parametric statistics (Nanna & Sawilowsky, 1998). Third, the standard formulas for determining p values with parametric statistics assume that the findings are based on random samples, which are rarely obtained in dream research.

The best way to deal with these problems is to use the combination of nonparametric statistics and randomization strategies explained in chapter 3. This approach is especially well suited for the nominal data produced by the Hall–Van de Castle coding system. It also eliminates any need to worry about the level of measurement, the randomness of samples, or the shape of the sampling distribution. In addition, it eliminates the need for equal sample sizes and makes it unnecessary to use different statistics for analyzing longitudinal data from individual dream journals.

The Issue of Sample Sizes

Statistical problems in dream research are compounded by the frequent use of sample sizes that are far too small to allow for the detection of statistically significant differences. There is a tendency for researchers to use only from 30 to 60 dream reports in each sample, partly because it is difficult to collect large samples of dreams using the 2-week dream diaries on which many researchers tend to rely. In addition, introductory courses in statistics emphasize that a sample size of 30 makes it possible to use simple parametric statistics, such as the t test. However, the use of small samples in dream research overlooks a major problem: Not all dreams contain the elements being studied. In actuality, then, the sample sizes in many dream studies are even smaller than they appear to be.

According to Cohen's (1977, p. 205) detailed work on the sample sizes necessary for attaining statistical significance with various magnitudes of difference between samples, it takes a large number of observations to detect small differences with any degree of certainty. For example, with a real difference of 20 percentage points, which is about as large a difference as is generally found in dream studies, 125 observations are needed to have an 80% chance of attaining statistical significance at the .05 level. For differences of 10 percentage points, it takes a sample of 502 observations to have an 80% chance of attaining significance at the .05 level. Thus, drawing one dream from longer dream diaries provided by 30 Mexican Americans and comparing them with 30 dream reports from Anglo Americans chosen in the same way almost guarantees no differences will be found (Kane, Mellen, Patten, & Samano, 1993). Similarly, comparisons of women who work at home with women in the paid work force are not going to yield results that can be replicated when they are restricted to 30 to 40 dreams per sample by using only one dream per dream diary (Lortie-Lussier et al., 1985).

THE QUALITY OF THE LITERATURE ON DREAM CONTENT

This chapter provides a benchmark for assessing the literature on dream content. Generally speaking, the literature is anecdotal, contradictory, and dispute ridden and is based on clinical case studies, poorly collected and overly small samples, unreliable and unvalidated rating scales, and inappropriate statistical methods. As the comments in this chapter on several studies suggest, most published studies are not substantial enough to be used in developing a neurocognitive model. However, rather than providing a long and tedious critique of the many weak studies in the literature, this book proceeds by building on the few solid studies that exist. For comments on many of these inadequate studies, see Domhoff (1996, 1999b).

The critique that Roth et al. (1979) made of nine studies on medication and dream content can be applied to many other parts of the content literature. They noted that "few if any of the existing studies were more than pilot studies" and that "there has been a failure to examine even one drug in depth" (Roth et al., 1979, p. 221). Although they concluded that some medications may affect dream content, they also say that "the lack of standardization of methods of assessing quality of dream content has resulted in isolated bits of information that do not yet form a coherent picture" (Roth et al., 1979, p. 221). Kramer and Roth (1979) reached similar conclusions about the literature on dream content and mental illness. In a follow-up assessment of the literature on dreams and mental health since 1975, Kramer (1999, 2000b) noted that the literature has not improved.

CONCLUSION

Despite the poor quality of the literature, this chapter nonetheless illustrates the potential for rigorous studies of dream content that can be used to test some of the ideas presented in chapter 1. First, there is every reason to believe that the quality of dream reports can be high if they are collected in a sleep laboratory or with the most recent dream method or if a long-term dream series can be obtained and authenticated. Second, solid evidence demonstrates that content analysis, when it is based on nominal categories, can be objective and useful. Third, good statistical methods are available for analyzing the data that derive from content analysis. These positive conclusions set the stage for a detailed presentation of the Hall–Van de Castle system.

3

THE HALL–VAN DE CASTLE SYSTEM

The purpose of this chapter is to show that the Hall–Van de Castle system of content analysis has the necessary reliability and validity for research that links dream content to the neural network for dreaming, on the one hand, and to waking cognition, on the other. The chapter includes additions to the system that can be used to study highly memorable dreams and describes the statistical methods and new software that now make the system even more accurate and powerful. The system is accessible to dream researchers anywhere in the world because everything needed to carry out a modern Hall–Van de Castle analysis is available on the Internet at http://www.DreamResearch.net: coding rules, aids for learning the coding system, a spreadsheet for rapid and accurate data analysis called DreamSAT, and programs for using randomization statistics to determine *p* values and confidence intervals (Schneider & Domhoff, 1995). Printed copies of the coding rules and normative findings can be found in Hall and Van de Castle (1966) and Domhoff (1996).

As briefly mentioned in chapter 2, the system rests on the nominal level of measurement, thereby avoiding the many problems with rating scales. The original eight general categories are as follows:

- Characters (subdivided into animals, humans, and mythical figures/creatures)
- Social Interactions (subdivided into friendly, aggressive, and sexual)
- Activities (often analyzed in terms of physical and nonphysical activities)
- Striving (success and failure)
- Misfortunes and Good Fortunes
- Emotions (anger, apprehension, confusion, happiness, and sadness)
- Physical Surroundings (settings and objects)
- Descriptive Elements (modifiers, temporality, and negativity).

Two categories have been added: Food and Eating and Elements From the Past. They were originally designed as theoretical categories to measure "orality" and "regression" (Hall & Van de Castle, 1966). However, as noted in chapter 2, no theoretical categories of any kind have proved useful in the study of dream content. Fortunately, the descriptive nature of these two scales makes it possible to adapt them into empirical categories. For example, the main categories of the Food and Eating scale are simply (a) eating or drinking, (b) being in a restaurant or bar, (c) preparing food, (d) purchasing or gathering food, and (e) seeing or mentioning food. The Elements From the Past scale consists of categories such as (a) being younger, (b) seeing a person who has been dead for at least a year, and (c) being in a location, seeing a person, doing an activity, or seeing an object that is mentioned as not being a part of the dreamer's life for at least a year. With both of these scales, it is also possible to eliminate one or more of the subcategories for specific research studies.

Extensive experience has shown that few aspects of dream content do not fit into one or another of the 10 Hall–Van de Castle categories. This finding, however, does not mean that all the categories need to be used in every investigation or that they have proven to be of equal value in developing hypotheses and testing theories. The Big Five of the coding system are Characters, Social Interactions, Emotions, Misfortunes, and Striving, but other categories have shown themselves to be valuable for specific investigations. In the dreams of Franz Kafka, for example, it is the high percentage of nonphysical activities and the attention to the human body that make his dreams distinctive. Moreover, the differences fit well with his waking preference for observation rather than physical activities and with his obsession concerning bodily defects (Hall & Lind, 1970).

Because the coding categories are clearly defined—the result of a 2-year process of trial and error in constructing them—the Hall–Van de Castle system has high intercoder reliability. This high reliability is determined by the percentage-of-agreement method, which means that all the similar codings by two independent coders are divided by the number of agreements plus the number of disagreements. For example, if coder A makes 51 codings for Characters and coder B makes 49 codings, and they make the same coding 48 times, then the intercoder reliability is 48 divided by 52 (48 agreements plus 4 disagreements), which equals .92. Although a slightly more complex formula can be used with categories with either very high or very low frequencies (Smith, 2000, p. 325), no Hall–Van de Castle categories are at these extremes.

Hall and Van de Castle decided to use the percentage-of-agreement approach to computing reliability by comparing its results with what they found with every other conceivable method. In fact, they showed that the outcomes from various methods of determining intercoder reliability can range from 0% to 100% with the same codings (Hall & Van de Castle, 1966, pp. 145–147). It is therefore meaningless in their eyes to report a reliability figure without stating the method used to determine it, and it makes little sense to use the other methods with this particular coding system (Domhoff, 1996; Hall, 1969a; Van de Castle, 1969). More generally, the percentage-of-agreement approach is now the one that is most frequently used in all areas of content analysis (Smith, 2000).

The Hall–Van de Castle scales for various types of social interactions avoid the untenable psychological assumptions often implicit in rating scales. Instead of constructing an ordinal aggression scale, for example, Hall and Van de Castle created eight separate nominal categories for types of aggression:

1. Hostile thoughts
2. Critical remarks
3. Rejections and refusals
4. Dire verbal threats
5. Stealing or destruction of possessions
6. Being chased
7. Being confined or attacked
8. Murder

Codings can be done reliably, and no information is lost when eight different frequencies can be noted and compared. For many purposes, the frequencies for the eight categories can be combined to create an aggression score.

As illustrated in chapter 2 with the example of the "animal percent," findings with the nominal categories are most useful and best understood when they are conveyed in an array of percentages and ratios that are called *content indicators*. In a similar fashion, the total number of known characters, divided by the total number of all characters, leads to the "friends percent," which has proven useful in distinguishing the dreams of people with mental illness from normative samples (Domhoff, 1996). The total number of male characters divided by the total number of human characters whose gender is indicated yields the "male/female percent," in which both the male and female percentages are presented to avoid sexism. The total number of references to various types of confusion, uncertainty, and surprise, when divided by the total number of emotions, provides the "confusion percent."

Aggressive and friendly social interactions can be analyzed by determining *rates per character*, a method that provides an excellent control for the number of characters. For example, the total number of friendly interactions (F) divided by the total number of characters (C) provides a ratio called the *F/C index*. This index also can be figured for specific characters or types of characters in dreams, leading to an F/C ratio index with parents, friends, or strangers. Mathematically speaking, the ratios differ from the percentage indicators in the previous paragraph. They therefore require different statistical treatment.

Table 3.1 presents all the indicators in the Hall–Van de Castle system and explains how they are calculated. The table includes several indicators that are a simple percentage of the dreams in the sample with at least one instance of a given category; they are therefore called "at-least-one" indicators. They are used for Aggression, Friendliness, Sexuality, Food and Eating, Misfortune, Good Fortune, Success, Failure, Striving, Negative Emotions, and Confusion. These indicators are useful for a quick comparison of two samples or for studies of large samples, but they have to be used with great caution because they do not include a correction for the variation in length of dream reports from sample to sample.

EMOTIONS IN DREAMS

The coding categories for emotions may prove to be particularly important in linking dream content to the neural network for dreaming. The coding system has five emotions categories: anger, apprehension, confusion, happiness, and sadness. The system is limited to these five categories because it was impossible to develop a reliable one with more categories. Hall and Van de Castle (1966) wrote that "the classification of emotions was one of our most difficult tasks" (p. 110). Coincidentally, good psychological reasons explain why it is hard to obtain reliable coding with more than these five categories. Several different kinds of psychological studies suggest that only a small handful of basic human emotions exist. The main five are basic level categories: anger, fear, love, joy, and sadness (Murphy & Lassaline, 1997; Shaver, Schwarz, Kirson, & O'Connor, 1987). Some lists also include contempt, disgust, and surprise (Ekman, 1992a, 1992b).

These categories correspond closely to those in the Hall–Van de Castle system. The love and joy categories are in effect collapsed into one category, happiness, for the simple reason that the relatively few positive emotions in dreams are difficult to distinguish in a reliable fashion. As noted in passing in chapter 1, only 20% of all emotions in dreams fit into the happiness category, a finding that has been replicated three times (Hall et al., 1982; Roussy, 2000; Tonay, 1990/1991). The waking emotions of sadness, anger, and fear (or apprehension) are exactly represented in the Hall–Van de Castle system. As for disgust and contempt, they are included within the anger category.

The category for surprise in the set of human emotions advocated by Ekman (1992b) corresponds with the category for confusion in the Hall–Van de Castle system. Although confusion was not considered an emotion at the time the coding system was created, it was included because it is a psychological state that occurs frequently in dreams. In fact, 12% of men's dreams and 13% of women's have at least one instance of confusion. More-

TABLE 3.1
Formulas for Calculating the Hall–Van de Castle Content Indicators

Characters

Male/female percent	Males ÷ (Males + Females)
Familiarity percent	Familiar ÷ (Familiar + Unfamiliar)
Friends percent	Friends ÷ All humans
Family percent	(Family + Relatives) ÷ All humans
Animal percent	Animals ÷ All characters

Social interaction percents

Aggression/friendliness percent	Dreamer-involved aggression ÷ (D-inv. aggression + D-inv. friendliness)
Befriender percent	Dreamer as Befriender ÷ (D as Befriender + D as Befriended)
Aggressor percent	Dreamer as Aggressor ÷ (D as Aggressor + D as Victim)
Victimization percent	Dreamer as Victim ÷ (D as Victim + D as Aggressor)
Physical aggression percent	Physical aggressions ÷ All aggressions

Social interaction ratios

Aggression/character index	All aggressions ÷ All characters
Friendliness/characters index	All friendliness ÷ All characters
Sexuality/characters index	All sexuality ÷ All characters

Self-concept percents

Self-negativity percent	(D as Victim + D-inv. Misfortune + D-inv. Failure) ÷ (D as Victim + D-inv. Misfortune + D-inv. Failure + D as Befriended + D-inv. GF + D-inv. Success)
Bodily misfortunes percent	Bodily misfortunes ÷ All misfortunes
Negative emotions percent	Negative emotions ÷ All emotions
Dreamer-involved success percent	D-involved success ÷ (D-inv. success + D-inv. failure)
Torso/anatomy percent	Torso, Anatomy, Sex body parts ÷ All body parts

Other indicators

Physical activities percent	(P, M, and L activities) ÷ All activities
Indoor setting percent	Indoor ÷ (Indoor + Outdoor)
Familiar setting percent	Familiar ÷ (Indoor + Outdoor)
Distorted setting percent	Distorted settings ÷ All settings
Unusual character percent	(Dead, imaginary, metamorphoses, and creatures) ÷ All characters
Confusion percent	Confusion ÷ All emotions

Percentage of dreams with at least one

Aggression	Dreams with aggression ÷ Number of dreams
Friendliness	Dreams with friendliness ÷ Number of dreams
Sexuality	Dreams with sexuality ÷ Number of dreams
Misfortune	Dreams with misfortune ÷ Number of dreams
Good fortune	Dreams with good fortune ÷ Number of dreams
Success	Dreams with success ÷ Number of dreams
Failure	Dreams with failure ÷ Number of dreams
Striving	Dreams with success OR failure ÷ Number of dreams

D = dreamer; inv. = involved; L = location change; M = movement; P = physical; GF = good fortune over, confusion accounts for 22% of the emotions in men's dreams and 18% of those in women's dreams, second only to apprehension, which constitutes 45% of the emotions in men's dreams and 37% in women's. Confusion in dreams is "generally produced either through confrontation with some unexpected event or else through inability to choose between available alternatives" and is indicated by such terms as "surprised, astonished, amazed, awestruck, mystified, puzzled, perplexed, strange, bewildered, doubtful, conflicted, undecided, and uncertain" (Hall & Van de Castle, 1966, p. 112).

It is likely that emotion knowledge is organized in at least two ways: by a positive–negative dimension and by intensity (Shaver et al., 1987). Both of these dimensions are reflected in the Hall–Van de Castle system. The positive–negative dimension is captured by the inclusion of a "negative emotions percent" as one of the content indicators in Table 3.1. As for the intensity of emotions, it can be coded with the Hall–Van de Castle system's Intensity scale for classifying any word modifiers that are used to describe force or the expenditure of energy. These modifiers may refer to either physical or mental energy or to emotions and sensations. In the case of emotions, the simple appearance of the emotion is not sufficient to code for intensity. The dreamer must use some intensity modifier, such as "very" or "extremely," for the emotion to be coded I+ (high intensity), or "mildly" or "a little" for it to be coded I– (low intensity).

NORMATIVE FINDINGS ON COLLEGE MEN AND WOMEN

To make the system more useful for studying individuals or unique population groups, Hall and Van de Castle (1966, chapter 14) created a set of normative findings that were based on five dreams from each of 100 male and 100 female students at Case Western Reserve University and Baldwin-Wallace College in Cleveland, Ohio, between 1947 and 1950. Table 3.2 provides the normative findings for most of the content indicators presented in Table 3.1. Other normative findings are available upon request through http://www.DreamResearch.net. These results, including a brief discussion of the gender similarities and differences, are presented later in this chapter.

The Hall–Van de Castle norms were replicated for men and women at the University of Richmond in the early 1980s; for women at the University of California, Berkeley, in the mid-1980s; at Salem College in the late 1980s; and at the University of California, Santa Cruz, in the early 1990s (Domhoff, 1996; Dudley & Fungaroli, 1987; Dudley & Swank, 1990; Hall et al., 1982; Tonay, 1990/1991). The norms for several of the character categories were replicated at the University of Cincinnati in the late 1960s

TABLE 3.2
A Comparison of the Male and Female Norms for the
Hall–Van de Castle System

	Male norms (%)	Female norms (%)	Effect size	p
Characters				
Male/female percent	67	48	+.39	.000**
Familiarity percent	45	58	−.26	.000**
Friends percent	31	37	−.12	.004**
Family percent	12	19	−.21	.000**
Animal percent	6	4	+.08	.037*
Social interaction percents				
Aggression/friendliness percent	59	51	+.15	.014*
Befriender percent	50	47	+.06	.517
Aggressor percent	40	33	+.14	.129
Victimization percent	60	67	−.14	.129
Physical aggression percent	50	34	+.33	.000**
Social interaction ratios				
Aggression/character index	.34	.24	+.24	.000**
Friendliness/character index	.21	.22	−.01	.852
Sexuality/character index	.06	.01	+.11	.000**
Self-concept percents				
Self-negativity percent	65	66	−.02	.617
Bodily misfortunes percent	29	35	−.12	.217
Negative emotions percent	80	80	+.00	.995
Dreamer-involved success percent	51	42	+.18	.213
Torso/anatomy percent	31	20	+.26	.002**
Other indicators				
Physical activities percent	60	52	−.38	.000**
Indoor setting percent	48	61	−.26	.000**
Familiar setting percent	62	79	−.38	.000**
Percentage of dreams with at least one				
Aggression	47	44	+.05	.409
Friendliness	38	42	−.08	.197
Sexuality	12	4	+.31	.000**
Misfortune	36	33	+.06	.353
Good fortune	6	6	+.02	.787
Success	15	8	+.24	.000**
Failure	15	10	+.17	.007**
Striving	27	15	+.31	.000**

Note. The p values are based on the formula for the significance of differences between two proportions. The effect size derives from Cohen's h. The h statistic is determined by the following formula:

$$h = \cos^{-1}(1-2P_1)-\cos^{-1}(1-2P_2)$$

P_1 and P_2 are proportions between 0 and 1, and the $\cos^{-1}$ operation returns a value in radians.
* significant at the .05 level
**significant at the .01 level

(Reichers, Kramer, & Trinder, 1970). The seeming exceptions to these replications (Bursik, 1998; Kramer et al., 1983; Rubenstein & Krippner, 1991) have major methodological problems that are discussed in detail elsewhere (Domhoff, 1996, 1999b).

The norms originally were calculated by pooling all 500 dreams in each sample, thereby ignoring the fact that they are not independent observations. The same results, however, are obtained when the figures for each of the 100 participants in each sample are computed and then averaged across individuals. Some of the evidence for this point is presented in Table 3.3. This recalculation answers the concern expressed by Urbina (1981) that determining the results for each person and then averaging them might lead to different results.

The Hall–Van de Castle system sometimes can be made more useful by combining two or more of its nominal empirical categories. Such combinations can be used instead of relying on theoretical rating scales of unknown reliability and validity to test new hypotheses. This point can be demonstrated first of all by looking at Beck and Hurvich's (1959) mislabeled and unvalidated Masochism scale, which is one of the few scales other than the Hall–Van de Castle system that has been used by independent investigators. The scale consists of a wide range of negative experiences ranging from physical discomfort to rejection to being punished, lost, or victimized. Using this scale, Cartwright (1992) came to the conclusion that divorced women who are not depressed are more masochistic than divorced men who are depressed. This is a surprising result that seems to raise more questions than it answers.

TABLE 3.3
Group vs. Individual Norm Comparisons for Selected Categories

	Collective male norms (%)	Average of 100 individual normative dreamers (%)	Difference (%)
Male/female percent	67.8	66.1	−1.7
Familiarity percent	45.0	44.9	−0.1
Friends percent	31.4	30.8	−0.6
Animal percent	6.0	5.9	−0.1
Aggression/friendliness percent	59.0	58.6	−0.4
Aggression/character index	.340	.371	.031
Friendliness/character index	.211	.210	−.001
Indoor setting percent	48.6	49.5	0.9
Self-negativity percent	64.7	66.0	1.3
At least one Aggression	47.2	47.2	0.0
At least one Friendliness	38.2	38.2	0.0
At least one Sexuality	11.6	11.6	0.0
At least one Misfortune	36.4	36.4	0.0

In a useful study, Clark, Trinder, Kramer, Roth, and Day (1972) hypothesized that the items on the Masochism scale are encompassed by three categories in the Hall–Van de Castle system: failures, misfortunes, and victim status in aggressive interactions. They then demonstrate this point by coding two different samples with both the Masochism scale and the three Hall–Van de Castle categories. They found that the masochism findings were encompassed by the Hall–Van de Castle categories, which also located several elements missed by the Masochism scale.

Because women are slightly more likely to fail when they strive in dreams and to be victims in aggressive interactions, the greater masochism that Cartwright reported in her women participants was really a combination of failures and victimizations, which are not manifestations of clinical masochism. Moreover, the Hall–Van de Castle misfortune categories, which might seem to be related to masochism, do not show any gender differences. The three categories are part of the "self-negativity percent" explained in Table 3.1. This category, along with a lack of friends and friendly interactions, distinguishes the dreams of people with mental illness from those of people without mental illness (Domhoff, 1996, 1999b, p. 127; Maharaj, 1997).

The usefulness of combining Hall–Van de Castle categories to encompass speculative theoretical rating scales also can be shown by looking at Krohn and Mayman's (1974) complicated system for determining the level of maturity in object relations, a concept drawn from a British variant of classical psychoanalytic theory. The scale calls for subtle judgments such as assigning an 8 if the dreamer reports "a sense of rapport with people and a well-developed understanding of their thoughts, feelings and conflicts" (Krohn & Mayman, 1974, p. 454). A 5 is assigned if the people in the dream have "no real identity"; a 3 if people are experienced as "insubstantial, fluid, more or less interchangeable"; and a 1 "if there are no other people and the subject's world seems to be completely lifeless, vacant, alien, strange" (Krohn & Mayman, 1974, pp. 452–454). Winegar and Levin (1997) applied the scale, which never has been validated, to 389 dream reports recorded by 115 adolescents between ages 15 and 18. They found that the girls showed more maturity in object relations than did boys and that the differences were greater at the older ages.

Winegar and Levin provided copies of the dream reports used in their study for reanalysis for this book. A sample of 12 reports coded "low" and 10 reports coded "high" on the Krohn–Mayman scale was coded with Hall–Van de Castle categories by two coders who had no knowledge of the Krohn–Mayman scale or of the fact that two sets of dreams were being used. They found that three easily coded nominal categories—friendly interactions, activities, and physical aggression—distinguished the two sets of dreams almost perfectly. Dreams with at least one friendly interaction were always in the high group, as were dreams with nonphysical activities like talking. Dreams with physical aggressions and physical activities were in the low group with one exception, in which a friendly interaction also took place. In effect, these results reveal the basis on which raters are making their judgments. They also suggest that the Hall–Van de Castle normative findings on physical activities percent, physical aggression percent, aggression/friendliness (A/F) percent, and the percentage of dreams with at least one friendliness could be used reliably to assess the relative maturity or immaturity of a group or individual.

PRESERVING SEQUENCES AND FINDING CONNECTIONS

The Hall–Van de Castle system contains two general categories for dealing with sequences of events in dreams. In the case of social interactions, it is possible to code for reciprocated aggressive, friendly, or sexual interactions, such as a character smiling back after being extended a friendly greeting. In the case of misfortunes, good fortunes, successes, and failures, it is possible to code for consequences. For example, a failure can be followed by a good fortune that reverses the failure, a new effort that leads to success, or a better outcome as the result of the friendly intervention of another dream character. The most interesting finding from sequential analyses is how rarely they occur. There are very few "reciprocities" for either aggressive or friendly interactions, and even fewer "consequences" of misfortunes, good fortunes, successes, and failures. However, these categories may prove to be useful in the study of individual dream journals.

Patterns and relationships among coding categories can be studied by means of contingency analysis, a nonparametric statistic designed for use with nominal data that provides the exact probabilities of relationships between two elements. It is ideally suited for content analysis studies (e.g., Osgood, 1959). Contingencies for any pair of Hall–Van de Castle coding categories can be found using the SearchCodings program available through DreamResearch.net. Once codings have been entered, the categories for which contingency information is sought are entered in designated input boxes. The program calculates the observed and expected frequencies of the overlaps and provides the p value for the difference that is found. For example, if the coding categories for strangers and physical aggressions are selected and both the male and female normative samples are searched, the results reveal a significant contingency between male strangers and physical aggressions for both men and women, but the contingency does not hold for female strangers. These results are displayed in Table 3.4.

TABLE 3.4
Contingency Between Physical Aggression and Strange Male Adult
Characters (xMSA) in the Male and Female Norms

	Contingency between physical aggression and male strangers			Contingency between physical aggression and female strangers		
	Observed (%)	Expected (%)	p	Observed (%)	Expected (%)	p
Male norms	7.2	3.4	0.008	1.6	2.5	0.324
Female norms	6.1	2.2	0.002	2.4	1.7	0.395

MEMORABLE DREAMS WITH AN IMPACT ON THE DREAMER

Most studies using the Hall–Van de Castle system have focused on everyday dream reports. However, the system can be adapted to study the occasional highly memorable dreams that have carryover effects into waking life and are of great interest to clinicians and humanists (Bulkeley, 1999; Knudson & Minier, 1999; Kuiken & Sikora, 1993). Then, too, the Hall–Van de Castle norms provide a basis for commenting on the frequency of such dreams.

Memorable dreams—dreams that have an impact on the dreamer—are often characterized by what Hall and Van de Castle call "good fortunes," which are defined as good things that happen to a dream character as a result of fate, rather than as a result of successful striving by the character or friendly actions by other dream characters:

> A good fortune is coded when there is an acquisition of goods or something beneficial happens to a character that is completely adventitious or the result of a circumstance over which no one has control. A good fortune is also scored if the dreamer appears in a bountiful environment. (Hall & Van de Castle, 1966, p. 105)

Hall and Van de Castle contrast good fortunes with misfortunes, which are bad outcomes that occur to characters independent of any aggressive interactions or failures. They found that misfortunes occur in 36% of men's dreams and 33% of women's dreams, whereas good fortunes appear in only 6% of dreams for both men and women. Because of the small number of good fortunes, they created only one general category for good fortunes. For purposes of studying memorable dreams, however, it is necessary to divide this category into six categories that parallel the six categories for misfortunes (Bulkeley, Dunn, & Domhoff, 2001).

The six expanded good fortune (GF) categories are defined as the mirror opposites of the six Misfortunes (M) categories, so it is useful to explain them in terms of that contrast. Because M6 is defined as "a character is dead or dies as a result of accident or illness or some unknown cause," GF6 is defined as a "character returns from the dead, acts as if he or she were alive, or transforms from an inanimate character (such as a puppet) into an animate character."

Just as M5 encompasses characters who are suffering injury, illness, pain, medical operations, bodily or mental defects, insanity, amnesia, or blindness, so GF5 encompasses recovery from illness or injury, miraculous healing, possession of extraordinary bodily powers, swimming under water for long periods without any need to breathe, enhanced mental and perceptual abilities, extrasensory perception, and dream lucidity. (The ability to fly under one's own power is not coded as a GF5 because it has its own category, GF2, to contrast with M2, which is for falling or the danger of falling.)

The category M4 focuses primarily on any character's lost, damaged, or defective possessions, but it also includes accidents without injuries that are experienced by any character. A lost ring, a house destroyed by a falling boulder, a broken computer, and a car crash because of an icy road are all coded as M4. Conversely, GF4 is defined by the possession of enhanced, magical, or supernatural objects and by experiencing miraculous events that are, in effect, the opposites of car crashes on icy roads, such as cars that fly over the traffic.

The category M3 includes all threats to a character's well-being and emotional stability that result from an impersonal force in the environment, such as walls or trees about to fall on the dreamer, boats about to capsize, hurricanes that might injure the dreamer, and tidal waves that might engulf the dreamer. GF3 therefore includes all situations in which an impersonal force in the environment may enhance a character's well-being or heighten emotional pleasure or satisfaction, such as waves that carry a person to the shore or beautiful rainbows that cause great joy.

M2, as already noted, is reserved for falling or the danger of falling. For symmetry's sake, GF2 is restricted to any situation in which a dream character is suspended above the ground or flying under her or his own power. This category also can include situations in which a dream character feels as though she or he has the potential to fly, live in the clouds, be in another universe, or be in any other state that is the opposite of "the danger of falling."

Finally, M1 encompasses all those frustrating situations in which dream characters encounter environmental obstacles, such as doors that won't open, or in which they are unable to move, are lost, or are in danger of being late. GF1 is therefore defined by the "bountiful environments" mentioned in Hall and Van de Castle's (1966) definition of a good fortune. These are environments with beautiful animals, imaginary creatures, beautiful vistas, and an abundance of resources. GF1 differs from GF3 in that the dream report itself contains no evidence that the dream character's well-being is heightened or emotional satisfaction enhanced.

In addition to the frequent presence of good fortunes, memorable dreams also seem to be characterized by particular patterns of Hall–Van de Castle indicators. This can be seen by looking at the patterns in the three types of such dreams—transcendent, existential, and anxiety—identified in studies using 1-month diaries from college students; these three types were then compared with everyday dreams (Busink & Kuiken, 1996; Kuiken & Sikora, 1993). The examples provided in these two studies suggest that the three types of memorable dreams fit the following coding patterns:

- *Transcendent* dreams are characterized by unusual or distorted settings, famous or mythical characters, friendly interactions, good fortunes, success, and positive emotions.
- *Existential* dreams are more likely to involve deceased characters, major misfortune, thinking instead of physical activity, and intense feelings of sadness or confusion.
- *Anxiety* dreams contain unfamiliar settings, unknown characters or animals, physical aggression directed at the dreamer, physical activities instead of thinking, and intense feelings of apprehension.
- *Ordinary* dreams are far more likely to have familiar settings, familiar characters, nonphysical aggressions, minor misfortunes, and no emotions.

CORRECTING FOR VARIATIONS IN REPORT LENGTH

As discussed in chapter 2, wide variations in the length of dream reports lead to seemingly contradictory findings in the literature on dream content. Thus, a good control for the differing lengths of dream reports is essential. In their original study, Hall and Van de Castle (1966) dealt with this problem by limiting their normative sample to dream reports of between 50 and 300 words.[1] However, experience since they wrote suggests that the percentages and ratios discussed earlier in the chapter are a better way to correct for dream length. These indicators eliminate the problem that some people are wordier than others and allow researchers to use dreams of more than 300 words.

The spreadsheet on DreamResearch.net makes it possible to conduct large-scale studies to demonstrate the power of percentages and ratios in

---

[1] Unfortunately, subsequent work with the original dream reports and coding cards showed that four male dream reports and one female dream report in the sample had fewer than 50 words, and one male report and three female reports had more than 300 words.

correcting for report length. Three different studies—one using the male norms, another the female norms, and a final one using the "Barb Sanders" series (analyzed at length in chapter 5)—show that the content indicators are successful in eliminating any biases created by report length. As a starting point, Table 3.5 presents the results of a correlational study of word length and raw frequencies. For most content categories, the correlations are low. As might be expected, however, there is a substantial correlation between the number of words in the dream reports and the number of activities, objects, and characters. There is also a correlation between the number of words and number of aggressions (.25) and between number of words and the number of friendly interactions (.21). Although not shown in the table, a correlation of .32 has been found between characters and aggressions and .31 between characters and friendly interactions.

Figure 3.1 shows that the content indicators control for these correlations. Comparing dreams with fewer than 175 words with those with more than 175 words in three different samples that range from 50 to 300 words reveals no systematic differences between short and long dreams on any of the percentages and ratios when the two samples are compared. The physical aggression percent for women is unexpectedly lower in the long dreams, and the familiar setting percent lower in the men's dreams, but the same differences are not found in the other samples. Similarly, the bodily misfortunes percent is lower for Barb Sanders in the long dreams, but the same difference does not show up with the other two samples. On the other hand, and as expected, the long dreams are more likely to have at least one incident of most elements, demonstrating that at-least-one indicators—and, by inference, the rating scales used in most dream studies—are extremely sensitive to dream length.

The largest study of the issue of dream length is based on the Barb Sanders series. It includes dreams that range in length from 2 to 500 words. This range encompasses a little more than 95% of her dream reports. The starting point was the random sample of 250 dream reports that ranged from 50 to 250 words in length. The dreams were coded for Characters, Social Interactions, Misfortunes, and Emotions. Then random samples of 200 short and 200 long dream reports were added; these samples were only coded for Social Interactions, the most important and sensitive coding categories, because of limited resources.

The study reveals that the at-least-one indicators rise consistently as word length increases, reaching a plateau at 400 words. This finding shows that long reports have a greater number of social interactions, as most researchers might expect. It is also likely that most other coding categories would show the same sensitivity to report length. None of the rates and percentages, however, is affected by dream length once a minimum of 50 words is reached. A selection of these results is displayed in Figure 3.2. At

TABLE 3.5
Correlation of Category Frequencies With Word Length for Males, Females, and Barb Sanders

	Male norms		Female norms		Barb Sanders	
	f per dream	Correlation with word count	f per dream	Correlation with word count	f per dream	Correlation with word count
Objects	4.89	+.57	5.33	+.58	n/a	n/a
Activities	4.78	+.59	4.95	+.60	n/a	n/a
Characters	2.36	+.46	2.88	+.45	3.68	+.64
Modifiers	2.26	+.39	2.89	+.43	n/a	n/a
Settings	1.27	+.24	1.29	+.24	n/a	n/a
Aggressions	0.80	+.25	0.67	+.20	1.20	+.18
Emotions	0.57	+.33	0.84	+.27	0.98	+.37
Friendliness	0.50	+.21	0.61	+.27	1.18	+.32
Misfortune	0.41	+.07	0.41	+.07	0.65	+.31
Failure	0.17	+.15	0.10	-.01	0.05	-.04
Success	0.16	+.17	0.07	+.08	0.06	+.06
Sexuality	0.15	+.01	0.04	-.01	0.34	+.05
Good fortune	0.07	+.09	0.06	-.06	0.02	+.03

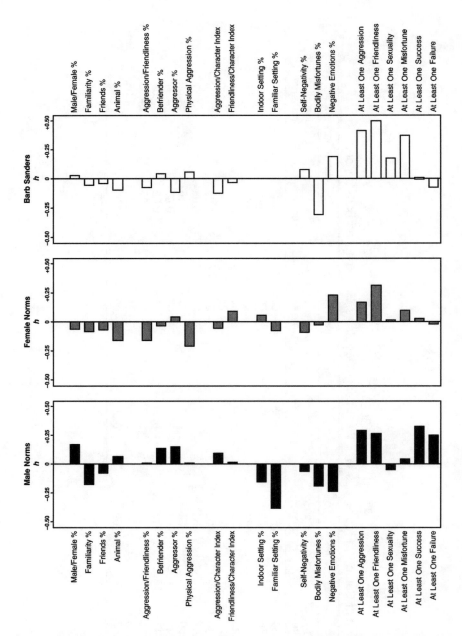

Figure 3.1. A comparison of long and short dreams from various dream series, with the shorter dreams serving as the baseline. The differences in this figure are expressed in terms of the effect size statistic *h,* which is a simple transformation of percentage differences. An *h* of .20 or less is considered small. For instance, the figure shows that the percentage of settings in the longer dreams that are familiar to the male dreamers is much lower than in the shorter dreams that are serving as the baseline, which is indicated by the vertical line in the middle of the figure. Conversely, the figure shows that more of the longer dreams have at least one aggression and at least one friendliness than the shorter dreams for male dreamers, female dreamers, and Barb Sanders.

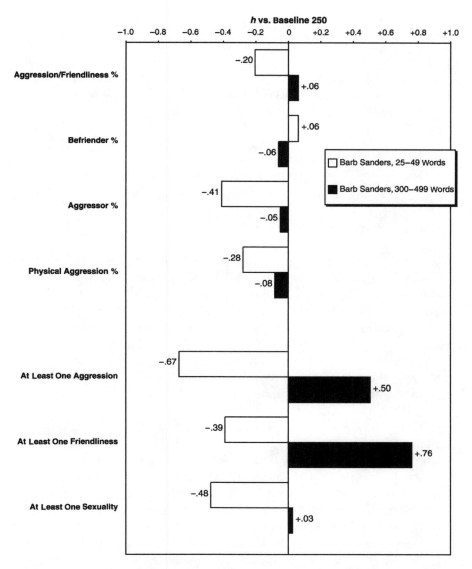

Figure 3.2. A comparison of Barb Sanders's long and short dream reports, compared with her dream reports containing 50 to 300 words. The differences in this figure are expressed in terms of the effect size statistic *h*. For instance, this figure shows that the aggressor percent is 41 *h* points lower in the shorter dreams than it is in the baseline sample of dreams with 50 to 300 words. Conversely, it shows that the longer dreams are 76 *h* points higher than the baseline sample of dreams with at least one friendliness.

the same time, the results in Figure 3.2 also clearly demonstrate that the content indicators do not do a good job of correcting for the distortions that appear in dream reports of 25 to 49 words. The findings for dreams under 25 words in length, which are not included in Figure 3.2, are even more distorted. This result reinforces the earlier decision by Hall and Van de Castle to exclude dream reports shorter than 50 words. It also fits with Hobson, Pace-Schott, and Stickgold's (2000a, p. 1024) impressionistic conclusion that it takes at least 50 words to describe a dream experience. Thus, it seems unlikely that repeatable and scientifically useful results can be obtained with short reports.

THE STATISTICAL ANALYSIS OF HALL–VAN DE CASTLE DATA

Testing for Statistical Significance

Many psychologists believe that the usefulness of determining p values has been vastly overrated because statistical significance is simply a function of sample size if even a small difference exists (Cohen, 1994; Meehl, 1997; Thompson, 1999a). Significance levels may be so misleading that some psychologists have advocated their banishment from scientific journals (Hunter, 1997; Scarr, 1997; Schmidt, 1996). Nevertheless, p values are likely to persist for some time; studies of the statistics used in journal articles in the 1990s suggest that the critics have had little impact in deemphasizing significance levels and increasing the use of effect sizes (Thompson, 1999b, 1999c).

The statistical approach most compatible with the Hall–Van de Castle content indicators is simple but powerful and uses the latest techniques available for determining p values. A Hall–Van de Castle analysis begins with nonparametric statistics because they do not require any assumptions about the level of measurement or the shape of the sampling distribution. Although evidence indicates that parametric tests can be useful even when some of their underlying assumptions are violated, other evidence suggests that nonparametric tests are better when sample sizes are small or unequal (Sawilowsky & Blair, 1992). Moreover, parametric statistics are especially weak with ordinal or nominal data, even when sample sizes are relatively large, because such data are likely to deviate from a normal curve (Micceri, 1989; Nanna & Sawilowsky, 1998).

Given the lack of an underlying continuous distribution with nominal data such as the Hall–Van de Castle system provides, most statistics textbooks suggest the use of proportions or chi square (e.g., Siegel & Castellan, 1988). Fortunately, these two statistics are ideal for the percentage indicators used in the Hall–Van de Castle system (e.g., Reynolds, 1984). Moreover, the test for the significance of differences between two independent proportions and chi square provide exactly the same results for the 2 × 2 categorical tables most frequently used with the Hall–Van de Castle system. That is, the z score derived from a proportions test is equal to the square root of chi square (Ferguson, 1981, pp. 211–213). In addition, as Cohen (1977) explains, a proportion is merely a type of mean in which all the values in the distribution are either 0 or 1, so "the same kind of inferential issues" are involved with proportions as with means in general (p. 179). Nothing would be gained by determining the mean number of characters or emotions or aggressions per dream, even if the calculation of means did not have problems stemming from the differing lengths of dream reports from sample to sample.

The computationally intensive randomization strategies made feasible by programs available through DreamResearch.net are used to determine p values (Noreen, 1989). Like the nonparametric statistics to which they are closely related, randomization strategies have the great virtue of bypassing most of the assumptions necessary for the use of parametric statistics. First, they make random sampling unnecessary. Second, they do not assume a normal distribution, Third, randomization techniques are also useful because they work equally well with longitudinal studies of individual cases and other types of repeated-measures designs. Fourth, through the use of 1,000 or more resamplings from the original samples, they provide exact p values, not approximations. They do assume that the samples being compared have similar shapes and variances, but that is also true for parametric statistics (Franklin, Allison, & Gorman, 1997).

The p values for the percentage differences between samples are determined by the randomization strategy called *permutation testing* by statisticians and *approximate randomization* by social scientists. With this method, the difference between the two original samples is compared with a distribution of differences obtained by pooling the data from both samples and then creating 1,000 or more pairs of random samples. The p value is simply the percentage of times that the difference between a pair of randomly drawn samples is greater than or equal to the difference between the two original samples. For example, in a comparison of the normative male/female percents for men (67/33) and women (48/52), there were only 6 instances in 5,000 trials where the difference between the randomly drawn pairs of samples was greater than or equal to the difference between the two original samples, so the p value is .0012 (6/5000 = .0012).

When the results using approximate randomization are compared with the standard formula in a study of male/female percent, there is no disagreement as to the level of significance. However, when the same analysis is done with some of the other Hall–Van de Castle indicators, discrepancies between the two methods are revealed. The standard formula sometimes indicates that the results are significant at the .05 or .01 level of confidence, but approximate randomization shows that the results are not significant at either of those levels. In such cases, the formula is wrong because the frequency distribution is far different from the assumed normal distribution. Figure 3.3 presents examples of the highly skewed frequency distributions for several Hall–Van de Castle content categories. It also shows that the distribution for characters is considerably less skewed.

Statistical analyses for the aggression (A/C) and friendliness (F/C) indexes require a different rationale because they are ratios, not proportions. Statistically speaking, the Social Interaction indexes are ratios of two sample means. In the case of the A/C index, for example, the index in effect compares the mean number of aggressions in a sample to the mean number of characters. Because both of these means are determined by adding up raw frequencies and dividing by the total number of dreams, it is possible to add up the number of aggressions and divide by the number of characters to arrive at the same result. Once the ratios have been calculated for both samples and the difference between the two samples has been determined, the p value can be determined by approximate randomization in the same way as for percentage-based indicators. In other words, for significance testing the social interaction indexes "behave" as though they were proportions, even though they are not.

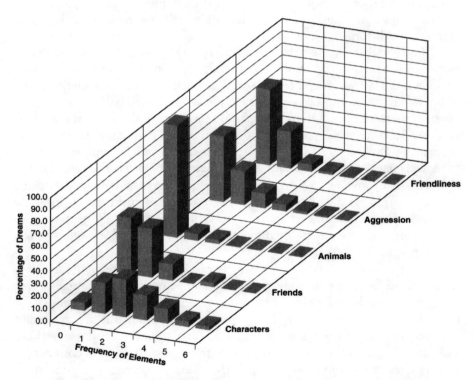

Figure 3.3. Frequency distributions for selected Hall–Van de Castle categories.

Determining Confidence Intervals by Bootstrapping

Confidence intervals provide an indication of the precision of the findings with any given sample. Cohen (1994) and Meehl (1997) believed it would be more useful—and more sobering—if 95% confidence intervals were provided, rather than p values. Cohen (1994) suspects that confidence intervals are seldom reported because they are "embarrassingly large" in most psychological studies (p. 1002). This point holds true for some Hall–Van de Castle findings as well. In the case of the difference between men and women on the familiarity percent, for example, a 95% confidence interval of 18% to 36% does not sound as impressive as a p value of .000 (Domhoff, 1996, p. 56).

The randomization strategy called *bootstrapping* makes it possible to determine confidence intervals for individual samples. As with other randomization statistics, the basic idea is to draw 1,000 or more resamples and examine the distribution of outcomes. In the case of bootstrapping, the unique aspect is that random samples of the same size as the original sample are created by putting the score just drawn back into the sample before the next random pick is made (i.e., "resampling with replacement"). As a result of replacement, some of the original codings appear more than once in each new random sample, and some codings appear not at all. The basic assumption is that the resamples "are analogous to a series of independent random samples" (Mooney & Duval, 1993, p. 11). Simulation studies using samples with known parameters support this assumption. They also show that bootstrapping provides more accurate confidence intervals than do standard formulas that assume normal distributions based on randomly drawn samples. Bootstrapping also allows confidence intervals to be asymmetrical when a distribution is skewed, something not possible with the standard formula.

The approach to calculating bootstrapped confidence intervals most frequently used by applied statisticians, the percentile method, is ideal for use with the Hall–Van de Castle content indicators because it is consistent with the use of percentages for determining p values and effect sizes. In addition, the other methods either revert to parametric assumptions or require hundreds of thousands of resamples, with little gain (Mooney & Duval, 1993). Although the percentile method is of limited usefulness with samples of fewer than 30 and requires 1,000 or more resamples, these potential problems are not relevant for Hall–Van de Castle analyses because they use large samples and rely on resampling software available through DreamResearch.net.

Statistics textbooks usually suggest several hundred to 1,000 resamples to determine the 95% confidence interval. To set the 95% confidence interval, the bootstrapping program available through DreamResearch.net first generates a value for each of 5,000 resamples of the indicator being studied. Next, it counts down from the largest value in the distribution to the 125th largest value and then up from the smallest value to the 125th smallest value. The 125th largest value and the 125th smallest value are the 95% confidence interval with 5,000 resamples. (In other words, 5% of 5,000 equals 250, with half of the 250 at one end of the distribution, the other half at the other end.)

Determining Effect Sizes

Critics of conventional significance testing argue for an emphasis on the magnitude of differences between two samples and greater use of "effect size" statistics (Rosenthal, Rosnow, & Rubin, 2000). The Hall–Van de Castle system responds to this new emphasis by using Cohen's h statistic, which is ideal for use with percentage data. Conceptually, the effect size when comparing two percentages is simply the difference between them. Moreover, this difference is equal to phi and lambda, the two statistics used to determine effect sizes with chi square. This result might be expected on the basis of the earlier discussion of the equivalence of proportions and chi square with 2×2 tables (Ferguson, 1981; Reynolds, 1984). It is also important to note that the magnitude of the relationship between two percentages can be understood in correlational terms: As Rosenthal and Rubin (1982) show, the difference between two percentages is equal to Pearson's r for dichotomous variables, so nothing is gained by using a correlational approach instead of percentages.

Unfortunately, an effect size using differences between two percentages cannot be quite as simple computationally as it is conceptually. A correction has to be made for the fact that it is not possible to calculate the standard deviation of a distribution of scores that has been transformed into percentiles. To deal with this problem, Cohen (1977) created the h statistic, which is based on an arcsine transformation of the percentages calculated for the two samples. This correction can be made using tables found in Cohen (1977, p. 183) and Domhoff (1996, p. 315). Moreover, the h statistic itself is calculated by the DreamSAT spreadsheet on DreamResearch.net, making use of the table unnecessary. Generally speaking, h is a little more than twice as large as the percentage difference between two samples when the percentages for the two samples are between 20 and 80. It is only at the extremes that h becomes increasingly large.

The determination of what is a small, medium, or large effect size varies from research area to research area and is, in large part, a judgment that is based on experience. Cohen suggests that a sensible starting point is to consider $h = .20$ a small effect size, $h = .40$ a medium effect size, and $h = .80$ a large effect size. However, he also advises researchers to "avoid the use of these conventions" if they can substitute "exact values provided by theory or experience" in the specific area in which they work (Cohen, 1977, p. 184). The experience with Hall–Van de Castle findings to date has found that effect sizes up to .20 are small, effect sizes from .21 to .40 are medium, and effect sizes above .40 are large. Effect sizes of .50 or above have been extremely rare except in a few case studies (Domhoff, 1996, chapter 8; Domhoff, 1999b).

To provide some perspective on the relative magnitude of these effect sizes, Table 3.6 presents the mean effect sizes that Rosnow and Rosenthal (1997) calculated for several areas of psychological research, along with the equivalent h values calculated for this book. The table shows that the effect sizes in Hall–Van de Castle studies are in the middle of the range.

There is good reason to believe that h works just as well with the "repeated measures" of a long-term dream series as it does with independent samples. This claim derives from a simulation study using 10,000 resamples. The simulation shows that Cohen's formula for determining the effect size between two independent means, d, produced almost exactly the same results with correlated measures as did a more complex formula that takes into account the size of any correlation between two samples. Because proportions are simply a special case of the mean, this result holds for Cohen's h as well. Although the authors concluded that the more complex equation used in their simulation study is "consistently slightly more accurate," they also noted that "the differences are quite small and are trivial for the sample size of 50" (Dunlap, Cortina, Vaslow, & Burke, 1996, p. 172). Because the differences are small and the sample sizes are almost always greater than 50 in Hall–Van de Castle studies, it is feasible to use h for both independent and repeated-measures studies of dream content.

The h statistic also makes it possible to create a clear "graphic representation" of the kind Cohen (1990) advocates because the effect sizes for any

TABLE 3.6
Effect Sizes in Selected Areas of Psychological Research

	Mean effect size in Pearson's r	Mean effect size in Cohen's d	Equivalent effect size in Cohen's h
Laboratory interviews	.07	.14	.14
Reaction time	.08	.17	.16
Hall–Van de Castle studies			.20–.40
Learning	.26	.54	.52
Person perception	.27	.55	.54
Inkblot tests	.39	.84	.78
Everyday situations	.40	.88	.80

Note. From *People Studying People* (p. 47), by R. L. Rosnow and R. Rosenthal, 1997, New York: W. H. Freeman and Company. Copyright 1997 by W. H. Freeman and Company. Adapted with permission.

subset of the Hall–Van de Castle indicators can be placed on a bar graph that resembles an MMPI profile. This "h profile" immediately reveals the comparative size of the h differences between any two samples on the content indicators that are being used. When new samples are regularly compared with the norms, it is possible to determine quickly whether any consistent patterns exist for particular types of individuals or groups. Patterns that are based on comparisons of h profiles are the closest approximation to a multivariate analysis that can be achieved with the Hall–Van de Castle content indicators.

However, the h statistic cannot be used to determine effect sizes for the A/C and F/C indexes because h is based on a mathematical transformation that is valid only for distributions that vary between 0 and 1. The simple arithmetic difference between the two sample ratios is therefore used as the basis for estimating the effect size. Because the A/C and F/C ratios are between .20 and .80 in most samples, the lack of a correction for extreme scores in this method of determining effect sizes is not a problem. The effect-size findings for these two indexes are made comparable to h by multiplying by 2.36, a figure that was determined through an empirical analysis using many subsamples of Hall–Van de Castle indicators.

Figure 3.4 presents the h-profile for a comparison of the male and female norms; the profile is based on the methods described in this chapter for determining p values and effect sizes, using the female norms as the "baseline" group. The largest effect sizes concern the higher male/female and physical aggression percents, the higher percentage of dreams with at least one sexual interaction, and the lower familiar settings percent in men's dream reports. With regard to the guidelines for small, medium, and large effect sizes stated earlier, there is only one large difference: the higher male/ female percent in the dreams of men. For those who want to study gender differences, it also can be said that there is a pattern of small differences; but for purposes of developing a neurocognitive model of dreams, which is the goal of this book, the important point is that the norms provide a baseline for comparing new samples of men or women and for studying individual men and women.

The Importance of Replications

According to Cohen (1990), there is no substitute for replication studies in psychology no matter how large the sample size or how great the sophistication of the statistical analysis. This admonition seems doubly important for dream research, in which contradictory results are frequent because of the many small studies using different rating scales. It therefore should be taken as a rule that any result reported in the dream literature is considered tentative until it has been replicated at least once. This rule

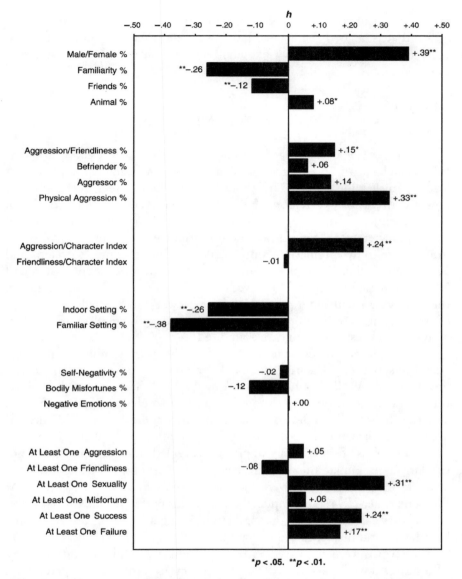

h

| | −.50 | −.40 | −.30 | −.20 | −.10 | 0 | +.10 | +.20 | +.30 | +.40 | +.50 |

Male/Female %   +.39**
Familiarity %   **−.26
Friends %   **−.12
Animal %   +.08*

Aggression/Friendliness %   +.15*
Befriender %   +.06
Aggressor %   +.14
Physical Aggression %   +.33**

Aggression/Character Index   +.24**
Friendliness/Character Index   −.01

Indoor Setting %   **−.26
Familiar Setting %   **−.38

Self-Negativity %   −.02
Bodily Misfortunes %   −.12
Negative Emotions %   +.00

At Least One Aggression   +.05
At Least One Friendliness   −.08
At Least One Sexuality   +.31**
At Least One Misfortune   +.06
At Least One Success   +.24**
At Least One Failure   +.17**

*p < .05. **p < .01.

Figure 3.4. The *h* profile for the Hall–Van de Castle male normative sample, using the female normative sample as a baseline. For instance, men are 26 *h* points lower than women in the percentage of human dream characters that are known to them, whereas they are 33 *h* points higher on the percentage of their aggressions that are physical in nature.

makes it possible to build on solid findings in working toward the ultimate goal—that is, a good theory—rather than spend time critiquing each rival study or developing unlikely explanations that span the range of disparate findings.

NECESSARY SAMPLE SIZES

Cohen's (1990) trenchant critique of the use of statistics in psychological research also notes that small sample sizes are a major problem that leads to misleading results. This problem looms even larger in the study of dream content for two reasons. First, the crucial issue for studies of dream content using nominal categories is the frequency with which various categories appear per dream report, not the total number of dream reports. If, for example, friendly interactions only occur in 42% of women's dreams and 37% of men's dreams, as the norms show to be the case, then a sample of 30 dreams actually contains far fewer than 30 friendly interactions. Second, the relatively small differences that exist between individuals and groups on most content indicators cannot be detected with small samples when conventional tests of significance are used.

Two earlier studies demonstrated that the average minimum sample size necessary for studies using the Hall–Van de Castle system is 100 to 125 dream reports if all the indicators are to be used. The first study making this point is based on many thousands of subsamples of 25, 50, 75, 100, and 125 dream reports drawn from the original codings of the 500 dreams used to establish the male norms. A determination of "average departures from the norms" for each subsample size revealed that subsamples did not regularly approximate the normative figure for most content categories until at least 100 dream reports were included (Domhoff, 1996, pp. 65–66). At the same time, 250 reports replicated the norms perfectly, and samples with 125 reports came close. In a second study, using a 3-month dream journal kept by a natural scientist, the results with the 178 dream reports with 50 or more words were compared with those from subsamples of various sizes. This study showed that it took 100 dream reports to come within 5 percentage points of the overall findings for most indicators (Domhoff, 1996, p. 148).

Because p values are a function of both the size of the difference between two groups and the sample size, it is possible to estimate the approximate number of dream reports that are needed for obtaining significant p values. For example, in testing for the significance of the difference between the male/female percents in two samples, each sample has to have 100 dream reports if an h difference of .20 is to be significant at the .05 level. Each sample would have to have 175 dream reports to reach significance at the .01 level. However, if the h difference for the male/female percent is

.40, as it is between the men and women who contributed to the normative samples, then only 25 dream reports would be needed in each sample.

The results in the previous paragraph were obtained by combining the findings with the 1,000 dream reports in the male and female normative samples to determine the mean number of elements that appeared in each dream report for each Hall–Van de Castle indicator. This *element rate* makes it possible to calculate approximately how many dream reports are needed for significance at the .05 or .01 levels for each indicator, depending on the size of *h*. The calculation involves the rate of elements per dream, the relevant *z* score (1.96 or 2.54, for significance levels of .05 and .01, respectively), and the hypothetical *h* value. Selected findings from this analysis are presented in Tables 3.7 and 3.8. Table 3.7 shows the sample sizes needed for significance at the .05 level when *h* is .20, .35, or .50; these values encompass the range for *h* in most dream studies. Table 3.8 presents the *h* difference that is necessary to obtain significance at the .05 level with samples of 30, 75, and 125 dream reports.

If these results are taken as seriously as they should be, then the shortcomings of the dream research literature should be readily apparent.

TABLE 3.7
Estimated Minimum Number of Dream Reports Needed
in Each Comparison Group to Find a Statistically Significant Difference
at the .05 Level

	Estimated rate of elements per dream	Critical *n* needed for these hypothetical *h* differences		
		h = ±.20	*h* = ±.35	*h* = ±.50
Characters				
Male/female percent	1.927	100	33	16
Familiarity percent	2.471	78	26	13
Friends percent	2.471	78	26	13
Family percent	2.471	78	26	13
Social interaction percents				
Aggression/friendliness percent	1.076	179	59	29
Aggressor percent	0.484	397	130	64
Physical aggression percent	0.739	260	85	42
Settings				
Indoor setting percent	1.177	164	54	27
Familiar setting percent	0.626	307	101	50

Note. The formula used to calculate these "critical *n*" values is as follows:

$$n_c = \frac{2 \, Z_c^2}{h^2}$$

Z_c is the critical *Z*-score for significance at the desired *p* level (in this table, Z_c = 1.96), *h* is the hypothetical *h* difference between the two groups being compared, and *r* is the rate at which the coding elements in question typically appear in a single dream.

TABLE 3.8

Estimated *h* Difference Needed to Find a Statistically Significant Difference at the .05 Level, Given Two Dream Series of Equal Length

	Estimated rate of elements per dream	Critical *h* needed for these sample sizes		
		n = 30	*n* = 75	*n* = 125
Characters				
Male/female percent	1.927	.36	.23	.18
Familiarity percent	2.471	.32	.20	.16
Friends percent	2.471	.32	.20	.16
Family percent	2.471	.32	.20	.16
Social interaction percents				
Aggression/friendliness percent	1.076	.49	.31	.24
Aggressor percent	0.484	.73	.46	.36
Physical aggression percent	0.739	.59	.37	.29
Settings				
Indoor setting percent	1.177	.47	.30	.23
Familiar setting percent	0.626	.64	.40	.31

Note. The formula used to calculate these "critical *h*" values is as follows:

$$h^c = \frac{Z_c}{\sqrt{nr/2}}$$

Z_c is the critical *Z*-score for significance at the desired *p* level (in this table, Z_c = 1.96), *n* is the number of dream reports in the two samples being compared (it is assumed that the samples are of equal size), and *r* is the rate at which the coding elements in question typically appear in a single dream.

First, similarities from group to group and person to person may have been overemphasized in some studies because of small sample sizes. Second, many interesting hypotheses probably have been rejected prematurely. Thus, large sample sizes are needed to construct a sound theory.

CONCLUSION

The Hall–Van de Castle system of content analysis is comprehensive, reliable, and easily adapted to modern statistical procedures. It has yielded sound findings on how dream content relates to age, culture, psychopathology, and individual differences when applied to samples of adequate size, and it has shown that dream content is generally consistent over time and continuous with either past or present waking emotional concerns. Furthermore, as chapter 4 shows, it now can be supported and supplemented with the aid of fast searches that use a Web site on the Internet.

4

A NEW RESOURCE FOR
CONTENT ANALYSIS

The biggest drawback with nominal categories such as those used in the Hall–Van de Castle system is that they are labor intensive. Part of this problem has been solved by DreamSAT, which provides instant and accurate data analyses once the codings are entered. Still more of the problem can be mitigated through the development of Internet-based resources that are accessible to all dream researchers. Such online resources have several advantages that stem from centralization: They can be used from any location without the need for extra software, only one database needs to be maintained, and any improvements to the program or additions to the database benefit everyone.

This chapter discusses one such resource, http://www.DreamBank.net, which was created by Adam Schneider in 1999. This site contains both a large collection of dream reports and a search engine, which is written in the Perl programming language. The site can be used in at least three ways. First, it can be used to identify subsamples in long-term dream series. Second, it can be used to conduct consistency studies for specific characters and elements in a dream series. Third, it can be used to explore possible new categories for doing content analysis with the search engine.

The search engine locates individual words, long strings of words, or phrases by means of *regular expressions*, which are codes used for pattern matching in computer programming (see Schneider & Domhoff, 1999, for a detailed discussion of regular expressions). Once the pattern is located, the search engine reports the identification number for each dream that contains the requested query, along with the percentage of dreams containing the words. Contingencies between patterns also can be calculated, such as the degree of relationship between the words "house" and "father."

The dream reports retrieved by the search engine can be viewed in full on the screen or in an abbreviated form that displays only the sentences with the requested words in them. The requested words are highlighted and in boldface when the dreams are brought up on the screen for viewing. When scrolling through the dreams on the screen, those that are not relevant can be eliminated before the dreams are printed or analyzed on the screen. It is also possible to draw random samples from DreamBank search results. The minimum and maximum number of words per dream in the random sample can be specified along with the desired sample size.

The site contains more than 11,000 dream reports from groups and individuals of all ages. The reports can be used for a wide range of studies, including those relating to figurative thought in dreams. They can be drawn upon to create new sets of dreams on specific topics, such as dreams that contain weddings, bridges, or murders. Researchers who want to use the search engine to study dream reports they have collected themselves but do not want those reports to be part of the DreamBank site may arrange for a confidential site. Although every effort has been made to ensure that the dream reports on DreamBank.net are accurate and authentic, some of the dreams from children and teenagers may be the product of poetic license. The best defense against this possibility is to use the largest sample size that is feasible. Table 4.1 presents an overview of the dream reports available on DreamBank.net.

FACILITATING A HALL–VAN DE CASTLE CONTENT ANALYSIS

The coding of large dream samples using the Hall–Van de Castle categories can be aided in several ways that save many hours of reading through dream reports. Simple word searches are most valuable in facilitating the coding of social interactions with specific dream characters. For example, in the 3,116 dreams of the Barb Sanders series analyzed in chapter 5, one of her brothers appears 97 times and one of her daughters appears 165 times. Her aggressive and friendly social interactions with them were coded at the rate of one or two per minute by entering their names into the search program and scrolling through the dream reports online.

Word strings are most useful when they are based on phrases or expressions that are found to be frequent in an individual dream series. For example, most dreamers use only a few phrases for sexual interactions, such as "made love" or "had sex." These phrases then can be combined with a standard string of sexual interaction terms created by using "pipes," which are the means for signifying "or" in the language of regular expressions. Thus, a string like "kiss|hug|intercourse|made_love|had_sex" might capture a representative sample of sex dreams in a given dream series. Word strings also can be useful for creating two subsamples that are based on different defining elements, which can be compared with each other. For example, the frequency of striving and the percentage of negative

TABLE 4.1
The Dream Series Available on http://www.DreamBank.net

	Gender	Years	N
Alta: a detailed dreamer	female	1985–1997	302
Arlie: a middle-aged woman	female	1992–1998	212
Barb Sanders	female	1960–1997	3,116
Barb Sanders: baseline	female	1960–1999	250
Bay Area girls	female	1996–1997	388
Betty: a college student	female	1993	28
Blind dreamers	male and female	mid–1990s	381
Chuck: a physical scientist	male	1991–1993	75
College men and women, 1999	male and female	1999	320
College women, late 1940s	female	1946–1950	667
David: teenage dreams	male	1990–1999	156
Dorothea: 53 years of dreams	female	1912–1965	900
Edna: a blind woman	female	1948–1949	19
Emma's husband	male	1940–1998	72
Emma: 48 years of dreams	female	1949–1997	1,221
Female norms	female	1940s–1950s	491
Jeff: a lucid dreamer	male	2000	87
Joan: a lesbian	female	mid-1980s	42
Male norms	male	1940s–1950s	491
Mark: a young boy	male	1997–1999	23
Melissa: a young girl	female	1998–2000	67
Miami home/lab	male	1963–1965	445
The Natural Scientist	male	1939	218
Prospero: a blind man	male	1970	202
Prudence: a literary woman	female	1927–1998	209
Samantha: in her 20s	female	1992–1999	63
Santa Cruz multiethnic	male and female	1998	35
Seventh grade girls	female	1996	69
Swiss children	male and female	1989–1995	299
Teenage girls (West Coast)	female	mid-1990s	89
Teenagers (Midwest)	male and female	1998	194
Topwater: a violent man	male	1965–1980	301
Univ. California Santa Cruz women	female	1996	81
Wedding dreams	female	1940s–1950s and 1990s	65

emotions could be compared for dream reports with music- and sports-related terms in them.

There are also some dream elements that most people describe with common words or phrases. Any dream report that describes the experience of flying under the dreamer's own power is likely to contain the word "fly," "float," or "air," although those words also will appear in some reports that are not about the topic under discussion. Similarly, most metamorphoses or abrupt scene changes are likely to be captured by "turned into," "changed into," "become," "transform," and "suddenly." There will be many times when these words do not imply a metamorphosis or scene change, but those instances can be eliminated by reading through the dream reports before doing the analysis.

DreamBank also makes it possible in some cases to save time by entering large strings of words that are likely to locate most of the elements that might be coded for a particular Hall–Van de Castle category. Such strings seem practical for codings for food and eating references, emotions, and animals. However, even the longest of strings is likely to miss some dream reports that contain instances of the coding category, so there is a trade-off between efficiency and accuracy that must be taken into account. The loss of accuracy can be gauged in some cases by reading through random samples of the dream reports to determine what percentage of the codeable elements were missed. Moreover, it is still necessary to look at each instance brought to the screen in order to eliminate those that do not meet the coding rules for one reason or another. This latter point can be demonstrated here with a brief analysis of the animals that appear in the normative male and female dream samples.

For this demonstration, the dream reports coded by Hall and Van de Castle as containing at least one animal were located by entering the code for animals—ANI—into the SearchCodings program available through http://DreamResearch.net for use with already coded sets of dreams. Once the actual animals in the dreams were written down, this string of animal terms was then entered into the query box for a search of all the reports in the two normative samples. The search produced 8 more male reports and 10 more female reports than were coded for an animal character. This overshot stems from instances such as "soldiers in a *fox*hole," a discussion of "small words like '*cat*'," and the presence of a "*goose*-necked lamp." Moreover, the search retrieved figurative expressions, such as "flying like a *bird*," "making *pigs* of themselves," and "acting like maddened *animals*." Once those cases were removed, the findings were similar to the normative Hall–Van de Castle figures for the percentage of dream reports that have at least one animal. For future studies of animals in dreams, long strings of animal words could be used as a starting point, but they would have to be augmented by a reading of the dream series under study.

USING DREAMBANK.NET FOR CONTENT ANALYSIS

The search engine on DreamBank.net makes it possible to carry out all four steps of a content analysis: (a) create carefully defined categories that have high reliability, (b) determine frequencies for each category, (c) transform the raw frequencies into percentages or rates, and (d) compare the findings with norms or a control group. This approach is completely independent of the Hall–Van de Castle coding system. The phrases or strings of words entered into the search program in effect define the new categories. Because the same results are guaranteed each time the sample is searched, the categories have perfect reliability. The search engine also does the second step of a content analysis, which is to provide frequency counts. The program generates some of the necessary percentages, but this step has to be supplemented in most studies by separate analyses of the kind to be presented next.

The fourth step of a content analysis, a comparison with a normative or control group, can be carried out by drawing on other sets or series in the DreamBank. For many studies, the ideal comparative sets may be the dream reports that Hall and Van de Castle used in creating the male and female norms discussed in chapter 3. Using these dream reports as a baseline gives a study some comparability with Hall–Van de Castle findings. However, in some cases it might make more sense to use another series as the comparison group. For example, one or two dream series from adult women might make good comparison groups for studying a new dream series from a woman of about the same age. The comparison samples can be searched for the phrase or word string at the same time the main sample is being searched.

These points can be demonstrated with a simple study of pet animals in dreams. The categories first determine the frequency with which people mention the two most common house pets: cats and dogs. These findings are then used to create percentage-based indicators that distinguish between "cat people" and "dog people." To begin, the search program is put on the "OR" mode. Next, two strings of words are entered that include regular expressions of various kinds to ensure a focused and quality search:

$$\wedge(cat||kitten|kitty|kittie|feline)s?\wedge\wedge(dog|doggy|doggie|puppy|puppies|canine)s?\wedge.$$

Then the dreams of two cat lovers, "Alta" and Barb Sanders, are selected for searching, along with those of a young girl, Melissa, who loves all animals, and an older woman, Arlie, who has little or no interest in animals. In addition, the dreams used to create the female and male norms for the Hall–Van de Castle system are selected to provide comparison groups. The male normative dream sample is included to see whether a gender difference exists in the preference for cats and dogs. The search produces the results that are presented in Table 4.2.

As can be seen in the table, the results reveal the number and percentage of dreams that contain a mention of at least one cat, at least one dog, and at least one dog or cat. The third column from the left, which contains the summary information for the presence of a cat or dog, provides an indication of a general interest in house pets. It can be tentatively called the "pet percent." As expected, Arlie, with only 1.9% of her dreams containing a cat or a dog, is below the female norm of 3.9%; the other three dreamers

TABLE 4.2
Findings on Pets With Selected Dream Series on DreamBank.net

	Cats	Dogs	"Pet percent"	"Cat percent"
Female norms (*n* = 491)	9(1.8%)	11(2.2%)	19(3.9%)	45%
Male norms (*n* = 491)	2(0.4%)	11(2.2%)	13(2.6%)	15%
Alta (*n* = 422)	55(13.0%)	21(5.0%)	67(15.9%)	72%
Arlie (*n* = 212)	1(0.5%)	3(1.4%)	4(1.9%)	25%
Barb Sanders (*n* = 250)	12(4.8%)	8(3.2%)	18(7.2%)	60%
Melissa (*n* = 67)	9(13.4%)	11(16.4%)	18(26.9%)	45%

are above the female norm, suggesting that they are interested in pet animals. There is a small but trivial difference between the male and female normative dreams on the pet percent.

An indication of the degree to which a person dreams about cats as opposed to dogs is obtained by dividing the total number of dreams with at least one cat by the total number of dreams with at least one cat or at least one dog. Recalling the assumption that frequency reveals the intensity of interest or concern, this "cat percent" reveals that Alta and Barb Sanders are more concerned with cats than dogs, whereas young Melissa seems to be interested in both cats and dogs. The normative sample for women suggests that Alta and Barb Sanders are well above the average woman on cat percent. The comparison of the female and male normative dream samples shows a large difference between women (45%) and men (15%). The results of this simple study, in the context of the continuity principle discussed in chapter 1, lead to a substantive prediction: The pet percent and the cat percent will be continuous with waking interests and concerns in future studies using these scales.

More generally, the two scales show the possibilities for creating scales for parents, family members, and friends. They would by no means be perfect, but it is easy enough to figure out just how accurate they are by making comparisons with hand tallies. Their justification is that they make possible overview studies of long-term dream series that would not otherwise be feasible. However, it remains essential to tailor each scale on the basis of a careful examination of the dream series to which it is to be applied.

The development of useful scales that are independent of the Hall–Van de Castle system also can be demonstrated through a "sensory references" coding scale that was created to study 372 dream reports from 15 blind men and women (Hurovitz et al., 1999). This example also provides an entry point into the issue of identifying possible instances of figurative thought in dreams, because many sensory terms are used metaphorically (e.g., "I see what you mean"; "the taste of victory is sweet"; and "that deal smells fishy to me"). In this study, the researchers compared the dreams of people who were congenitally or adventitiously blind and examined differences in the percentage of visual, auditory, olfactory, gustatory, and tactile references. All forms of the words "see," "saw," "watch," "look," and "notice" were used to provide a starting point for coding visual imagery. All forms of "hear" and "listen" were used to locate possible auditory imagery. All forms of "taste," "smell," "aroma," "scent," "feel," "felt," and "touch" were used as a starting point for the other three senses. This list of words is based on a careful reading of the dream reports for all sensory terms.

After the dream reports with possible sensory references were located by the search program, two coders studied each boldface word and its context to determine which sensory mentions seemed to be literal and which might be figurative. The distinction between the literal and the figurative use of terms is important in most studies, but it is especially crucial in a study looking for visual imagery in the dreams of blind participants. The sensory references were divided into three categories: visual, auditory, and taste/smell/touch, and the percentage of each type was determined. The findings were analyzed in terms of a "taste/smell/touch percent" because earlier studies showed it to be the distinguishing sensory feature in the dreams of blind people. As expected, the taste/smell/touch percent was high in the dream reports of the congenitally blind participants. On the other hand, for two women who lost their sight after age 8, only 1 of 36 sensory references was in the taste/smell/touch category. Five of the women's sensory references were auditory, and the rest (86%) were visual. The findings with the adventitiously blind participants were similar to those for sighted adults in large-scale studies (Snyder, 1970; Zadra, Nielsen, & Donderi, 1998).

The seeming visual exceptions in the dreams of two congenitally blind people turned out to be metaphoric in nature; they used a common metaphor in which "knowing" or "experiencing" is "seeing" (Matlock, 1988; Matlock & Sweetser, 1989; Sweetser, 1990). For example, a 52-year-old woman reported a dream in which she and her husband (also blind since birth) visited with Thomas Jefferson himself on a trip to Monticello. She first says in the dream report that Jefferson "was glad to meet us and he didn't care if we couldn't see," a statement that confirms her lack of vision. However, she then reports that Jefferson took them to "see" the plants in his garden, a statement that appears to be an instance of "experiencing is seeing."

Scales aside, DreamBank.net provides a quick and powerful way to study consistency in dreams. Such studies are most clear-cut for the consistency with which a specific character appears, but they can be done as well for objects such as cars or activities such as running. The frequencies that are found can be turned into percentages in one of two ways: by dividing the frequency for a given year by the number of dreams for that year, or by using the number identifications for each dream to determine frequency per 50 or 100 dream reports. A example of such consistency studies is provided in the final section of this chapter.

STUDYING FIGURATIVE THOUGHT IN DREAMS

The DreamBank search engine, especially when used in conjunction with the Hall–Van de Castle categories, provides an entree into the difficult problem of studying figurative thought in dreams. Two brief examples, which concern dreams about weddings and dreams about bridges, are provided here and are only meant to suggest possibilities.

Wedding dreams are of potential interest for two reasons. Women have more of them than men, and women experience more mishaps and mistakes in them than men do. In terms of the Hall–Van de Castle coding system, previous studies suggest that women's wedding dreams have an unusually high number of misfortunes—the wrong groom, the wrong church, or the wrong dress, for example (Domhoff, 1996). These misfortunes may be a useful starting point for the question of figurative thought in dreams because many of the phrases that are characterized as misfortunes in the Hall–Van de Castle system can be construed as metaphoric (e.g., "I was lost" or "I was overwhelmed by a tidal wave"). The possibility therefore arises that wedding dreams might provide a collective metaphoric portrayal of how American women think about weddings.

The first step in such a study would be to search all the adult dreams on DreamBank.net using a word string like wedding|married|marriage|groom|bride. The search would provide a frequency for each individual and group. As a second step, random samples of wedding dreams could be created for both individuals and groups and then coded with the Misfortunes scale. Then the findings for men and women could be compared with each other and with the male and female norms. If the previous finding of more misfortunes in women's wedding dreams is upheld, more detailed and qualitative studies of the specific misfortunes in those dreams could be undertaken.

Dreams about bridges are of potential use for two reasons. First, they are central to some waking metaphors for personal transitions, such as "cross that bridge when you come to it," "don't burn your bridges," and "that's water under the bridge." Second, there are few or no synonyms for the word that designates these structures. Circumstantial evidence that bridges may serve as metaphors for personal transitions in dreams can be found in a detailed discussion of "bridgeness" in a dream report by Boss (1958), a phenomenological dream theorist who professed to be adamantly opposed to the idea of symbolism. If bridges have a metaphoric meaning in dreams, then perhaps they would be more likely to be associated with misfortunes and negative emotions than they are in waking life, where they are matter-of-fact, easily crossed, and seldom in danger of breaking. So, after eliminating the relatively few instances of the word "bridge" that designate a card game or dental work, the contingencies between bridges and misfortunes and between bridges and apprehension could be determined. If the results of an earlier study using a small sample are any indication, it is likely that relationships will be found (Hall & Nordby, 1972, pp. 136–137).

USING DREAMBANK.NET TO STUDY THE EMMA SERIES

Many of the points made in this brief overview can be demonstrated with several analyses of the "Emma" series. The findings with this series also serve as an introduction to the extensive analysis of the Barb Sanders series in chapter 5.

Emma is a 77-year-old woman who first wrote down her dreams when she was in a Jungian analysis as a young woman. Several years later, when married and the mother of young children, she began writing down her dreams again, with the intent of studying them for symbolism and archetypes at some later point. She eventually lost interest in analyzing the dreams but continued the journal out of habit. The journal contains 1,221 dreams in all, most of them written down between ages 40 and 77. There are no dreams for 1981, 1988, and 1989, and only 47 dreams for 1993 to 1997, when the series ends. Her dreams came to the DreamBank because she asked a Jungian author familiar with content analysis if anyone might want them. Emma wrote down her dreams for another 3 years after she first gave her dream journals to the DreamBank.

Reading through the part of the journal that is relatively continuous over 37 years, the most striking impression is the frequency with which her husband and the minister at her church appear. This impression led to a search of the dreams for the number of appearances by various friends and relatives. It confirms that her husband and minister are by far the most frequent characters in the series. Her husband appears in 30% of the 1,137 dreams during this time period and her minister in 23%. Taken together, they appear in 48.3% of those continuous dreams. If frequency is an indicator of "intensity," as all past studies indicate, then these two men are her greatest concern. Because Emma knew both of them over the entire time period, the question arises as to how consistently she dreamt about them. This analysis shows that she was more likely to dream about her minister in each of the years from 1960 to 1971 and was increasingly likely to dream about her husband until 1990, after which the two men appear more equally in the small number of dreams that were recorded. Table 4.3 summarizes the results.

TABLE 4.3
Number of Dream Reports That Include Emma's Husband or Minister,
by Time Period

Years	Husband	Minister
1960–1971	117	169
1972–1989	201	70
1990–1997	25	17
Total	**343**	**256**

A reading of the dreams about the husband and the minister suggests that they do not often appear in the same dream. This possibility can be studied by using the contingency program that is part of the search engine. Because her husband appears in 30% of the dreams and the minister in 23%, the expected value for their joint appearances is .069 (.30 × .23), or 78 dreams. In fact, they appear together only 51 times. This difference has a p value of .02, suggesting that the two men occupy somewhat separate spheres in the dreamer's mind. Although the effect size is not large, this finding fits with the fact that Emma's husband is not religious and does not go to church with her.

The question naturally arises as to the nature of Emma's interaction with the two men, which can be explored by using the Hall–Van de Castle categories for friendly and aggressive interactions. To answer this question, Thomas Van Rompay first used the search engine to draw two random samples of 100 dreams that contained one of the two dream characters. Then the dreams were coded for friendly and aggressive interactions between Emma and either of the two men. The contrast is striking: Her interactions with her husband are aggressive, but her interactions with her minister are friendly. Furthermore, Emma usually initiates the aggressive interactions with her husband, which mostly consist of angry thoughts, critical comments, and yelling. She and the minister both initiate friendly interactions when they interact. Some of the specific findings from this analysis are presented in Table 4.4.

TABLE 4.4
Emma's Social Interactions With Her Husband and Minister

	Husband* (%)	Minister* (%)
At least one social interaction	26	52
Proportion of social interactions that are friendly	11	93
Proportion of social interactions that are aggressive	89	7

*n = 100 dream reports for each sample.

The findings with the two men are all the more interesting in the context of the findings from a random sample of 100 of Emma's dreams, which Van Rompay (2000) had coded earlier for another project. Compared with the female norms, the most atypical aspect of her dream life is the high rate of friendliness and the low rate of aggression, which makes the pattern with her husband even more striking.

Three inferences about Emma's waking thoughts can be drawn from the analyses of her dream series. First, Emma is intensely concerned about both her husband and her minister in waking life, as shown by the large number of times they both appear in her dreams. Second, her interest in the minister, which reached a high point when she was in her 30s and 40s, has declined. Third, Emma has a greater number of positive feelings about her minister than she does about her husband. Emma's responses to questions that were based on these inferences are discussed in the next chapter, after a method for evaluating dreamer responses is introduced.

CONCLUSION

This chapter has demonstrated some of the possibilities for studying dream reports by using the Hall–Van de Castle system and DreamBank.net in conjunction with each other. It also has shown that DreamBank.net can be used to make analyses that are independent of the Hall–Van de Castle system. In addition, the large number of dreams that are available for searching makes it possible for a wide range of researchers to study dreams without having to develop samples of their own. Researchers also could work together on in-depth studies of a single series, such as the Barb Sanders series discussed in chapter 5. At the least, the dream reports on Dream-Bank.net can serve as control groups in studies by other researchers. The existence of DreamBank.net leads to the possibility that fewer and fewer studies in the dream literature will have small sample sizes or use dream reports that are shorter than 50 words in length.

5

NEW WAYS TO STUDY MEANING
IN DREAMS

The methods and discoveries discussed in chapters 1 through 4 are a solid foundation for future studies that attempt to link dream content to both the neural network for dreaming and waking cognition. Researchers can now focus on atypical cases that make it possible to test specific hypotheses relating to the neurocognitive model. To do this, researchers need good dream recallers who are willing to supply candid responses to inferences derived from blind analyses of their dream reports. The necessary dream reports can be obtained in the laboratory, through home-based monitoring using the Nightcap, or from personal dream journals.

There are several reasons why in-depth analyses of individual dream series, in conjunction with neuropsychological or neuroimaging studies, may be the best research strategy for the development of the neurocognitive model. First, as argued in chapter 2, experimental studies of dreams have been of limited usefulness. Second, it is difficult to collect a large representative sample of thorough dream reports from a group of people or to obtain the amount of nondream information from them that is usually needed. Third, the many findings on the relationship between dream content and age, gender, culture, and psychopathology provide a context within which specific hypotheses can be tested through detailed examinations of themes and coding categories in a dream series. Fourth, a long-term dream series can be studied expeditiously by many different people from many different angles with the help of DreamBank.net.

As useful as individual dream series can be, most of the early case studies have limitations of one sort or another. Although they showed that information can be extracted from a series of dreams, the case studies did not reveal whether all aspects of dreams are coherent and sensible. They demonstrated that many aspects of dreams are continuous with waking personal concerns of the past or present, but they did not show whether or how all elements in a dream relate to waking cognition. Most of all, they did not include a way to deal with disagreements between the inferences of the dream researcher and the replies of the dreamer.

STUDYING A DREAM SERIES

The purpose of this chapter is to present a new approach to studying individual dream journals that might make it possible to understand dream content in great detail and to determine the degree to which it is based in figurative thought. This approach is demonstrated with several different analyses of a series of 3,116 dreams written down by an adult woman known by the pseudonym "Barb Sanders." The study is, in many ways, the most detailed examination of a dream series that ever has been undertaken, but it is not an exhaustive examination of the series. There are many more analyses that would need to be conducted to provide a complete picture of the dreamer and her dreams. To make such investigations possible, all the dreams in the series are available to other researchers on DreamBank.net, along with the codings for several Hall–Van de Castle categories in more than 400 of the dream reports. Future researchers also can apply their own coding systems to the dreams or use the search engine on DreamBank.net to study aspects of the series that the present study does not cover. In addition, the results of interviews with the dreamer and several of her friends are available on request.

In the several blind analyses of dream series carried out by Hall, replies from the dreamers were the main source of information concerning the inferences made on the basis of the dream reports (Domhoff, 1996, chapter 8). This approach makes it possible to focus on what seems to appear most directly in dreams, namely, concerns and interests, by developing questions that are based on inferences that arise from the analysis of the dream reports themselves. This approach makes it possible to bypass personality tests, which so far have not proven to be fruitful in the study of dreams (Domhoff, 1996). The usefulness of this method is demonstrated by the frequency with which Hall's inferences were corroborated, leading to the idea of a continuity principle.

A sole reliance on the dreamers themselves for information has two major problems, however. Sometimes dreamers do not have an answer for a question, and sometimes they provide an answer that is not convincing on the basis of past studies. Disconfirming replies are reassuring, in the sense that they increase confidence in the affirmative replies, but they also generate a further question. How certain is it that the dreamers' negative answers should be used to reject an inference that seems to be based on a solid generalization, namely, the continuity principle?

The problem can be demonstrated with the case of "Lucille," a woman in her 50s who began sending Hall her dream reports after reading one of his books. This series of several hundred dreams over a 10-year period revealed strong consistency from year to year and an h profile close to the norms on most indicators (Schneider & Domhoff, 1995). For the most part, the few deviations from the norms are consistent with her waking life. For example, Lucille has a high percentage of dreams with at least one friendly interaction ($h = +.37$); in her dreams, she shows kindness to her family, her supervisor, and little children, behavior that mirrors her waking behavior. Then, too, she is above the norm in dreams with at least one misfortune ($h = +.45$) as a result of her dreams about the infirmities of both her husband and work supervisor, who did in fact suffer from infirmities.

The analysis of the Lucille series also reveals that she dreams about some people far more than others and has different patterns of friendliness and aggression with each of them, as shown in Table 5.1. These patterns parallel her feelings about them in waking life, with one important exception that is discussed shortly. Lucille dreams most often about her husband, whom she saw every day until his death about 4 years after she started to send dreams to Hall. She has a high rate of both aggressive and friendly interactions with her husband, as shown by the A/C and F/C indexes (described in chapter 3, this volume), and the dreams have a greater number of aggressive than friendly interactions, as shown by an aggression/friendliness percent of 58. This finding fits with the couple's interaction pattern of small annoyances and rejections in waking life.

Although Lucille sees a great deal of both her sisters, who live together, she dreams far more of sister X (110 appearances) than sister Y (53 appearances) and has a far higher rate of both aggressive and friendly interactions with sister X than sister Y. Lucille reports greater emotional involvement with Sister X than Sister Y, which fits with the dream content. In like fashion, Lucille is close to her daughter, of whom she dreams frequently, and has many more friendly than aggressive interactions with her, which—according to her replies to Hall's inquiries—is also the case in waking life. She also was close to her mother, whom she visited daily until the mother

TABLE 5.1
Lucille's Social Interactions With the Main Characters in Her Dreams

Character	Number of appearances	A/C index	F/C index	A/F (%)
Husband	134	.66	.47	58
Sister X	110	.41	.43	49
Daughter	103	.25	.58	30
Supervisor	83	.42	.61	41
Sister Y	53	.10	.07	59
Mother	51	.04	.30	12
Brother	8	.00	.00	n/a
Father	2	.00	.00	n/a

Note. A/C index = aggressions divided by characters; F/C index = friendliness divided by characters; A/F% = aggressions divided by aggressions plus friendliness.

died, and their interactions were far more positive than negative in both dreams and waking life. Lucille dreams least often of her brother and her father and does not have any friendly or aggressive interactions with them. Her brother lives in a distant city, and she rarely sees him. Her father died when she was 9 years old.

The dream patterns match extremely well with her replies concerning her relationships to these family members in waking life, but such is not the case with her work supervisor. This man appears more often than all but three other dream characters. He is involved in more friendly than aggressive interactions with the dreamer, which is a different pattern from that involving her husband. On one or two occasions, the dreamer and her supervisor are hugging or kissing. These contrasting findings with the supervisor and husband are reminiscent of a similar situation in the Emma series discussed at the end of chapter 4, in which it was found that Emma had positive interactions with her minister and negative interactions with her husband. In Lucille's case, Hall inferred that she had romantic feelings toward her supervisor, but she strongly rejected that idea.

Similarly, it now can be added to the information presented in chapter 4 that Emma does not agree that she has strong negative feelings toward her husband. Emma agrees that her husband and minister are the two most important people in her life and that she has positive feelings about her minister, especially in the 1960s when she dreamed of him more frequently. She is reluctant to say anything critical about her relationship with her husband. She reports that they had times of tension between them but that those tensions were transitory and are largely in the past.

But how can we be certain that Emma's dreams about her husband and Lucille's dreams about her supervisor do not follow the continuity principle? It is easy enough to say that they have chosen to report what they know is not the truth or to claim, as clinical theories that are based on defense mechanisms can readily justify, that the dreamers may have repressed their feelings in those specific instances. However, that also means that inferences cannot be falsified, leading to the justified criticism that the theorist is always right no matter what the dreamer says.

There are two ways to deal with this dilemma. The first is to seek out letters and diaries from the dreamer's recent past. The second, and better, approach is to pose the same questions asked of the dreamer to people who know the dreamer well. If those people are in general agreement, they can serve as judge and jury in the case of disagreements between the dreamer and the researcher. If they agree with the dreamer, the researcher is wrong. If they agree with the researcher, then the dreamer is unwilling to answer truthfully for some reason or has a *blind spot* on the issue. The phrase blind spot has been carefully chosen to avoid any implication of what process or processes might be leading to an inaccurate comprehension of one's feelings.

It is also a metaphor that expresses the common understanding that everyone has beliefs or opinions on some personal issues that are at variance with what others judge to be the case.

This study of Barb Sanders makes use of interviews with four of her close women friends, who proved to be knowledgeable about her personal relationships, interests, and potential blind spots. As already noted, the summaries of those interviews are available upon request to researchers who are doing their own study of the series. However, the present study is limited in its demonstration of the power of this approach: There were no major disagreements between the dreamer and the researcher or between the dreamer and her friends. The dreamer rejected some of the researcher's inferences, but the inferences involved issues about which the friends had no information; in any event, it was sufficiently clear that the inferences were wrong.

A PORTRAIT OF BARB SANDERS

Born in the 1940s and raised in a small town, Barb Sanders is the oldest of four children. She has a brother 2.7 years younger, a second brother 4.7 years younger, and a sister 6 years younger. Both of her parents earned college degrees at a small, denominational college and worked all their lives in education and social work. Her parents also had a strong interest in music, and all the children sang and played musical instruments. Sanders was an average high school student who married after 1 year of college and had three daughters in the space of 4.5 years. Her husband was a good student who earned an M.A. and then went to work in a technical profession for a natural resources corporation. Sanders earned a B.A. degree in her mid-20s from a state college and left her husband at age 30, when her daughters were 7, 4.5, and 2.5. Her daughters stayed with her ex-husband, and she returned to her home state, where she earned an M.A. in a helping profession and worked in a community college setting for several years. She had several boyfriends after her divorce and never remarried. She became involved in local theater productions as an actress and director, and she developed a strong interest in dreams and participated in dream groups.

When the interviewees were asked about Sanders's possible blind spots, they had only a few reactions, but two of the four said that she has a blind spot when it comes to understanding her relationships with men:

> *First Friend:* "I think it's generally with male relationships, she doesn't see them for what they are. She doesn't see them for what they are at the time that she starts a relationship. And she, I think that she fantasizes more in the beginning than what it is, and tries to make it what she

wants it to be. And Ginny (her other closest friend) and I share that understanding about her."

Second Friend: "Well, I think probably in relationships with men, she has a certain naiveté about her. I think of her more as like a young teenager in relationships with men in her development . . . when it comes to her own personal life, I would say there's a certain naiveté, this certain blind spot, yeah."

Barb Sanders reported that she has always been fascinated with dreams but did not start a dream journal until a few years after her divorce, at a time when she was having disturbing dreams, including some relating to the divorce and its aftermath. She hoped to gain insight about herself from keeping the journal and perhaps enhance her efforts at creative writing. Soon after she began recording her dreams, she also included in the journal several dreams she had written down in her late teens. She also wrote down more than 100 dreams from memory. The early dreams that she wrote down at the time she had them are included in the dream series that is analyzed here, but not the dreams written down from memory. Although the journal is continuous from the late 1970s to 1996, the number of dreams written down or entered into the computer in each year varies. Figure 5.1 illustrates the number of dreams by year.

As with most dream series, the dreams vary in length, but 66% are between 50 and 300 words. Sixteen percent have fewer than 50 words; a

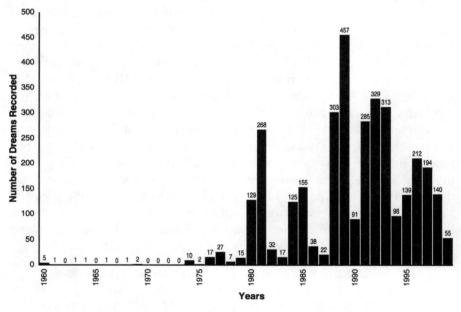

Figure 5.1. The distribution of Barb Sanders's dream reports by years.

disproportionate number of the short reports come from the 1960s and early 1970s. Figure 5.2 presents the complete distribution of dream reports by length.

The analysis of the Barb Sanders series began with a Hall–Van de Castle content analysis of a random sample of 250 dream reports (the "baseline 250") ranging in length from 50 to 300 words. This baseline sample was coded for Characters, Social Interactions, Misfortunes, Successes and Failures, and Emotions by Sarah Dunn, Melissa Bowen, and Heidi Block, who worked in different pairs on different categories. Several reliability checks yielded the high percentages of agreement shown in Table 5.2. All differences of opinion were resolved by discussion among the coders to provide a uniform result for entry into DreamSAT.

The first important finding is a methodological one: The codings from any 125 of the 250 dreams in the random sample replicate the results almost exactly, as determined by the approximate randomization program available to researchers on request through http://www.DreamResearch.net. However, there are many deviations from the overall results with subsamples of 100 dream reports, and the drop-off is large at 75 and 50, demonstrating once again how risky it is to accept or reject hypotheses on the basis of inadequate

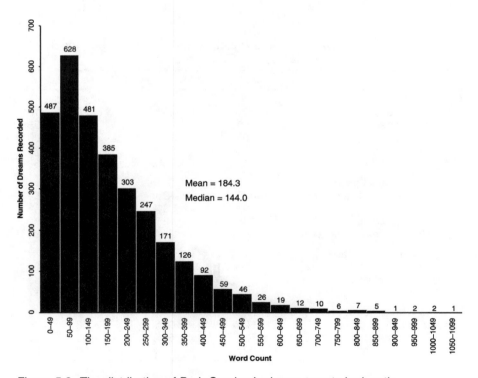

Figure 5.2. The distribution of Barb Sanders's dream reports by length.

TABLE 5.2
Reliability Figures for the Codings of the Barb Sanders Baseline Sample of 250 Dreams

Category	Agreements	Disagreements	% of Agreement
Characters	425	38	92
Aggression	188	17	92
Friendliness	106	20	84
Sexuality	11	0	100
Misfortune/Good fortune	109	15	88
Striving	45	13	78
Emotions	185	25	88

sample sizes. For example, the A/C index of .33 is usually between .30 and .35 with randomization samples containing 125 dream reports, but it ranges from .27 to .39 with samples of 75 dreams.

The first substantive analysis concerns the consistency in the dream series (Table 5.3). A comparison of the first 125 dreams in the baseline sample with the second 125 found the dreamer to be consistent within 5 or 6 percentage points in all but two or three categories. Her male/female

TABLE 5.3
Consistency in the Barb Sanders Baseline 250 Sample When the Two Halves Are Compared

	First half	Second half	h	p
Characters				
Male/female percent	58%	49%	−.20	.013*
Familiarity percent	38%	33%	−.10	.135
Friends percent	20%	11%	−.26	.000**
Family percent	15%	20%	+.12	.076
Animal percent	07%	06%	−.05	.430
Social interaction percents				
Aggression/friendliness percent	49%	49%	−.00	.984
Befriender percent	49%	56%	+.16	.251
Aggressor percent	53%	48%	−.10	.480
Physical aggression percent	29%	33%	+.08	.484
Social interaction ratios				
Aggression/character index	.31	.35	+.09	.408
Friendliness/character index	.29	.35	+.14	.060
Sexuality/character index	.09	.10	+.02	.817
Dreams with at least one				
Aggression	52%	56%	+.08	.526
Friendliness	53%	54%	+.02	.899
Sexuality	22%	18%	−.08	.527

*significant at the .05 level
**significant at the .01 level

percent fell from 58/42 to 49/51, placing her close to the female norms of 48/52. It is also interesting that she dreamed less of friends and more of family members in the second half of the series. The findings on consistency support several previous studies demonstrating consistency in dream content over decades (Domhoff, 1996, chapter 7). The result is now so well established that deviations from it are of interest in developing a better theory or in understanding a specific person. The finding can be used as one litmus test for determining the adequacy of any dream theory.

Characters and Social Interactions

Characters and social interactions are usually the most psychologically revealing aspect of a detailed content analysis, and the Sanders series is no exception. The random sample contains 884 human characters, 3.4 per dream report. Because the female normative figure is 2.7, this finding suggests that Sanders is more intensely involved with other people in her dreams than the typical woman is. This presumption is supported when the 679 social interactions are analyzed in terms of rates per character, that is, the A/C, F/C, and S/C ratios. As shown in Table 5.4, the dreamer is 19 to 24 h points higher than the normative figures for these three ratios. The effect sizes are small but statistically significant; what makes them noteworthy is that all three indicators are elevated (Bowen & Dunn, 1999).

Although Barb Sanders has a higher rate of social interaction than the normative sample, she is typical in her A/F percent (49) which means that she is equally involved in friendly and aggressive social interactions when all dream characters are considered. However, she does differ in that she is far more likely to be the aggressor (50 to 33), which is 36 h points above the norm, a moderate effect size. Most of these aggressions are angry thoughts toward a person, critical comments, or rejections. She is about average on befriender percent (53).

TABLE 5.4
Barb Sanders's Social Interaction Percents Compared With the Female Norms

	Barb Sanders baseline 250	Female norms	h	p
Aggression/character index	.33	.24	.21	.000**
Friendliness/character index	.32	.22	.24	.000**
Sexuality/character index	.09	.01	.19	.000**
Aggression/friendliness percent	49%	51%	−.05	.400
Aggressor percent	50%	33%	+.36	.000**
Befriender percent	53%	47%	+.11	.255

To provide an indication of her patterns of interaction with key people in the dreamer's life, Ryan Harvey coded all of the friendly and aggressive interactions in the entire dream series with her parents, favorite brother, daughters, and two close women friends. The findings, which are summarized in Table 5.5, correspond to how the dreamer and the four interviewees describe her relationships with these people in waking life. For example, her mother is the most important and difficult person in Barb Sanders's life. Sanders provided the following portrayal of her mother:

> My mother is an angry, isolating person, and she also has good things too, don't get me wrong. But she and I have had a personality clash as long as I can remember. I feel that she keeps herself so distant that I didn't feel I was getting nurturing mother love. I told one of my women friends that the love of my mother is like carrying a barbed blue baby blanket, you know, with barbs in it. It's supposed to be soft and cuddly and loving, but in fact, she was sharp and critical and negative and physically distant.

Her mother appears in 239 dream reports, or 7.7% of the total, which is more than any other familiar character. The A/C ratio with her is .70, well above Sanders's .33 average in the baseline 250 for all characters. The A/F percent between them is 72, well above the dreamer's normative figure of 49 (h = .48). This A/F percent is consistent over the entire series, as shown when the dreams are divided into thirds.

On the other hand, Sanders stated that she has a more positive attitude toward her father, a claim that was corroborated by her friends. He appears in 213 dream reports, second only to her mother. The A/C ratio with him is .36, not far above her normative figure with all characters, and the F/C is .37, once again slightly above her normative figure. The A/F percent for their interactions is 50. Although nothing stands out about Sanders's

TABLE 5.5
Barb Sanders's Social Interactions With Significant People in Her Life,
Compared With the Baseline 250 Sample

	N	A/C index	F/C index	A/F (%)	Aggressor (%)	Befriender (%)
Baseline 250	884	.33	.32	49	50	53
Mother	239	.70	.27	72	46	48
Father	213	.36	.37	50	47	42
Oldest daughter	81	.51	.65	44	73	77
Middle daughter	165	.92	.52	64	79	70
Youngest daughter	83	.36	.81	31	63	61
Favorite brother	97	.23	.69	25	59	60
Friend Ginny	96	.26	.89	23	52	53
Friend Lucy	59	.39	.63	38	78	78

relationship with him, the relationship is dramatically different from her relationship with her mother.

Sanders's middle daughter is almost as problematic for her as her mother. This daughter was 4.5 years old at the time of the divorce and was the child most upset by it. At age 14 she ran away from her father's home and came to live with Sanders. She did poorly in school, cannot hold a job, and suffers from severe psychological problems. She had a daughter when she was a teenager and soon left her to Barb Sanders to raise. She still returns to live with Barb Sanders from time to time. Sanders worries about her constantly, and there is great tension between them.

This daughter appears in 165 dream reports. The A/C ratio is .92, even higher than with the mother, and the F/C ratio is also high (.52, well beyond Sanders's average for all characters). Most of the friendly interactions involve Sanders helping her daughter in one way or another. Taken together, the two ratios show a high rate of interaction between them. The A/F percent is 64, with Sanders initiating 79% of the aggressive interactions and 70% of the friendly interactions, far above her averages for all characters. These indicators provide an accurate summary of how Sanders conceives of their relationship.

By contrast, Sanders dreams only half as often of her oldest and youngest daughters, who adjusted to the divorce better, went to school in their father's home state, saw their mother primarily during summer vacations, and live normal adult lives. The A/F percents, 44 with the older daughter and 31 with the younger daughter, show that she has more friendly than aggressive interactions with both of them, which reflects her more positive relationship with them. As with the middle daughter, Sanders is more likely to be the initiator of both aggressive and friendly interactions.

The dream reports also capture Sanders's positive relationships with the favorite people in her life. For example, Sanders has great affection for the brother closest to her in age. He appears in 97 dream reports, which is the same as the total for her other two siblings combined. The A/F percent for their interactions is 25, almost the mirror opposite of her interaction pattern with her mother. Positive patterns also are apparent with two women friends, but differences emerge on some indicators, which reflect her different pattern of interaction with each of them. Sanders met her closest friend of long-standing, Ginny, when she returned to college for her master's degree. After college Ginny married, moved to a city more than 100 miles away, and raised a family, but she and Sanders remained in close touch. Her husband and children are also friendly with Sanders, who has visited their home frequently over the years. Ginny appears in 96 dream reports and has an A/F percent of 23, the most positive balance with any known dream character. The comradely nature of their relationship is seen in the fact that they are equally likely to initiate friendly or aggressive interactions.

Sanders met another close friend, Lucy, when Lucy was a student at the community college where Sanders worked. Lucy, who is several years younger than Sanders, is outgoing and dramatic, and she and Sanders soon ended up working together in musicals and theatrical productions. She appears in 59 dream reports. Sanders is the big sister in this relationship; she gives Lucy instructions, helps her, and becomes annoyed when Lucy is late or resists direction. This pattern is reflected in the fact that Sanders initiates 78% of the many friendly interactions between them as well as 78% of the relatively few aggressive interactions.

These analyses of Sanders's dreamed social interactions with several of the significant people in her life are only a starting point in understanding her waking conceptions of them. Highly detailed studies with any of the characters would be likely to yield rich findings because of the large number of dream reports. To demonstrate this claim, somewhat more detailed analyses are next presented on two different subsets of dream reports. One subset concerns her ex-husband, the other a man she was infatuated with for nearly a year in the middle 1990s.

The Ex-Husband Dreams

Barb Sanders first met Howard, her future husband, when they were in high school, where they had lockers near each other. They sometimes danced or flirted, but he had a steady girlfriend. In her senior year, Barb fell in love with Darryl, the person she still considers the true love of her life. However, that relationship did not work out for reasons that she explained in the interview[1]:

> Okay, so then Darryl went off to the Navy and that kind of ended it? What happened was that we decided we would not go steady, but we were still going to get married, but we could explore with other people, that kind of thing. It kind of broke my heart, and I found out in an indirect way that he, when we were going steady, he was going out with some other woman at the Navy base, and so I felt terribly betrayed. So I started going out with Howard, and then there was a third gentleman by the name of Pete, and all three of them asked me to marry them, so it was quite a. . . . But by then you didn't want to marry Darryl? I was so angry and felt so betrayed that at that point, I don't know what it is about this, but I, when I said, "That's it, we're done. I'm dating these other guys, you know," it's like, "Oh no, please take me back, you know, and I'll be, forgive me, etc., etc." But by then I was done, I was out, and very, very angry and was not willing to trust him again. So he was

---

[1] Sentences in italics in this and subsequent interview segments in this chapter are the questions asked by the author.

going to buy the engagement ring and we were going to get married, but that's it. I wouldn't talk to him, wouldn't answer his letters back.

At this point, Howard was attending a major university far from their hometown and was no longer seeing his high school girlfriend. He and Sanders reconnected when he came home for the summer, and they were married after an 18-month courtship. Although it is risky to rely on memories of 35 years earlier, especially after a painful divorce, Sanders recalls that she harbored some doubts about the relationship even then. Perhaps this is not surprising in the context of the highly mixed feelings she harbored about Darryl and the end of the relationship with him. She also remembers Howard as a person who was insensitive to her need for tenderness and expression of feeling, as a person who just wanted sex. She felt that their sexual interactions sometimes felt more like rape than seduction.

Howard appears in 164 of the 3,116 dream reports. He is surpassed only by her mother, father, and middle daughter in the frequency of his appearances.[2] These dreams have a fairly regular structure (Block, 1999). They usually start with Sanders noticing that Howard is back, causing her considerable apprehension or annoyance. At the outset he is often seeking reconciliation, although on occasion she is the one who is thinking about the possibility of getting back together. As the dream unfolds, Howard usually tries to initiate a sexual interaction, through a touch or a kiss, but Sanders is either hesitant or repulsed. Sometimes she is tempted, but then changes her mind. For example:

> *July 13, 1976:* Howard wanted back with me. I put my arm around him but it was a terrible effort. Then he started to kiss me and I pulled away, feeling sickened and disgusted. "Don't ever touch me again," I said. I woke up feeling good that I can leave it, and sick that I spent 10 years with him.
>
> *November 26, 1980:* Howard, hovering around, wanting us to be together. I have a tight smile on my face. I keep turning away from him, but I'm tempted.
>
> *March 4, 1981:* I'm in a house, getting ready to go home. Howard is there. He wants to kiss me and go home with me. I want to be nice to him but I don't want him back. If I'm nice to him, he'll move right in. I feel trapped.

---

[2] The analysis of the ex-husband dreams extends through the middle of 1999, 3 years after Barb Sanders gave the first 3,116 dreams to the DreamBank, when she provided 376 more dream reports. All other analyses in this chapter (except for the Derek dreams discussed in the next section) are based on the original series of dreams so as to avoid the possibility that the dream reports might be influenced by the fact that the dreamer was now helping with a research project. An exception was made with the ex-husband and Derek dreams to see whether a process of gradual change could be detected. This decision added 32 additional Howard dreams for a total of 196.

September 9, 1990: I am in bed with Howard again. It's been so long since we've made love and he wants it real bad. I agree. I lie down and try to pretend I'm asleep. I am turned away from him. He slowly and gently comes close to me. He's afraid I'll pull away or refuse him and so he's being very hesitant and careful. He licks my cheek. I feel some revulsion. He touches my nipple. I want to cringe. I try to tolerate it but can't, it is so repugnant to me. I sit up, crying and sobbing. He is heartbroken and runs from the room.

May 8, 1991: Howard and I are in bed. He wants to make love. He tries to kiss me. I am repulsed and sad. I feel empathy and sadness for him because he wants it/me so badly. I feel so sad for me too. I want sex, love, and relationship, and to say "no" to him means saying no to myself as well. But I can't get over the repulsion I feel. He cries and says "You used to be so beautiful," meaning when I was younger. I am surprised. Maybe he is finally able to express his emotions. But as he continues to talk he clearly stays in a logical, digital conversation. I am disappointed.

In 1996 and 1997, the Howard dreams seem to become somewhat more benign. They appear to contain more reflection and regret as well as more discussion between the two of them. In one or two dreams, she even entertains the idea of reconciliation, an idea for which there was no basis in her or his waking reality. They lived far apart, never saw each other, and rarely communicated. In addition, Howard had been remarried for many years. This impression of a change in the tone of the Howard dream reports is borne out by the large decline in the A/F percent when they are divided into four chronological segments; proportionately more friendly interaction occurs in the later years. This result is shown in Table 5.6.

Sanders's reflections on her feelings about Howard in March 2000 parallel the main themes in the dreams as well as the changes, as shown in these excerpts from the interview with her:

> In the earlier years the dreams were just exact experiences of my life with him, so it was real-life stuff. He really did beg, and he really did try to get me back in the relationship. He really wanted the relationship to stay. I was unable to do that. My anger at his closed emotional stuff was very strong in the dreams, it was very strong in my life.

TABLE 5.6
Barb Sanders's Dreams of "Howard":
Changes in the Aggression/Friendliness Percent Over Time

	Barb Sanders baseline	1st segment	2nd segment	3rd segment	4th segment
Aggression/friendliness percent	49	57	59	61	34

It took a lot of years of evolution, but in fact I watched myself go from extremely painful anger, hardly able to mention the word marriage or Howard without practically spitting, just being dramatic about the whole thing. That was at the beginning, and the nightmares of Howard wanting me, or finding myself back in the relationship. Oh man, they were just, oh. And now I have Howard-is-back dreams and they're okay. I had a couple more even in the year 2000. He's still there. But it is changed. A forgiveness phase happened. Years and years and years, anger, anger, anger, and slowly over that time learning more about myself, how I operate, how he operates, and through the dreams themselves I was able to let go of a lot of the anger and get more in touch with the sadness.

Then, in the midst of this apparent softening of attitude toward Howard, he died unexpectedly of a heart attack in April 1997, without any history of serious illness. At this point the dreams about him seem even more reflective, and sometimes include the awareness that he is dead, even though she is interacting with him in the dream:

> *May 5, 1999:* I am lying on a bed, trying to sleep. Howard is seated near me. We talk. He is being helpful, trying to help me understand something that would be good for me to know. Later, he is lying in the bed with me. I "wake up" in the dream and realize that Howard is dead. He can't be there in my bed. I turn and look. He is not there. Then he talks to me. So now I'm wondering if I really looked or if I dreamed I looked. I am confused if he's really there or if I am dreaming it.

Despite this trend toward a more positive resolution of her feelings about Howard and the divorce, the negative dreams still appear on occasion. On November 13, 1997, for example, about 6 months after his death, Sanders has a dream that is similar to the five from 1976 to 1991 excerpted earlier:

> I am in bed with Howard and he feels sexual desire for me. He's looking at me; he groans and says you're so beautiful. I move away from him and say, "Please don't." He looks sad and says "Please." And I say I'm sorry. I pull away from him so we're not touching and I say to him, sometimes I think about just letting you do it, to give you relief, but I just can't, after all those 10 years of marriage and I begin to cry. He gets out of bed and comes around and tries awkwardly to help me feel better. I feel very sad.

Sixteen months later, on February 13, 1999, Sanders has a dream in which Howard suddenly appears and asks for sex. She thinks about it, but then "I pull back and say 'no.'" He then "gets angry and grabs my arm and forces me over the wall of a house and tries to rape me violently." She hits him and knocks him unconscious. When he starts to regain consciousness, she escapes in a car.

In all, the dreams about Howard are a classic example of the operation of the repetition principle over the space of nearly 25 years. There is some decline in the negative aspects of these dreams, and there are changes in her waking reactions to them, but the issues they reflect remain essentially unchanged. It is as though the themes are embedded in her vigilance–fear system and are subject to reactivation under circumstances that cannot be determined with the information that is available for this study.

Moreover, the repetitive patterns seem to persist even though Sanders feels she has gained greater perspective on her failed marriage in waking life. Her belief is supported in the interviews with her friends, who note that she talks about him less and expresses less anger than in the past. But the dreams do not change quite as much as her thoughts about him. This fits with Foulkes's (1985) cognitive view that dreams reflect mental encodings of past waking experience, not the experiences themselves, so they are not likely to be changed by further reflections. It also fits with the idea that the updated aspects of a conception are no more likely to appear in dreams than the older one, because of the lack of reality constraints during sleep. Taken together, these ideas lead to the hypothesis that waking feelings may change more, or more quickly, than dream feelings.

The dreams about Howard could be said to contain a "wish," in the Freudian sense, in that they clearly show a regret that the marriage was not successful and sometimes express a hope for reconciliation as well. There is also a wish for sexual gratification in several of the dream reports. At the same time, the dreams have a traumatic quality that overwhelms the wishful dimension. The fears and negative emotions persist, yet periodically, dreams occur that clearly seem to "resolve" the issue and signal that the dreamer is ready to move on. Those dreams are eventually followed by another negative dream. This finding should be given consideration before accepting claims in the clinical literature about the frequency and importance of "resolution" dreams. Such claims often suffer from the lack of longitudinal follow-up.

Dreams of a Failed Infatuation

In late September 1994, several years after she had dated anyone regularly, Sanders met a man at a party whom she found attractive. She and Derek had a common circle of friends and a mutual interest in the theater and dreams. They struck up a friendship, and a few months later they were in a small playwriting group together. Later they were in the same dream-sharing group as well. Derek is 12 years younger than Sanders and did not seem interested in more than a friendship, which Sanders basically understood. Nonetheless, she became infatuated with him and entertained the hope of a romantic relationship.

Her friends were sure that nothing would come of the relationship and worried about her. However, two of them felt that the relationship would have positive aspects because it would add new zest to her life no matter how it ended up. The friendship blossomed over the space of a year. Perhaps Derek gave some indications that he did care for her romantically more than she realized at first, mostly through heartfelt conversations. Whatever the signals, Sanders came to feel betrayed when the relationship did not go further. She became upset when he showed affection toward another woman in her presence. When he came to a meeting of the dream group with a date, Sanders expressed her annoyance to him, to the great surprise of his date, and in effect ended the friendship in early April 1996. She saw him only once or twice in passing after that.

Derek appears in 43 dream reports during the time period covered by the systematic analysis, then in another 4 dreams in the portion of the dream journal written after this study began.[3] The first dream occurred on October 7, 1994, just a few days after she met him. Thereafter, the frequency and content of the dream reports reflect the rise and fall of her hopes about him. The dreams have a high rate of friendly and sexual interactions and a low rate of aggressions, especially physical aggressions, as shown in the h profile in Figure 5.3. This h profile compares dreams concerning Derek to dreams with Howard in them and to the baseline sample (Dunn, 2000).

Thirteen of the first 16 dream reports in which Derek appears contain sexual or intimate physical interactions with him, such as warm hugs or resting her head on his lap. These early sensual dreams are in general very positive and full of anticipation, but they also express her fear that he does not care about her; in one dream, he even chases her after he has an orgasm:

> *November 11, 1994:* Derek kisses me. I am disappointed because his mouth is hugely wide and it doesn't feel good. He French kisses and it is intense, our tongues intricately intertwining. I feel him have an orgasm and I am untouched with sexual passion. It feels very cold and self-serving. Now I am being chased by him and other people. I run for my life.

As Sanders accepted that the relationship was not going to develop in the way she hoped, her sexual interactions with Derek become less frequent in her dreams. She also has dreams in which she is angry with him or jealous that he is having sex with someone else. He is more peripheral in the dream reports in which he does appear, and some characters are now described not as "Derek," but as "like Derek." On May 2 and 3, 1996, about

---

[3]Once again, as with the Howard subseries, this part of the analysis includes dream reports from after the first 3,116 dream reports were received in order to make the subseries even more useful.

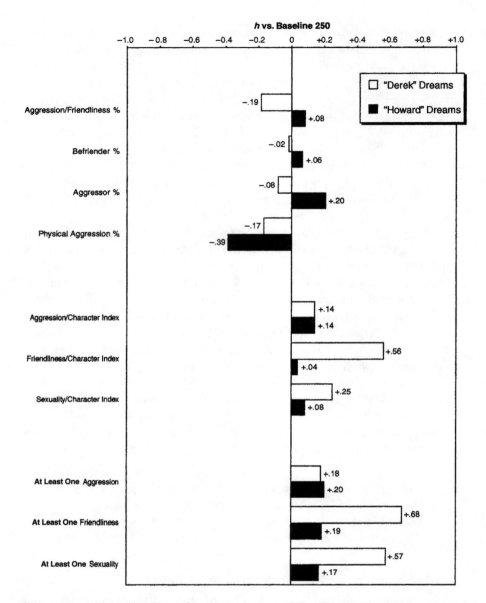

Figure 5.3. An *h* profile of Barb Sanders's dreams of "Derek" and "Howard," compared with the Barb Sanders baseline 250 sample.

a month after she broke off their friendship, Sanders describes dreams in which she is upset because he is with another woman:

> I am sobbing. My heart is broken. Derek has betrayed our relationship with another woman. Now he follows me around begging me to forgive

him. I can't stop crying. Derek is with someone else or is ignoring me. I am sitting next to his brother and decide to hell with Derek, I will chase his brother. We hug and flirt. Derek is jealous and moves between us, and now I am having dinner with Derek and then a helicopter comes and picks me up in the middle of dinner.

Then, after a period of 5 months in which she records 72 dreams, but none of Derek, Sanders has one that she calls "the kiss of forgiveness":

September 26, 1996: I am sitting on a couch. A male friend who is also a friend of Derek's comes in, and Derek is walking behind him. I am surprised. He comes in and talks a bit. I respond back in a friendly manner. He is still uptight about our break-up and non-connection of the last few month. The friend comes over and sits beside me on the couch. Derek walks over and puts his face between our faces. I kiss him on the cheek. He is still distant, but then he keeps talking and I keep talking and then he kisses me on the lips in a genuine kiss.

A week later, she has a dream that implies they are still friends, even though she has not seen him in months:

October 3, 1996: Derek approaches me and begins to talk quite friendly and I respond back. It's like we are pretending the last few months of no communication never happened. I feel glad we are talking again.

After this pair of dreams, Derek appears in only 4 out of the next 461 dream reports. By contrast, he appeared in 43 of the previous 334 dream reports. Two of the dreams after the apparent resolution dreams are relatively benign, but in one someone like Derek is betraying her, and in the other he is tormenting her, so he is not entirely gone from her mind:

February 16, 1998: I am trying to do something. To get something done. Derek interferes, teasing me and stopping me from accomplishing what I am trying to do. I am very angry at him, but I choose not to blow up. I hold in my anger because I know he is deliberately trying to provoke me. He is acting like one of my granddaughters does. I am trying to be loving in spite of the provocation.

The Derek dreams are striking for the fact of sexual intercourse and other sexual intimacies that have no correspondence to her waking reality. They are clearly wishful dreams: They are continuous with her waking hopes, but not with her waking life. The dreams also directly reflect her fears about him and the relationship. Unlike the Howard subseries, they decline greatly in frequency once the wishes are gone. This pattern leads to a testable hypothesis for future studies: It is only possible for a significant person to disappear from dream life if no real-life intimate interactions have been involved.

For several reasons, the Derek subseries is deserving of much more thorough study than has been possible here. It is long enough to make detailed analyses possible, but not so long as to be overwhelming. It occurs in a relatively circumscribed period of time and is mixed with 334 other dream reports between October 1994 and October 1996. It has been coded for several Hall–Van de Castle categories, the results of which are available in the SearchCodings section of DreamResearch.net. In addition, it contains much material that might lend itself to a blind metaphoric analysis that could be compared with the coding results. Finally, the interviews with Sanders and all four friends provide highly detailed commentary on the relationship. More generally, it is possible that highly focused analyses of subseries such as this one may be an excellent way to study dream meaning in great detail.

For now, though, enough analysis has taken place with the Howard and Derek subseries and the other character studies presented in this section to show that Barb Sanders's dream reports present an accurate portrayal of her relationships with the important people in her life. The findings support a hypothesis that derives from the studies of the Lucille series and many other dream journals: People's dreams about family and friends enact their conceptions and concerns in regard to them. Such dreams are like dramas that reflect waking relationships; they are miniature soap operas.

Although this is an important and useful conclusion, it does not follow that all the other elements in these dreams are equally accurate and informative. Nonsense may be mixed in with the coherent aspects in dreams about family members and close friends. Nor does it follow from these findings that the many dreams that do not include known characters are consistent with waking conceptions. Thus, a great deal of dream content remains to be explained.

Theater Dreams

It appears from reading through Barb Sander's dreams that she has a strong interest in theatrical performances, whether as an actor, singer, or director. When a word string containing all relevant theater-related terms is entered into DreamBank.net, it retrieves 169 dream reports from the series, 77 of which actually involve Sanders auditioning for, taking part in, or directing a theatrical production. This large number of theater dreams is, in fact, continuous with Sanders's waking interests. She acts and sings in productions, some of which she writes herself. She also enjoys directing theatrical performances.

In half of the theater dreams in which she is involved as a performer or director, Sanders sees herself as giving an excellent performance. Sometimes she comes out of the audience to give an unexpected performance that is met with great approval. In others she is "discovered" at the last minute to be worthy of a starring role. It is clear from these positive theater dreams that Sanders has, or once had, high hopes and ambitions. She would like to be in the public limelight as an esteemed artistic figure. Her desire is shown most dramatically in a dream report in which she, her middle daughter, and another woman find themselves singing on stage to great acclaim. Sanders reports that she loves the applause but wants to do a solo, and she ushers her daughter and the other woman aside:

> June 8, 1985: I see a stage, with musicians there. I go out on stage, to the mike. I remember that my sister and daughters are there too. I start to talk to the audience, who are far away, seated at tables. I say, "everybody get up and go to the dance floor." Most do. . . . I turn to the musicians, "Hit it boys, some hot boogie. . . . " I start singing and it's good. My middle daughter and another woman join in, three-part harmony. It's great. Audience loves it, I love, it except I want to do it solo. I tell my daughter and the other woman to go away and I sing ballad. It's great.

This inference of great ambition is supported in the interview with her friend Lucy, who often performs with her:

> I think she's incredibly ambitious and overachieving, and it's like it's never enough. Nothing is ever enough for her to feel good enough about herself, and yet she's so wise and good and strong and able, and it's just never enough for her to make herself feel, I think that's why she goes out and does theater because she wants to make herself feel positive and beloved.

But an equal number of the theater dreams contain rejections and misfortunes. Sanders does not win the part, or people leave as she is about to perform. She misses a rehearsal, can't find the theater, or nearly falls off the stage. In seven instances, she forgets her lines or is afraid she will forget them, and in two others she does not have a script. The negative events are consistent with two of her waking concerns in regard to her public performances. First, Sanders is indeed afraid she will forget her lines, as attested to by both her and her friends. Second, she does feel that she is often ignored or unappreciated, a point that is stated most frankly by two of her friends.

So, just as Sanders's dreams featuring significant others enact her conceptions of her relationships with them, the theater dreams seem to be variations on a few of her major concerns about artistic performances. She wants to be noticed and thinks she deserves far more attention than she receives, but she worries that she will forget her lines and that people will ignore her. These concerns are the "themes" that are acted out to various degrees in each dream relating to the theater and performances. That is, each dream can be seen as a specific instance from which generic information can be extracted. This instantiation of generic information may be based on an abstract conceptual metaphor, "the generic is specific" (Lakoff, 1993a; Lakoff & Turner, 1989). The existence of this metaphor is inferred from the fact that people can understand parables so readily, including parables from other cultures that they have not heard before. If the "generic is specific" metaphor could be shown to be operative in generating at least certain types of dreams, such as ones that are variations on a theme, it might account for a significant minority of dream reports.

Dream Elements That Are Not Continuous

Although the several analyses presented so far support the continuity principle, some elements in Sanders's dream reports are not continuous with her waking life. They may provide an interesting exception to the continuity principle that could lead to a better understanding of dream meaning, or perhaps they reveal the limits of the conceptual systems available to the neural network for dreaming (Foulkes, 1999; Hobson, 1988). For example, Sanders has several dreams about cats, especially kittens, that are neglected, deformed, or starving. The appearance of cats fits with her interest in cats in waking life, but contrary to the continuity principle, she does not worry about the health of cats in waking life, nor does she fear that they might starve or be neglected.

An example of how the contradictory findings on neglected cats might be approached using DreamBank can be seen through the mention of "stray kittens." Five of the eight uses of the term "stray" occur in conjunction with kittens, a contingency with a p value of .000. Four of these instances— in January 1981, October 1982, and twice in October 1986—occur in reference to men who are lost souls who do not amount to much in her eyes. The fifth, which occurred in December 1981, concerns two actual stray kittens. The dream report begins as follows, then moves to unrelated topics having nothing to do with kittens or inadequate men:

> The stray kittens plead for food. They are very hungry. I feel badly for them. I look in the refrigerator. I find some sugar cakes and some cheese. I am dressing up to go out on a date. It's a conservative outfit, but as soon as I'm out the door, I'll readjust the front and it will be very sexy.

In waking life, the equation of "stray kittens" and "lost men" is understandable to most people, given their general knowledge of the world, as a conceptual blend. They see the connection due to their instantaneous comprehension of the characteristics of stray kittens that can be applied to at least some men—helplessness and lack of attachment to an important source—while ignoring the kittens' irrelevant properties—needing to be breast fed, furriness, claws, and mewing (Teenie Matlock, Department of Psychology, Stanford University, personal communication, August 15, 2001). With regard to Sanders's dreams, the research question is: Does her understanding of rootless men as stray kittens underlie her dream of actual stray kittens? This example merely poses the question and in no way begins to answer it.

Unlike kittens, horses are portrayed in a positive light in Sanders's dream reports. She has 24 dreams in the series in which she is riding a horse. In all of those dreams, she portrays herself as an excellent rider. In one dream she rides like the wind, in another she learns quickly and becomes an excellent rider, and in another her father praises her for her riding skills. Taken together, the dreams give the impression that she learned to ride as a child and likes horses, but that is not the case. The following excerpts from the interview with her give the flavor of her reactions to inferences about her conceptions and waking experiences concerning horses:

> *When you were growing up, did you learn to ride horses?* I had some experiences with riding horses, yes, but I didn't have a lot of it. I loved doing it. They scared me; they were awfully big and they had a tendency to bite. But other than that, it was fun. I do remember a couple of incidents where we were galloping away, and it was such, out of control, but fun kind of, you know, I was just hanging on for dear life, hoping I don't fall. *But you wouldn't say you did a lot of riding or were a good rider?* No, I was not a good rider.
>
> *But you're a good rider in your dreams.* I am, aren't I, yes. *Did you think they are pretty positive dreams, your horse dreams?* Yes, I think most of my animal dreams seem to be really positive dreams, yes. *But yet, in this case we're seeing then an example of where your proficiency in riding and your use of horses and all really doesn't reflect reality.* It's very metaphorical. It's not, it's not a real life experience. I think I have ridden horses max eight times in my whole life, you know, and I can remember the specific times. Somebody else held the horse, one had a tendency to bite and I was very afraid of him, and we sort of walked slowly around the pasture. Another one, that one was okay, but it got spooked by another horse that started running, so I was just hanging on for dear life. And when they did trotting, it was just disaster city because I never learned how to do the posting.

Although the dreamer begins by saying she "loved" the few occasions on which she rode a horse as a child, the general thrust of the interview contradicts the expectations of the continuity principle. She later says that horse dreams are "not reality." The point could be stretched to say that the dreams are continuous with her wishes, but the problem is that the continuity principle would predict that her negative experiences with horses should be reflected in the dreams as well. Later in the interview, she recalled more about horses as follows:

> One more thing about horses—my father became a part owner of a race horse, and for a while this beautiful race horse was in our back pasture, and so it wasn't like an animal I could ride or anything, but it was quite exquisite and I would like to look at it as it ran around, and we would go to the races and cheer for the horse. Yeah, and he was beautiful, and that was a special arena, horse racing, so he was supposed to go out there and make money. [she laughs]

Beautiful horses are part of Sanders's pleasant memories and a plausible basis for her positive dreams of riding horses. The horse dreams seem to be based on her early thoughts about horses with little regard for her few and often negative waking experiences. Thus, the research issue is how to tell these possible wish dreams from realistic dreams.

Sanders's dreams also show a lack of continuity in relation to her use of guns and rifles in her dreams. In 33 dream reports in the series, she is holding or shooting a gun, always with confidence. She fixes and reloads guns, kills dangerous animals, and fights off human attackers. In one dream she captures seven men at gunpoint. In another she grabs a woman's gun and kills her. Based on the continuity principle, these assertive dream actions led to the inference that she might have learned to shoot guns as a child and still enjoys doing so. However, the inference is incorrect, as seen in the following interview material:

> *How about guns? Were there guns around?* Don't like guns. There weren't a lot of guns around. Now in extended family—uncles and cousins and things, you know, a bunch of rednecks and guns are part of that culture— but in my family, no. *But as far as you shooting them and shooting with them. . . .* I did some target work when Howard and I were first starting, because he was interested in guns. He had guns all the time and loved hunting. *Did you ever do any hunting with him?* He wanted me to, and he took me out target shooting, but I balked at actually shooting animals. I have the Bambi syndrome. *Did you do much target shooting? Did you feel proficient with a gun?* Umm, no, not a lot.

The unexpected answers to questions about horses and guns may provide a starting point for future studies: Dream content that is not continuous with waking memories and past experiences may be indicative of figurative thought. In exploring such a possibility in the Barb Sanders series, it would have been useful to start with questions relating to her thoughts and fantasies concerning horses and guns. That is, the focus should have been on how she organizes and uses her knowledge and feelings about horses and guns before turning to her actual experiences with them. This conclusion could be of use in future investigations of figurative thought in dreams

Unusual Elements in Dream Reports

The unusual elements in dreams—distortions in familiar settings, impossible acts like flying under one's own power, and metamorphoses—immediately come to mind when most people in Western cultures think of dreams. Although such elements are less frequent in representative samples of dream reports than popular stereotypes suggest, they do happen in 10% to 35% of dreams (Hall, 1966b; Revonsuo & Salmivalli, 1995; Rittenhouse, Stickgold, & Hobson, 1994), and they once again raise the possibility that dreams have nonsensical aspects resulting from the limited capabilities of the conceptual systems available during sleep.

It also may be that some unusual elements are nonsensical and others are metaphorical, meaning that distinctions among various types of unusual elements might be useful. For example, composite characters that are based on two different people sometimes appear in the Sanders dream reports, usually designated by a slash, as in "Dwight/Howard," a composite of her favorite brother and ex-husband. Composite characters lend themselves to study as possible conceptual blends (Grady et al., 1999). In the 43 dreams in which Derek appears, for example, 8 of those appearances characterize him as "like" someone else or as a combination of himself and another person. Most strikingly, he appears as "Derek/Darryl" in three dream reports, which yokes him with the true love that she rejected for unfaithfulness at age 18. In this case, there are two pieces of information that suggest that this composite character may represent a conceptual blend. First, Sanders said in the interview that they were the two men she loved the most. Second, they are also similar in that she never had sexual intercourse with either of them.

Interestingly, 5 of Darryl's other 31 appearances in the dream series involve comparisons or composites in addition to the three composites with Derek. The network of likenesses and composites centering on Derek and Darryl is presented in Figure 5.4. It is another example of how the study of unusual elements in dreams might proceed.

Character metamorphoses are relatively rare in dreams; they occur only 12 times in the 1,000 dream reports comprising the Hall–Van de Castle normative samples. However, they often strike dreamers as remarkable and mysterious when they occur. Although it is common in waking life to say that a person is like someone or for an object or event to remind someone of some other object or event, metamorphoses nonetheless seem far removed from waking thought patterns, even though they are often seen in movies

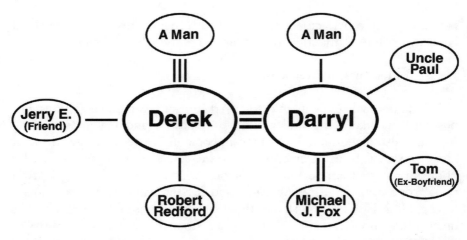

Figure 5.4. Composite characters involving "Derek" and "Darryl" in Barb Sanders's dreams. Each line represents an instance in which two characters were "combined."

and videos. They therefore provide an interesting challenge and opportunity for researchers who hope to find meaning in all aspects of dream content.

There are only four instances of character metamorphoses in the Sanders baseline 250, not enough for a systematic study. To find a sample of metamorphoses in the entire Sanders series, the terms "changes into," "turns into," "becomes," and "is now" were entered into DreamBank.net. It is unlikely that the four terms capture all the metamorphoses in the series, but they do provide a large sample that is probably representative of the population of metamorphic changes in the series. The sample has the added advantage of including metamorphoses of objects, which are not coded for in the Hall–Van de Castle system. After eliminating phrases such as "the argument turns into a fight," "he becomes angry," and "the food is now ready to serve," the initial yield of 132 dream reports boiled down to 50 instances that qualify as metamorphoses in 49 dream reports.

Thirty of the 50 metamorphoses include a human or animal character at the beginning or the end of the transformation. Thirteen of those changes are human-to-human transformations, but in seven dream reports people change into animals, creatures, or objects; in another seven, the animals or objects turn into people. On two occasions, one animal turns into another, and in one case, a male puppet turns into a female puppet. Thus, character transformations involve no one pattern.

A few of the changes seem to be similar to the cases of composite characters discussed in the previous section, such as when Sanders's ex-husband is now one of her brothers, or a man is now like Derek, or a woman turns into Faye Dunaway. It is also interesting that nine cases involve babies or young children, who are obvious instances of relatively rapid transformation. However, there are several changes that do not seem to have any immediate plausibility, even when the context of the dream is added. For example, a yellow wooden horse turns into an artistic man; a horse becomes a cat; a large pig becomes a piglet; and a spider becomes a miniature man, who in turn becomes a light bulb.

In addition to the 30 transformations that involve dream characters, there are 20 cases where one object turns into another. Fourteen of those changes involve objects that are linked to travel or movement, a finding that may suggest a possible underlying pattern connected to one of several conceptual metaphors. For example, "change is motion," as in "his mood jumped from morose to ecstatic in less than a minute," and "processes are movements," as in "the meeting goes for two hours" (Teenie Matlock, Department of Psychology, Stanford University, personal communication, August 15, 2001). Both metaphors are pervasive in everyday thinking, and they are compatible with a metaphor closely related to issues of self: "life is a journey," as in "she's come to a fork in the road" and "they have one more mountain to climb." According to Lakoff (1987), these and other motion metaphors are connected to an "umbrella" (i.e., higher level) concep-tual metaphor called *event structure*.

Regarding the specific object-to-object metamorphoses in the Sanders series, several of the transformations are fairly straightforward, such as when a small car becomes a big, flashy car; a car becomes a house trailer; or a car becomes a hearse. Other changes involving vehicles seem less straightfor-ward, as when a bus becomes a series of kiddie cars, a table becomes a circus train, or a pickup truck becomes a tape recorder that has to be pushed up a hill. In addition, interesting changes that may relate to "change is motion" or "life is a journey" occur in passageways: A bridge becomes a stairway, another bridge becomes a boat, a road becomes a hallway, another road becomes a staircase, a waterfall becomes a freeway, and a hallway is suddenly the inside of a diesel truck.

Although the 50 cases suggest some possible metaphoric meanings, it was not possible to develop convincing evidence that any of the metamor-phoses relate to the systematic findings presented earlier in this chapter, despite the context provided by the series. It will take further investigations and, perhaps, new approaches, if a case is to be made for meaning in these elements.

CONCLUSION

This chapter has only scratched the surface of the Barb Sanders series. It is a demonstration of possibilities, not a definitive analysis. However, enough has been said to illustrate that the main characters, social interactions, and activities in the dreams reveal Sanders's waking conceptions and concerns in relation to the significant people and interests in her life. On the other hand, there are elements in the dreams that do not immediately seem continuous with her waking conceptions, such as her excellent riding and shooting. Those elements may reveal the limits of cognitive capabilities during sleep, or they may be the products of figurative thinking. Similarly, the unusual elements in the dream reports, such as composite characters and metamorphoses, may define a dimension that goes from the metaphorical to the nonsensical. The resolution of these seeming anomalies will require many further studies.

Most important, this chapter illustrates a methodology that could be applied to a wide range of interesting cases. Perhaps it would be especially revealing with people who were keeping a dream journal before they suffered a brain injury or a personal trauma or had to go on one or another medication. If such people were then able to resume their dream journals, the original journal could serve as a baseline for trying to determine what effects, if any, the sudden alteration in their life circumstances is having on their dreams.

The new findings in this chapter, along with the many empirical studies cited in previous chapters, provide a basis for future advances in the study of dream meaning. They also make it possible to develop an assessment of traditional dream theories, which is the main task of the final chapter.

6

A CRITIQUE OF TRADITIONAL DREAM THEORIES

This chapter brings together all systematic findings on dreams, including some of the new material presented in earlier chapters, to address the main hypotheses in the best known traditional theories of dreams, and concludes that all of these theories have failed on one or another key issue, suggesting that it is time to find a new starting point. To begin, the chapter discusses every major claim made by Freud and Jung, none of which stands up against the empirical evidence that is available. However, the chapter does not consider the clinical theories of the neo-Freudians, phenomenologists, or existentialists because their theories are either combinations of Freudian and Jungian ideas to one degree or another or deductions that are based on a philosophical tradition. The neo-Freudians Adler and Fromm, for example, drew on Marxism to make general statements about the continuity between dreaming and waking thought that turn out to have validity in the light of later research, but their writing inspired no systematic work on dreams and had no lasting impact.

Following the discussions of Freudian and Jungian dream theories, the chapter addresses the problems with both the original and revised versions of activation–synthesis theory. This theory has the most commonalities with the neurocognitive model presented in this book, but significant differences remain. Finally, the chapter points out the weaknesses of the many theories that assume one or another problem-solving function for dreams. Some of those theories hypothesize that recalled dreams have problem-solving functions, whereas others claim that the functions are carried out during sleep, whether the dreams are recalled or not. Either way, problem-solving theories have been extremely difficult to test, so they rest primarily on analogies with new discoveries in other fields or on anecdotal examples.

The evidence used in assessing the theories comes from a wide range of areas within empirical dream research, including experimental studies in sleep laboratories, content analyses of dream reports, neuropsychological studies of the effects of brain lesions on dreaming, and correlational studies relating dream recall to cognitive and personality variables.

THE FREUDIAN THEORY OF DREAMS

During the late 19th century, dream theorists generally believed that dreams are brief and that they are usually a reaction to an internal or external stimulus or occur during the process of awakening. Freud (1900) tried to blend these perspectives by comparing dreams to "a firework that has been hours in the preparation, and then blazes up in a moment" (p. 377). He agreed that they last for only a brief time and perhaps occur only during awakening, but he added the new idea that the thoughts underlying dreams develop slowly during the day. However, contrary to Freud, laboratory studies have revealed that dreaming takes place longer, more frequently, and more regularly than he or any other theorist ever imagined before the serendipitous discovery of REM sleep in 1953 (Aserinsky & Kleitman, 1953; Dement, 1955; Dement & Kleitman, 1957b).

Freud (1900) also asserted that "a reference to the events of the day just past is to be discovered in every dream" (p. 127), but five detailed studies later demonstrated that only about half of dreams contain even the slightest "day residue" that can be identified by the dreamer (Botman & Crovitz, 1989; Harlow & Roll, 1992; Hartmann, 1968; Marquardt, Bonato, & Hoffmann, 1996; Nielsen & Powell, 1992). As part of his emphasis on the large role of specific memories in shaping dream content, Freud (pp. 266–267) concluded that all significant speeches in dreams can be traced to memories of speeches heard or sentences read, but the analysis of hundreds of speech acts in dream reports collected in sleep laboratories has shown that they are usually new constructions appropriate to the unfolding dream context, not reproductions (Meier, 1993). Indeed, speech acts are sometimes so appropriate to the dream context that many bilingual participants in one laboratory study reported that they spoke in the language understood by the dream character with whom they were talking (Foulkes, Meier, Strauch, Kerr, Bradley, & Hollifield, 1993).

Freud's (1900) most famous and important claim is that "wish-fulfill-ment is the meaning of each and every dream" (p. 106). Although this hypothesis is based on his work with adult patients, he thought that the dreams of young children provide "invaluable proof" of his wish-fulfillment theory, and he used dreams from his own children as evidence, including a sleep-talking episode from his 19-month-old daughter. However, Foulkes (1982, 1999) found that young children have static and bland dreams, not at all like Freud's anecdotal examples, and concluded that there are no signs of wishes in children's cognitively impoverished dream reports. Moreover, examples from sleep-talking episodes no longer have any standing as evidence since the discovery that most sleep talking originates during the microawakenings of from 10 to 20 seconds that occur several times per night in both children and adults (Arkin, 1981; Boselli, Parrino, Smerieri, & Terzano, 1998; Mathur & Douglas, 1995)

Freud began the case for his wish-fulfillment theory with children's dreams because he believed that the wishes in most adult dreams are disguised in order to reduce their anxiety-arousing tendencies. This self-deception is especially the case for the infantile sexual wishes that Freud believed are the basis for most adult dreams. Dreams are disguised at the behest of a "censor" by four cognitive processes that together comprise the *dream-work* (1900, pp. 328, 389). *Displacement* is a process whereby highly charged thoughts are transferred to minor elements in the impending dream. *Condensation* compresses several different *dream-thoughts* (i.e., the embodiments of wishes) into a composite element, including dream characters who have the qualities of two or more people. The two processes produce most of the transformations that render dreams difficult to understand.

Although displacement and condensation are "the two foremen in charge of the dream-work" (Freud, 1900, p. 235), they are joined by two other processes that make the dream more coherent. The *regard for representability* changes abstract thoughts into a pictorial form that is more sensible and acceptable to the censor. This process can make use of the waking processes of figurative thought that generate jokes, legends, and proverbs (Freud, 1900, p. 259). Finally, the dream is shaped by *secondary revision*, a process that overlaps with waking thought and is responsible for the interpolations and additions that give the manifest content a somewhat intelligible pattern.

Freud (1900) brought forth numerous clinical examples to demonstrate how each of these processes works. He concluded by stressing that "the task of transforming the unconscious thoughts into the dream-content is peculiar to the life of dreams" and that this dream-work is "far more remote from the model of waking thought than even the most determined belittlers of the psyche's feats of dream-formation have thought" (pp. 328–329). No convincing nonclinical studies, however, have demonstrated the operation of the dream-work. Contrary to Freud's emphasis on the puzzling nature of dreams, two sympathetic reviews of all available experimental and correlational studies concluded that more information is available in the manifest content of a dream than would be expected if the dream-work had made the manifest dream-thoughts relatively meaningless (Fisher & Greenberg, 1977, 1996). This is also the conclusion of a careful study in which dreams were collected from two participants in the laboratory and then compared with material from their psychoanalytic sessions and structured interviews (Greenberg, Katz, Schwartz, & Pearlman, 1992).

The most consistent defense of Freud's ideas about the formation of dreams is based on an appeal to evidence from subliminal stimulation studies claiming that unconscious processes can be influenced significantly through the presentation of psychodynamically relevant stimuli (Shevrin, 1986, 1996; Slipp, 2000). In several studies between 1918 and 1960, participants were exposed to brief presentations of visual or auditory stimuli below the threshold of conscious awareness, and then asked to report their dreams the next morning and draw pictures that were based on those dreams. The evidence for incorporations in these studies was based on seeming physical resemblances and on symbolic interpretations of the kind the findings were meant to support. The method was therefore not independent of the theory. In a study by Fisher (1954), for example, it was necessary to believe, in the face of all the evidence showing the rarity of stimulus incorporation into dreams, that a vague drawing by the participant had some connection to a picture that was shown to her for less than a second below the threshold of awareness.

The most telling criticisms of the early studies have been provided by researchers trained in the tradition of subliminal psychodynamic studies by one of the original investigators, Charles Fisher. They noted that "suitable controls were often lacking, and the various clinical interpretations could be seen as equivocal and, at times, arbitrary" (Shevrin, 1996, p. 96). The same investigators claim that their own studies introduce the necessary controls, but their studies rely primarily on the production of waking mental images and free associations after laboratory awakenings from REM and NREM sleep, so they have nothing to do with dreams directly. In one later study, participants were exposed subliminally to a picture of a writing pen placed next to a person's knee, which presumably primes for unlikely cognitive associations like "pen-ny" through the clang association of "pen" and "knee." They then were awakened after REM or NREM sleep to provide free associations and dream reports (Shevrin & Fisher, 1967). No differences in the dream reports were found, but as predicted, there were more "conceptual" associations after NREM awakenings and more unlikely or "unusual" associations after REM awakenings. However, the same differences were found in other laboratory studies without the use of any presleep stimuli (Fiss, Ellman, & Klein, 1969; Fiss, Klein, & Bokert, 1966). In any event, a study of free associations after awakenings can provide no evidence about whether presleep stimuli influence the process of dreaming. Moreover, as Shevrin and Eiser (2000) acknowledged, "this study did not establish the disguising function of the primary process" (p. 1006).

Future attempts to use subliminal stimulation to study the process of dreaming are not likely to be of any use. A wide range of carefully controlled experiments has led most research psychologists to conclude that subliminal stimuli are limited to small priming effects for one or two words and have no ability to influence concepts; they therefore doubt that the processing of these stimuli could have anything to do with Freudian ideas (e.g., Fudin, 1999; Greenwald, 1992; Greenwald, Draine, & Abrams, 1996).

Freud (1900) did not discuss symbolism to any great extent in the first edition of *The Interpretation of Dreams*, and as already noted, he was careful to keep figurative thinking separate from the dream-work by maintaining that the dream-work sometimes makes use of this waking cognitive process. Given the lack of success in demonstrating that the dream-work is a unique psychological process during sleep and the success of recent work on waking figurative thought, it is difficult to sustain the distinction Freud tried to make. The distinction also breaks down with a close look at Freud's examples of the dream-work, which make frequent use of sexual slang, jokes, word etymologies, and proverbs. This appeal to the products of waking thought suggests that the dream-work, if it exists, is an instance of figurative thought, as convincingly argued by States (1987) and Lakoff (1997).

Freud's views on affect (i.e., emotion) in dreams are closely tied to his claims about the dream-work and have been challenged by more recent findings. According to Freud (1900), the emotions in dreams are often inappropriate to the content: "I dream I am in a frightful, dangerous, repulsive situation, but I feel no fear or revulsion at all; at other times, on the contrary, I am filled with horror at something harmless, and with delight at something childish" (p. 299). He attributes this mismatch to the fact that the contents of dreams are transformed by displacements and substitutions, but the emotions remain in place "unaltered" (p. 299). However, laboratory studies suggest that the emotions in dreams are "overwhelmingly appropriate to the dream content" (Foulkes, 1999, p. 68; Foulkes, Sullivan, Kerr, & Brown, 1988; Merritt, Stickgold, Pace-Schott, Williams, & Hobson, 1994).

Freud correctly anticipated that there would be objections to his wish-fulfillment theory based on anxiety dreams and punishment dreams. In the case of anxiety dreams, he claimed that they simply show that the censor has failed to disguise the wishes enough to make them acceptable. In the case of punishment dreams, he said that the wish came from the censoring agency within the personality. Those ideas are plausible enough within the context of his basic assumptions, but unlike actual scientific hypotheses, they also make it difficult, if not impossible, to falsify the theory. However, Freud did not try to explain away, or even discuss, the repetitive nightmares that are the hallmarks of posttraumatic stress disorder. Such dreams present the greatest problem for the wish-fulfillment dimension of his theory. If the theory cannot accommodate repetitive nightmares, then it is not necessary to become involved in an argument over his theory-saving claims about anxiety dreams and punishment dreams.

Freud did not consider traumatic dreams, an omission that is somewhat surprising because he had been impressed shortly before he wrote his book on dreams by the role that childhood traumas seemed to play in creating neurotic symptoms in adults. Although Freud soon abandoned his trauma theory of the neuroses, he never abandoned his interest in trauma as a key to the human psyche. Twelve years after he published *The Interpretations of Dreams*, he concluded in his first major work on culture, *Totem and Taboo*, that the trauma of patricide was the starting point for human society. In that volume, he explicitly debated the question of whether infantile wishes or real trauma is the central issue, concluding that historical trauma, not timeless psychological processes of human development, must be the starting point (Freud, 1912, pp. 159–161).

Even so, it was not until the recurrent "war neurosis" dreams suffered by combatants in World War I were brought to his attention that Freud focused on the issue of trauma in relation to dreams. At that time he conceded the main point, which is that "it is impossible to classify as wish fulfillments the dreams we have been discussing which occur in traumatic neurosis, or the dreams during psychoanalysis which bring to memory the psychical traumas of childhood" (Freud, 1920, p. 32). He decided that such dreams reveal an attempt at mastering overwhelming external stimuli. It is interesting that this explanation parallels what he originally thought about neurotic symptoms in the 1890s.

Although his concession clearly undermines the theory that all dreams are wish fulfillments, Freud (1933) claimed that the "exception does not overturn the rule" (p. 29). He argued that exceptions do not contradict his theory because they draw on a deeper level of the mind, one "beyond the pleasure principle" that shapes most dreams. His only modification of his theory was to say that dreams are a disguised attempt at wish fulfillment; he then concludes that "unconscious fixation to a trauma seems to be the foremost among these obstacles to the function of dreaming" (Freud, p. 29)

But such a resolution of the problem is not satisfactory. As shown in chapter 1, the accumulation of findings on the repetitive dreams of posttraumatic stress disorder since Freud suggests that they cannot be so easily isolated from dream life in general. More people have them, including victims of natural disasters, traffic accidents, rape and assaults, and they persist longer than Freud's dismissal implies (Barrett, 1996). They are experienced by 15% to 20% of the women and men who served in the Vietnam War, and not only by veterans who saw direct combat. Interviews and surveys suggest that young participants in the Vietnam War were more likely to suffer this syndrome and that those who experienced the unexpected loss of a close friend were more vulnerable than those who kept to themselves and formed no close attachments (Hartmann, 1984). Laboratory studies have found that these dreams occur in both REM and Stage II NREM (Kramer et al., 1987; Van der Kolk et al., 1984).

Far from being an exception to a general theory, the dreams of posttraumatic stress disorder are a strong test of the adequacy of any new theory of dreams. At the very least, traumatic dreams and recurrent dreams show that wish-fulfillment dreams are only a subset of all possible dreams. These dreams therefore stand as a refutation of the wish-fulfillment theory as a general theory. They lead to a rather mundane idea: Just as people have some waking thoughts that are wishful, so, too, do they have some dreams that are wishful. This conclusion fits well with the neurocognitive model outlined in chapter 1.

The main defense of the wish-fulfillment theory has come from Solms (1997). He sees his conclusion that the dopaminergic system is the trigger for dreams as support for Freud's idea, because this system is the basis for "appetitive interests." However, his strong emphasis on the dopaminergic system does not speak to posttraumatic dreams. It is greeted with skepticism by other neuropsychologists and neurophysiologists because dopamine production is about the same in waking and REM and is probably only one aspect of a complex neurochemical mixture (Doricchi & Violani, 2000; Gottesmann, 1999, 2000; Perry & Piggott, 2000). Moreover, dopaminergic blockers do not eliminate dreams (Hobson et al., 2000a, pp. 1028–1029); in a complex system like the neural network for dreaming, it is unlikely that only one location can stimulate it into action:

> As neuroimaging studies make clear, dreaming is a complex process occurring in a system of multiple interacting units across the brain. In such a distributed system, lesion studies cannot provide any means for deciding on a single location as the controller, because in fact there need be no such clearly defined module. (Bednar, 2000, p. 908)

Freud (1900, pp. 337–338) thought that people forget most of their dreams due to a hypothetical cognitive process called "repression," a process for which little or no convincing experimental evidence exists (Loftus, Joslyn, & Polage, 1998; Loftus & Ketcham, 1994; Loftus & Polage, 1999). Moreover, investigations of the relationship between frequency of recall and various personality and cognitive variables cast doubt on the notion that any process of denial or self-censorship is involved in dream forgetting (Cohen, 1979; Goodenough, 1991). Similarly, the results from several different laboratory studies demonstrated that the classic memory variables— recency, length, and intensity—best predict which dreams reported after awakenings in the night also are recalled the next morning (Baekland & Lasky, 1968; Meier et al., 1968; Strauch, 1969; Trinder & Kramer, 1971).

Freud's (1900) most controversial claim is that "impressions from the earliest years of our life can appear in our dreams, which do not seem to be at the disposal of our memory when we are awake" (p. 144). Once again, the memories can be varied in nature, but his greatest emphasis is on infantile sexual desires from "up to about the end of our third year"; he demonstrated his point by claiming that the "nakedness-dreams" experienced by many adults are "exhibition-dreams," which are based on childish desires to prance around naked (Freud, 1900, pp. 188–189). Such an assertion about early memories is highly unlikely in the light of modern-day research on memory, which shows that few or no conscious episodic recollections occur from before age 3 (Howe, 2000; Loftus & Ketcham, 1994).

In what may be his most sweeping and elegant construction, which builds on the wish-fulfillment theory and the fact that most dreams are forgotten, Freud theorized that dreams are the "guardians" of sleep, arising to deal with any bodily urges that may develop during the night (1900, p. 180). He used "dreams of convenience," such as those of going to the bathroom or having a glass of water, as simple examples of how dreams preserve sleep by providing a hallucinatory satisfaction to an urge. However, his greatest emphasis was on the role of dreams in preserving sleep in the face of infantile sexual urges.

The once plausible idea that dreams are the guardians of sleep is now contradicted by several different kinds of findings. First, the frequency and regularity of dreaming in most people suggests that the process cannot be primarily a way to deal with urges that emerge episodically during sleep. Second, the systematic study of dream content through laboratory awakenings contradicts Freud's theory because dream life so rarely includes the less threatening but nonetheless urgent desires, such as hunger and thirst. Although dream reports sometimes refer to eating and drinking, the striking fact is how infrequent those incidents are if the function of dreams is to guard sleep against wishes that may lead to awakenings. Third, as discussed in chapter 1, there is every reason to believe that preschool children seldom dream, but they sleep soundly nonetheless (Foulkes, 1982, 1999). Fourth, leucotomized schizophrenics show normal sleep in the laboratory, but they rarely report dreams even from REM awakenings (Jus et al., 1973).

In the face of these objections, the main defense of the guardian-of-sleep theory has come from a claim by Solms (1997) that the neural network may involve the "backward projection" of impulses arising in the dopaminergic system to the inferior parietal lobes and visual association cortex, thereby preserving sleep. There is, however, little or no evidence that such a mechanism is responsible for dreaming (Antrobus, 2000a, p. 905; Doricchi & Violani, 2000). It is more likely, as stated earlier in this section, that no single area generates all dreams (Bednar, 2000).

Solms (1997, p. 165) also defended Freud's functional hypothesis with his finding that study participants who reported the cessation of dreaming more often said that they had disrupted sleep than the control sample did. However, the findings are not impressive in that 51% of the 101 participants with global loss of dreaming indicated that their sleep was not disrupted. If dreaming is necessary to preserve sleep, then virtually everyone reporting global cessation of dreaming should be suffering far more from disturbed sleep than Solms's results suggest they do.

Because standard empirical methods have not been able to show support for any aspect of Freud's theory, his conclusions about the nature of dreams rest exclusively on his method of free association, in which the dreamer produces uncritical, unreflective trains of thought to each part of the dream. Freud assumed that free associations reveal the latent wishes on which dreams are based. The seeming discovery of latent dream-thoughts through free association then led to his inference that the cognitive processes called the dream-work transform these latent wishes into the manifest dream content.

However, there is no evidence that free association has any specific usefulness for examining Freud's hypotheses, even though it seems to be helpful in getting people to talk about their emotional memories and current concerns. As Fisher and Greenberg (1977) noted in their first assessment of Freud's work on dreams, "there is not a shred of empirical or reliable evidence that they [free associations] provide a unique 'true' solution concerning what is contained in the dream" (p. 66). In addition, it can be recalled from chapter 2 that the large-scale attempt by Foulkes (1978) to make use of free associations to understand dreams collected in the laboratory setting ended with the conclusion that the method is inherently arbitrary (Foulkes, 1996a, p. 617).

Contrary to the claim that the method is free of any suggestive influence by the psychotherapist, experimental evidence indicates that subtle suggestions from an experimenter–therapist can falsely convince many people on the basis of dream interpretations that they were once lost or abandoned as young children (Mazzoni & Loftus, 1998; Mazzoni et al., 1999). These and many other findings on the power of suggestion in a therapeutic context (Ofshe & Watters, 1994) take on greater importance when Freud's (1900, pp. 114–119) several reports of arguments with patients concerning the wishful and infantile bases of their dreams are added to the picture. What Freud saw as overcoming "resistance" can be understood from the vantage point of social psychology as a process of persuasion and conversion. This finding does not mean that all psychoanalytic sessions have been shown to be exercises in suggestion. However, it does mean that the burden of proof is now on Freudians to demonstrate that any therapeutic data they use to make claims about dreams are not confounded by this extremely important variable.

Despite the failure of all of his specific hypotheses, Freud deserves considerable credit for championing the general idea developed in the 19th century that dreams have personal psychological meaning. It also seems likely that his idea of wish fulfillment holds true for some unknown number of dreams. In addition, he is responsible for the idea that dreams may be the product of figurative thought.

JUNG'S THEORY OF DREAMS

The Jungian theory of dreams is based on four main ideas, which can be addressed with modern-day research on metaphor, on the one hand, and the large literature on dream content, on the other. Jung's (1963, 1974) best-known and most central idea is that highly significant dreams are the products of a *collective unconscious*, which contains the inherited experiential record of the human species in the form of *archetypes*, or highly energized patterns or concepts that must be expressed through the personality. However, as a comprehensive analysis and synthesis by Neher (1996) argued, this concept is unscientific because it (a) is based on the discredited notion of the inheritance of acquired characteristics; (b) does not allow for the variation in specific archetypes that would be expected on the basis of modern-day genetics; and (c) is not grounded in a convincing elimination of the possible influence of socialization and culture in the personal, therapeutic, and cross-cultural anecdotes on which it is based.

In addition, as the first point in Neher's (1996) critique implies, the concept is not able to escape the charge of circularity because the origins of the collective unconscious are said to be in repeated human experience, which is the phenomenon the concept is supposed to explain. If experience is the basis for the collective unconscious, there is no need to invoke a collective unconscious to explain commonalities of experience that are most likely based on the similar human situations that recur in each individual lifetime. This viewpoint also can better explain the variations in thinking styles that are found from culture to culture (Rogoff, 1990).

Second, Jung argued that the archetypes of the collective unconscious express themselves through a set of inherited symbols that also appear in myths, religious ceremonies, and other waking practices. Thus, the main focus of Jungian dream analysts is on interpreting these symbols using both individual dreams and cultural parallels. Jung's observation of some commonality in dream content across individuals and cultures is more parsimoniously and plausibly encompassed by the idea that metaphorical concepts are acquired through both developmental experiences shared by all human beings and gradual linguistic socialization into the huge treasure trove of conceptual metaphors that are part of a group's cultural heritage (Gibbs, 1994; Lakoff, 1987; Lakoff & Turner, 1989). This idea is supported by findings showing similarities in conceptual metaphors in many different cultures, including China and Japan (Lakoff & Johnson, 1999; Nomura, 1996; Yu, 1999).

The usefulness of thinking about symbolic interpretations as metaphoric analyses can be seen by looking at the dream that Jung (1963) claims to be the basis for his idea of a collective unconscious. In that dream, from a time when he was having grave doubts about Freudian theory, Jung found himself exploring a house that belonged to him but did not seem at all familiar. He was impressed by the elegant decor of the upper floor, and then descended to a lower floor with medieval furnishings. He next saw a heavy door that led to a stone stairway and an ancient vaulted cellar. On the cellar floor he saw a stone slab leading down another set of stairs to "a low cave cut into the rock," which contained remains from a primitive culture (Jung, 1963, p. 159). Jung interpreted the dream as "a structural diagram of the human psyche," with the deepest level of the house representing a collective unconscious of an impersonal nature (Jung, 1963, p. 161).

This interpretation makes "intuitive" sense to many people because it is based on a shared conceptual metaphor: The "mind is a container" (Lakoff, 1987; Lakoff & Johnson, 1999). The same conceptual metaphor makes it possible to say that there are "skeletons in the closet" or "bodies buried in the basement" when a person has a secret, or to say "there is no one home" when a person is absentminded or not interacting properly, or to characterize mental illness by saying a person has "bats in his belfry" or "bees in her bonnet." In fact, all of the "functional" or "subjective" symbols said by Jungians to represent the psyche, or aspects of it, can be linked to one or more of several conceptual metaphors.

Jung's third major idea is that most dreams, especially those with roots in the collective unconscious, have a *compensatory* function—that is, they express those aspects of the personality, including the archetypes, that are not adequately developed in waking life. This idea is difficult to support or refute in a definitive way because there may be subtle forms of compensation, even in dreams that do not seem compensatory on the basis of objective methods. Still, the idea seems to be contradicted by every relevant systematic study since the beginning of modern-day dream research in the late 19th century, when psychologists who wrote down their own dreams found considerable continuity between dream content and waking cognition (Calkins, 1893; Weed & Hallam, 1896). This finding was repeated in nonlaboratory investigations summarized by Fisher and Greenberg (1977, 1996), and it finds further support in laboratory studies by Fiss (1983, 1986) that used clinical assessments as well as in two laboratory studies that analyzed correlations between dream content and objective personality measures (Foulkes et al., 1969; Foulkes & Rechtschaffen, 1964). In both of the laboratory correlational studies, the young men who had the most unpleasant dreams also tended to have the highest scores on MMPI psychopathology indicators.

As stressed throughout this book, the continuity between dream content and waking life is one of the most striking findings from content analysis studies by Calvin S. Hall and his co-workers (Hall & Nordby, 1972). People dream most often about the people and interests that preoccupy them in waking life. They show the most aggression in dreams toward the people with whom they have the most conflict in waking life. The results are so consistent for these kinds of continuities that Hall adopted the term *continuity principle* to contrast his findings with Jung's compensation hypothesis. Hall's blind analyses of the dreams of a child molester, a neurotic patient in psychotherapy, Franz Kafka, and numerous average people who kept dream journals provide strong evidence for this alternative hypothesis (Bell & Hall, 1971; Domhoff, 1996; Hall & Lind, 1970). This evidence is now supplemented by the new findings presented in chapter 5.

Fourth, and finally, Jung claimed that gradual changes in dream content occur beginning in the middle years of adult life that reflect the psychological need for the "individuation" and "integration" of the personality, under the direction of the "self" archetype. However, as mentioned in chapter 1, there is considerable evidence that adults, unlike children, are consistent in what they dream about over months, years, or decades. The evidence is of two types: cross-sectional and longitudinal. Several cross-sectional studies, most in the United States, but one in Canada and one in Switzerland, demonstrated that dream content shows consistency, not change, as people grow older, with the possible exception of declines in aggression and negative emotions (Brenneis, 1975; Cote et al., 1996; Domhoff, 1996; Hall & Domhoff, 1963b, 1964; Howe & Blick, 1983; Inge Strauch, Department of Psychology, University of Zurich, personal communication, April 5, 2000; Zepelin, 1980, 1981).

Although the longitudinal studies were not large in number, they were similar in their results for both ongoing dream journals (Domhoff, 1996; Domhoff & Schneider, 1998; Hall & Nordby, 1972; Smith & Hall, 1964) and 2-week journals collected 10 to 17 years apart from 21 women (Lortie-Lussier et al., 2000). The analyses of the Barb Sanders series in chapter 5 now add an important new dimension to this body of evidence because of the number of dreams that were studied and the different types of analyses that were conducted. Few changes occurred in most of the coding categories or in various subseries, even though the dreams cover the years when the process of individuation is supposed to be unfolding.

Within this context of consistency, a study of dreams from women before, during, and after menopause is of special interest because it was designed to test ideas derived from Jungian theory concerning changes in dream content during and after menopause (Abel, 1994). The investigator created seven theoretical scales derived from Jungian theory that were used by three coders naïve about Jungian theory and blind as to the age of the dreamer. Even more important, an expert on Jungian theory coded all dreams on a scale for the degree to which the dreams expressed archetypal symbols.

Thirty-two of the women were still menstruating (average age = 39.6); 24 women were perimenopausal (average age = 49.2); and 20 women were postmenopausal (average age = 58.6). Women in the first group averaged 32 dream reports over a 1-month period; women in the second group averaged

21 dream reports; and women in the third group averaged 16 reports. This decline in dream recall parallels the decrease in dream recall with age in a study of 2,328 adults ages 17 to 92 (Giambra, Jung, & Grodsky, 1996). The only significant difference in dream content concerned an "initiation" scale, but the difference was not for the predicted group. Contrary to expectations, the codings by the Jungian expert did not show any difference in the degree of symbolic expression in the three samples.

Once again, then, the findings relevant to the theory under investigation provide no support for any of its most important claims. In the end, Jungian dream theory boils down to the idea that dreams can be understood in terms of waking conceptual metaphors. No evidence supports that claim, and no rules or guidelines determine which conceptual metaphors should be applied to which dreams. As the study of metamorphoses in the Sanders series shows, developing such rules and evidence will not be easy.

ACTIVATION–SYNTHESIS THEORY

As the first modern-day neuropsychological theory of dreams that draws on sleep research, activation–synthesis theory is a forerunner of the kind of neurocognitive model presented in this book. However, it differs from a neurocognitive theory in that it starts with studies of brain stem lesions in cats and extrapolates to human dreaming without considering any of the findings concerning dreaming and dream content that are based on laboratory awakenings (Foulkes, 1966, 1985). The activation–synthesis theory is distinguished by its emphasis on cells in one region in the pons as the only trigger for dreaming and as the main determinant of some of the unusual formal aspects of dreams. According to the original version of this theory, which became popular as the antithesis of Freudian theory, a dream is a catch-as-catch-can synthesis by the forebrain, which is "making the best of a bad job in producing even partially coherent dream imagery from the relatively noisy signals sent up to it from the brainstem" (Hobson & McCarley, 1977, p. 1347). The theory offers no suggestion that any cognitive processes are operative. More specifically, phasic stimulation from the brain stem, primarily in the form of ponto-geniculo-occipito (PGO) waves, is responsible for sudden scene changes, unusual juxtapositions, and other improbable constructions in dreams (Hobson, 1988; Mamelak & Hobson, 1989). The activation of the visual system in REM sleep is assumed to be "formally similar to that of the waking state," which is said to account for "the clarity of our dream vision" (Hobson, 1988, p. 205).

Even some types of dream content are claimed to be direct reactions to brain stem signals, such as being unable to move while being chased, which is described as an accurate cortical reading of the contradictory state created by the high activation of the motor-pattern generator in conjunction with the paralyzed state of spinal neurons. Similarly, "flying dreams may thus be a logical, direct, and unsymbolic way of synthesizing information generated endogenously by the vestibular system in D [dreaming] sleep" (Hobson & McCarley, 1977, p. 1339). The poor recall of dreams is said to reflect a "state-dependent amnesia," which may be a result of the low level of "aminergic neuronal activity and the resulting effects on second messengers and macromolecules" (Hobson & McCarley, 1977, p. 1347).

From the point of view of many of the early laboratory dream researchers, this theory was contradicted by several types of data that already had been collected in laboratories in the 20 years before it appeared. First, the presence of dreaming in many awakenings from NREM sleep is strong evidence against an exclusive emphasis on REM sleep as the context for dreaming (Foulkes, 1962; Foulkes & Schmidt, 1983; Foulkes & Vogel, 1965; Herman, Ellman, & Roffwarg, 1978). Although these studies show that many NREM dream reports are less "dreamlike" and more "thoughtlike" than typical REM dream reports, more than enough NREM reports contain full-blown dream content to contradict the strict equation of REM sleep and dreaming. Indeed, this evidence was so convincing to most dream researchers by the late 1960s that they had already abandoned the REM-equals-dreaming equation that was central to the original version of activation–synthesis theory (Berger, 1967, 1969; Foulkes, 1966; Hall, 1967).

Second, dreams at sleep onset, long before there are signs of REM, contradict the theory (Vogel, 1991). Although dreamlike mental activity is brief during the transition to sleep, it is extremely important theoretically because the highly regular sequence of mental changes discovered in the laboratory does not correlate strongly with the physiological changes that index the transition from waking to sleep. For example, hallucinatory imagery can even occur when the EEG pattern still indicates wakefulness (Foulkes, 1985, pp. 70–71).

These longstanding results were later supplemented by activation–synthesis theorists themselves in a study of 16 participants over a 2-week period, who were paged while awake or aroused by means of the Nightcap while sleeping in their homes. The study found that the prevalence of "hallucinatory content" ranged from 3.6% in quiet waking to the higher figures of 35% at sleep onset, 60% in NREM, and 82% in REM (Fosse et al., 2001, p. 33). The percentages for the NREM and REM awakenings are similar to what has been found in laboratory studies, but are only about half of what has been found for sleep onset through carefully pinpointed laboratory awakenings (Foulkes, 1985; Foulkes & Vogel, 1965; Vogel, 1991; Vogel, Barrowclough, & Giesler, 1972).

A third type of evidence against activation–synthesis theory comes from studies that attempted to link a range of phasic activities during REM—

such as bursts of eye movements, muscle activity, or bursts of theta waves—to dream content through immediate awakenings when the signs appeared. The findings of some of the studies suggest that dreaming is more vivid during phasic events, thereby supporting the idea that the level of activation may be indexed by them. However, there is little or no connection to dream features or dream content according to most reviewers (Antrobus, 2000b; Foulkes, 1985; Pivik, 1986, 2000). Still, the relationship is described as "weak but consistently positive" by activation–synthesis theorists (Hobson et al., 2000b, p. 799).

Fourth, the neuroimaging and lesion studies discussed in chapter 1 contradict the passive role assigned to the forebrain in the first version of activation–synthesis theory. They show that the forebrain is more active than the theory assumes and that it is selectively active in ways not anticipated by the theory. In addition, and contrary to activation–synthesis theory, the primary visual cortex and motor cortex do not seem to be part of the neural substrate for dreaming, according to the lesion studies, and they are not active during REM sleep, according to the neuroimaging studies (Conduit, Crewther, & Coleman, 2000, p. 925).

In the face of these accumulated findings, along with strong new evidence for the presence of full-fledged dreaming in NREM just before morning awakenings (Antrobus et al., 1995; Cicogna et al., 1998), activation–synthesis theory has been altered and expanded in several ways. In particular, the forebrain has been given a much larger role in regulating the pontine activation responsible for REM and in shaping dream content, especially through limbic structures (Hobson et al., 1998, 2000b). The revised theory also includes greater attention to two factors that were only briefly noted in the original formulation: the "input source" and the nature of the neurochemical "modulation."

The expanded model has three dimensions that are meant to account for all states of consciousness, not just dreaming: *activation, input,* and *modulation* (AIM). Activation now refers to both total and regional brain-activation levels. Input concerns the degree to which activation is being generated internally or externally. Modulation refers to the ratio of aminergic (i.e., serotonin and norepinephrine) to cholinergic (i.e., acetylcholine) neuromodulators in each consciousness state. The ratio is high in waking, but it is reversed during REM, when the levels of serotonin and norepinephrine fall to near zero (Fosse et al., 2001, p. 30; Hobson et al., 2000b, p. 805). In the full AIM model, waking is said to be characterized by high levels of brain activation, external sources of input, and aminergic neuromodulation, whereas REM is characterized by high levels of brain activation, internal sources of input, and cholinergic modulation. NREM is characterized by low levels of brain activation, internal sources of input, and a mixture of aminergic and cholinergic modulation. The model can account for a variety of unusual states of consciousness, such as REM sleep-behavior disorder, sleep paralysis upon awakening, and drug-induced hallucinations.

Cholinergic neuromodulation during REM, through its stimulation of PGO activity, is assumed to be the primary causal factor in accounting for the "hallucinatory" imagery of dreaming. The "ubiquity of motion" in dreams is said to be caused by the high level of activity in basal ganglia during REM, and plot discontinuity and incongruity are the result of "deficient executive functions including working memory" (Hobson et al., 2000a, p. 1030). Dreaming in NREM is now attributed to subtle stimulation by the same regions of the brain stem that generate REM. This stimulation is sometimes called "covert REM sleep" (Hobson et al., 2000b; Nielsen, 2000a, 2000b). In other words, the revised theory has somewhat less emphasis on the REM stage, but it has a continuing emphasis on brain stem stimulation from the pontine tegmentum as the key to dreaming. To make this point, Hobson (2000) argued that "all sleep is REM sleep (more or less)," a statement that implies that states of sleep are not as discrete as they were once thought to be (p. 952). The fact that relatively few dreams are remembered is now explained as an "organic amnesia" caused by the combined effects of low aminergic levels and decreased activity in the dorsolateral prefrontal cortex.

These alterations narrow the distance between activation–synthesis theory and a neurocognitive model on issues concerning the neural substrate for dreaming. However, those who have collected dreams from NREM have noted that no direct evidence connects NREM dream content to any potential indicators of covert REM sleep (Bosinelli & Cicogna, 2000; Cipolli, 2000; Feinberg, 2000; Vogel, 2000, p. 1015). These researchers especially believe that the large number of dream reports from spontaneous NREM morning awakenings (Cicogna et al., 1998) are probably best explained by general brain activation. Moreover, a research group that has collected dreams at sleep onset has suggested that the remnants of waking activation are a more likely explanation for these dreams than any stimulation from covert REM sleep (Ogilvie, Takeuchi, & Murphy, 2000). There are indications that activation–synthesis theorists concur with a primary emphasis on activation for sleep onset and spontaneous NREM morning awakenings, as in the comment that their model works best for "intense dreaming" in the "first 4 to 6 hours of the night" (Hobson, 2000, p. 951; Hobson et al., 2000a, p. 1023).

The gap could narrow even further if neurophysiological critics of activation–synthesis theory are right that the theory still overstates the role of the pontine tegmentum in REM regulation by not giving enough weight to growing evidence for control of this sleep state by the hypothalamus (Morrison & Sanford, 2000; Salin-Pascual, Gerashchenko, & Shiromani, 2000). Regulation by the hypothalamus includes control of the PGO waves that are central in activation–synthesis theory. As Steriade (2000) argued, hypothalamic and forebrain structures "may be the most effective in driving PGO neuronal generators" (p. 108). The gap could almost be closed in terms of differences of opinion on the nature of the neural substrate for dreaming if other neurophysiologists are correct that the theory has too exclusive an emphasis on cholinergic systems in the creation of dream mentation. As Gottesmann (1999, 2000), Perry, Walker, Grace, and Perry (1999), and Perry and Piggott (2000) argued on the basis of a range of evidence in animals and humans, it seems more likely that, at the least, it is the combination of acetylcholine and dopamine, in the absence of serotonin and norepinephrine, that modulates REM. As the mixture becomes more complex, neuromodulation shades toward the emphasis on "general activation" favored by cognitively oriented theorists.

Over and beyond these strictly neurophysiological issues, the AIM model has four other problems, all of which relate to the continuing neglect of the cognitive dimension, which remains underdeveloped in the theory. The first of these additional problems concerns the relative absence of dreaming in young children, which is denied by activation–synthesis theorists. To deal with young children's low recall from REM periods, the researchers could have modified their view to say that REM is necessary but not sufficient, as they did on the basis of the findings from adults with brain lesions. Instead of acknowledging that cognitive development is also necessary for dreaming, they argued that the children in Foulkes's (1982; see also Foulkes, Hollifield, Sullivan, Bradley, & Terry, 1990) studies felt uncomfortable and inhibited in the laboratory (Hobson et al., 2000b). They presented their own evidence of full-fledged dreams from preschool children on the basis of home-reported dreams collected by parents (Resnick, Stickgold, Rittenhouse, & Hobson, 1994). Some of the dreams were collected after having the children tell themselves at bedtime that they would remember a dream in the morning, which Foulkes (1996b, 1999) sees as an implicit pressure to comply that may have led to made-up dreams.

As if to underscore their differences with Foulkes's emphasis on the need for a certain level of cognitive development for dreaming to occur, the activation–synthesis theorists assert that they can imagine dreaming in neonates:

> Similarly, we specifically suggest that the human neonate, spending as it does more than 50 percent of its time in REM sleep, is having indescribable but nevertheless real oneiric experiences. An infant's waking experience remains essentially indescribable and speculative to us older persons but we do not doubt that infants enjoy some sort of waking conscious experience. For us, it is not at all difficult to imagine that an infant might be experiencing hallucinosis, emotions, and fictive kinesthetic sensations during REM sleep. (Hobson et al., 2000b, p. 803)

Contrary to these claims, Foulkes (1982, 1999) presented detailed evidence that his extensive efforts to make the children comfortable in the laboratory setting did prove successful. In addition, during the second and fourth years of his study, he tested for the possible effects of awakenings by allowing the children to sleep throughout the night in the laboratory. They then reported any dreams they recalled in the morning. This procedure found no differences with dreams collected after morning awakenings at home. Foulkes's finding means that any differences found in other studies between dreams collected from awakenings in the laboratory and at home are due to selective recall for atypical dreams at home, rather than to any alleged inhibitory effect in the laboratory (Foulkes, 1979, 1982, 1996b). The finding that two boys ages 11 to 13 who had low visuospatial skills unexpectedly showed low levels of REM recall also suggests that the issue is lack of dreaming, not lack of reporting skills (Foulkes, 1982, pp. 180–181, 225–226).

Second, the activation–synthesis theory of dream forgetting does not consider the cognitive factors that seem to be involved in low levels of dream recall. A strictly neurophysiological explanation does not take into account that waking recall also can be poor in some circumstances, such as when a person's mind is drifting while performing a routine task. From a cognitive point of view, the problem may be the lack of "an external narrative to which memories for internal events can be tied" (Chapman & Underwood, 2000, p. 917). Moreover, more forgetting in waking life occurs than is commonly assumed (Chapman & Underwood, 2000). The fact that high recallers tend to have a stronger interest in dreams than nonrecallers (Tonay, 1993) and that recall can be improved with training and encouragement (Schredl, 2000) also suggest that there is a cognitive dimension to dream recall.

Third, there are unresolved questions related to claims by activation–synthesis theorists about "bizarreness" in dreams. Although activation–synthesis theorists are highly critical of all clinical theories of dreams, they continue to talk about the normal process of dreaming as though it were a psychiatric phenomenon (Hartmann, 2000). For example, they call dream imagery "hallucinatory" and liken the dream experience to "religious conversion, near-death experience, functional psychosis, delirium, drug-induced conditions, and other altered states of consciousness" (Hobson et al., 2000b, p. 802). They attribute this alleged bizarreness to forebrain stimulation from the pontine tegmentum, but as Antrobus (2000a) stressed, "assumptions about how the pons determines the features of dreaming are completely without empirical support" (p. 905). He also pointed out that he and his co-workers have collected instances of unusual dream imagery when phasic activity originating in the pontine tegmentum was minimal (Antrobus et al., 1995).

Several different scales have been developed to assess bizarre elements, but there is no general agreement as to their usefulness or their methodological soundness (e.g., Bonato, Moffitt, Hoffmann, & Cuddy, 1991; Hall, 1966b, p. 40; Ogilvie, Hunt, Sawicki, & Samahalskyi, 1982; Revonsuo & Salmivalli, 1995). The scales developed by activation–synthesis theorists (Hobson, Hoffman, Helfand, & Kostner, 1987; Rittenhouse et al., 1994) emphasize sudden shifts in scenes that may not be unique to dreams if jumps in relaxed waking thought are used as the relevant comparison. In addition, most of the scales are compromised because they include no control for dream length and their reliability is uncertain.

The coding categories that activation–synthesis theorists have created for the study of bizarreness are no more reliable or convincing than any of the other bizarreness scales. Recognizing reliability problems with their first scale (Hobson et al., 1987, pp. 161–162), which showed only 55% agreement between two raters when used by another researcher (Abel, 1996, p. 10), Hobson and his colleagues modified the scale for later studies. In a study using the revised scale on 200 dream reports with 4,674 lines of text, it was reported that two of three coders designated 737 lines as containing bizarre features, but no indication of the number of lines on which they disagreed was provided, a piece of information that would make it possible to determine the percentage of agreement. Moreover, only 456 (62%) of the identified lines were agreed on by all three coders (Merritt et al., 1994, p. 53).

In addition, the boundary between features and contents is not always as clear as activation–synthesis theorists' coding system suggests. What they consider a bizarre feature, such as one character changing into another or one character being a combination of two people, may be "content" that is the product of a conceptual blend (Fauconnier, 1997; Grady et al., 1999). This possibility is demonstrated with some of the composite characters in the Barb Sanders series discussed in chapter 5. In effect, Hobson's theory and coding system rule out any study of figurative thought in dreams.

The most frequent bizarreness that activation–synthesis theorists find in dreams is in the number of abrupt scene changes, which occurred in 34% of 200 dreams in one of their studies (Rittenhouse et al., 1994). By contrast, using a scale that focused on unusual activities, unusual occurrences, distorted objects, and metamorphoses, Hall (1966b, p. 41) found that only 10% of 815 home and lab dream reports had at least one bizarre element, with no differences between the two types of reports. Moreover, there is far more discontinuity, drift, and inattention in waking thought than is implied by the claim that changes in dream scenes or settings are inherently bizarre (Chapman & Underwood, 2000). The relevant comparison for studying dream bizarreness is with reports of waking memories, not waking reality (Bednar, 2000, p. 909; Chapman & Underwood, 2000, p. 917).

Not all studies agree that there are frequent discontinuities within dream reports. In a detailed study of this issue, Foulkes and Schmidt (1983), divided REM dream reports into a series of "temporal units," which were defined by the appearance of a new activity in the dream, such as the sequence of "coming out of school/opening the gate/children saying goodbye to each other/walking down the street" (p. 267). They found that only 1 in 8 temporal transitions was accompanied by a discontinuity in both setting and characters. They argued that the relatively small discontinuities in dreams are consistent with, and probably necessary for, the considerable degree of narrative and thematic development that is found in most REM reports (cf. Cipolli & Poli, 1992). If the findings are accurate, then it is likely that the AIM model overemphasizes bizarreness due to its focus on the brain stem as a direct cause of unusual dream features.

Fourth, and finally, activation–synthesis theory has little to say about dream content due to its lack of attention to the cognitive dimension of dreaming. Its main proponents agree that the relative "mundaneness" of dream content is compatible with their emphasis on the bizarreness of dream form and that there is at least some information and pattern in individual dream journals. However, they raise questions about the accuracy and usefulness of dream reports and about the possibility of doing scientific studies of dream content (Hobson et al., 2000a, pp. 1020–1021). Consequently, they do not take seriously the need to add a content dimension to their theory. They therefore have little or nothing to contribute to the study of dream meaning at the cognitive level.

Contrary to their doubts, the arguments and evidence in chapter 2 show that the quality of dream reports can be excellent, and chapters 3, 4, and 5 demonstrate that it is possible to conduct scientific studies of dream content. Several Hall–Van de Castle categories for types of activities easily accommodate the activation–synthesis theorists' focus on sensory references and movement in dreams better than the activation–synthesis theorists' own scales. The categories for emotions are also better suited than their scales for studying the questions of interest to them, including their concern with confusion, surprise, and uncertainty.

The way in which issues concerning form and content might be integrated into the new neurocognitive model can be shown through two separate studies of the same dream series, taken from a 3-month journal of 233 dream reports. The journal was kept out of intellectual curiosity in the summer of 1939 by a 46-year-old natural scientist who had no training in psychology or psychiatry and no investment in any dream theory. He wrote in the preface that he was a frequent dreamer who had been frightened by some of his nightmares as a child and that he wanted to see for himself if there was anything to the general claims by Freud. The journal is exceptionally interesting in that it includes drawings that relate to many of the dreams.

For those who want to see the dream reports for themselves, they are available under the name "The Natural Scientist" at http://www.DreamBank.net.

Hobson purchased the dream journal from a medical book catalog in 1980; he used the drawings to study the sensory references, fictive movement, and bizarre features in the dream reports, claiming that his findings showed the influence of pontine stimulation on dream features (Hobson, 1988; Hobson et al., 1987). From his theoretical vantage point, the dreams seemed to be peculiar and incongruous, as indexed by sudden scene changes or uncertainties as to the identity of people or settings. However, no evidence linked these features to the neural network for dreaming except their apparent frequency.

The same dream journal yielded different information when it was studied from the content point of view by Adam Schneider, as first reported in Domhoff (1996, pp. 147–150). First, as shown in Table 6.1, when the first 93 reports with 50 or more words are compared with the second 93, the content is strikingly consistent over just this short period. Second, a blind analysis of the characters, social interactions, settings, and emotions in the dreams provides a good portrait of the dreamer's waking concerns and interests, as demonstrated through a later comparison of the dream findings with a four-page obituary that contains personal information.

For example, as shown in the *h*-profile in Figure 6.1, the dreamer scores low on aggressiveness and even lower on dreamer-involved aggression and

TABLE 6.1
Consistency in the Natural Scientist's 3-Month Dream Journal

	Total (*n* = 187)	1st set (*n* = 93)	2nd set (*n* = 93)
Characters			
Characters per dream	3.08	3.08	3.02
Male/female percent	70	70	70
Familiarity percent	38	38	37
Animal percent	11	14	9
Social interaction percents			
Dreamer-involved aggression percent	59	51	66
Dreamer-involved friendliness percent	70	68	72
Aggressor percent	35	38	32
Befriender percent	52	44	57
Physical aggression percent	45	42	45
Social interaction ratios			
Aggression/character index	18	15	21
Friendliness/character index	16	14	18
Settings			
Indoor settings percent	43	45	41
Familiar settings percent	73	76	70

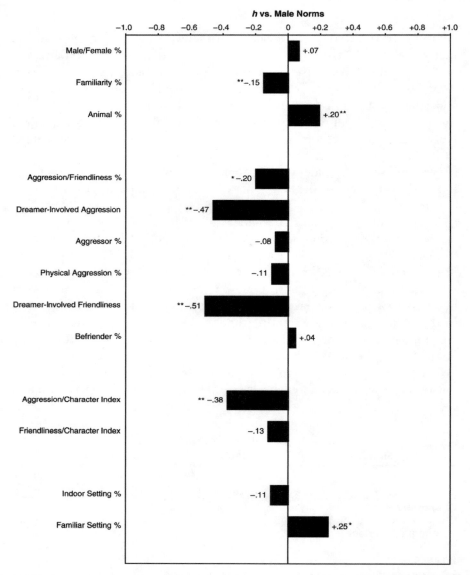

Figure 6.1. The *h* profile for the dreamer known as "The Natural Scientist," using the male normative sample as a baseline.   *p < .05. **p < .01.

dreamer-involved friendliness. These findings fit with his low-key personality and his focus on observation in waking life. In addition, there are no sexual interactions in his dreams, which is consistent with his status as a life-long bachelor. On the other hand, he is slightly elevated on animal percent, which fits with the fact that he was raised in a small farm town, liked to fish and hunt, and became an entomologist. The animals in his dreams are primarily birds, barnyard animals, and the insects he studied in his professional life. He is also somewhat above the norm on familiar settings percent, which means, in his case, that the dreams are located in his home, his office, and the family homestead.

The dreams demonstrate great attention to detail, a characteristic that fits with the monumental taxonomic task he had undertaken with the type of insect he studied. Thirteen dreams refer to golf, which the scientist enjoyed in waking life as part of a lifelong involvement in competitive sports. Contrary to what might be expected from activation–synthesis theorists' emphasis on vestibular influences on dreaming, in only one dream is the scientist flying. More exactly, in this dream he is floating a few yards above the ground, thanks to a small rectangular platform that he thinks may be a carpet and that looks somewhat like a magic carpet in the accompanying drawing. As to chase dreams and dreams in which he cannot move, which figure prominently in the examples used by activation–synthesis theorists, he describes none, although in one dream he watches a dog chase a mountain lion. Generally speaking, then, the connections between dream content and his waking life are more solid than any alleged connections between dream features and his brain stem.

Activation–synthesis theorists insist on the need for a "whole-brain isomorphism" in studying dreams, but their isomorphism is premature at best, as evidenced by the many changes in their specific claims on the basis of unexpected neurophysiological findings (Feinberg, 2000; Morrison & Sanford, 2000). Moreover, their isomorphism does not include any consideration of the cognitive dimension of dreaming. The connections between brain events and dream features that are claimed in their model remain entirely hypothetical. There is no more reason to believe, for example, that flying in dreams is due to vestibular disturbances than there is to believe that it is based on one or another conceptual metaphor. However, as previous chapters in this volume show, it may be possible to demonstrate empirically that an interaction occurs between physiological and cognitive levels: Brain variables can affect cognitive variables, and cognitive variables can affect brain variables. In fact, as this book argues, good studies of dream content in relation to brain lesions and medications might contribute to a closer theoretical articulation between brain and mind. Such an articulation would fully incorporate findings at the cognitive level and create a neurocognitive model of dreams.

FUNCTIONAL THEORIES OF DREAMS

Innumerable theories of dream function have been developed (Dallett, 1973). All of them are highly speculative and difficult to refute in a definitive way, and they therefore linger despite a lack of evidence for any of them.

This situation also provides a fertile terrain for new and unlikely theories that are based on analogies drawn from each development or discovery in other areas of research. This search for a function seems necessary and sensible to most people, but it rests on the false "adaptationist" assumption that "all the things that have form have function" (Thompson, 2000, p. 1014). In fact, many structures and processes persist even though they have no function; dreaming may be one of them (Flanagan, 1995, 2000a).

Aside from Freud's guardian-of-sleep theory and Jung's compensatory theory, which were refuted earlier in the chapter, the most prominent theory of dream function is that dreams provide solutions to current problems, especially emotional problems (Barrett, 1993; Greenberg et al., 1992; Greenberg & Pearlman, 1993). In one variant, Fiss (1993) suggested that dreams are especially good at registering subtle internal and external signals that often go undetected in waking life, making them potentially useful for picking up early signs of physical illness.

There are many empirical findings about dreams that do not fit well with any problem-solving theory. To begin with, the idea that dreams have a purpose originated at a time when it was thought that people rarely dream. In that context, it was plausible to believe that the occasional recalled dream could be a reaction to a specific event or emotional problem. But if most adults dream at least four to six times per night, then most people are recalling less than 1% of their dreams. Even the best dream recallers remember only a small proportion of their dreams. This lack of recall suggests that dreams in general are not an evolutionary adaptation to provide information or insight to people when they are awake.

In addition, only about half of recalled dreams seem to have even the slightest connection to the events of the previous day (Botman & Crovitz, 1989; Harlow & Roll, 1992; Hartmann, 1968; Marquardt et al., 1996; Nielsen & Powell, 1992). Kramer (2000a) claimed on the basis of one small clinical study that the concerns of the day are incorporated into dreams, but more recent and larger studies, in which judges try to match expressed daytime concerns with dream reports from laboratory awakenings, have proven unsuccessful (Roussy, 2000; Roussy, Brunette, et al., 2000). It is therefore unlikely that dreams often deal with immediately relevant issues, although this book suggests that they dramatize ongoing emotional preoccupations in many instances.

If dreams contain important information for consideration in waking consciousness, then it might be predicted that people who do not remember or pay attention to their dreams might suffer some disadvantages. People who rarely recall dreams, however, do not differ in personality or mental difficulties from those who recall dreams regularly (Antrobus, 1993; Blagrove & Akehurst, 2000; Cohen, 1979; Goodenough, 1991; Tonay, 1993). Generally speaking, it is difficult to distinguish "recallers" from "nonrecallers" with either personality or cognitive tests. If incorporating and dealing with the content of dreams mattered for psychological well-being, a different set of findings might be expected. In fact, contrary to any theory that emphasizes the problem-solving nature of dreams, dream recall is often as disturbing as it is helpful, as shown most dramatically with people who suffer from posttraumatic stress disorder. Many people who have recurrent dreams suffer from them (Zadra, 1996; Zadra & Donderi, 2000a).

It is also unlikely that dreams contain new information on physical illnesses. The few dream studies cited by Fiss (1993) are clinical studies with small samples. Those studies claim to find differences in themes concerning hostility or separation, but no direct indications of illness, as Fiss acknowledged. His signal-detection theory of dream function therefore rests on an extrapolation from the literature on subliminal stimulation. As noted earlier in the chapter, most research psychologists remain highly doubtful that any strong effect for subliminal stimulation has been demonstrated or that what has been demonstrated relates to psychodynamic claims about the unconscious (Fudin, 1999; Greenwald, 1992; Greenwald et al., 1996).

Faced with the findings on the rarity of recall and of dream content related to current events, some proponents of problem-solving theories now claim that only important and strongly emotional dreams have a problem-solving function. There are two important distinctions that must be made in analyzing this claim. First, it is one thing for a dream to "reflect" a problem; it is quite another for it to offer a "solution." Second, a distinction has to be made between solutions that are present within a dream, on the one hand, and waking realizations that are based on thinking about the dream, on the other. Realizations in the waking state are a much more plausible alternative because evidence indicates that conscious attention is usually needed for problem solving (Blagrove, 1992, 1996; Foulkes, 1985). Viewed in this way, human beings have developed "uses" for dreams in the course of history, including personal development (Fiss, 1983, 1991; Hunt, 1989); cultural uses, however, are not the same as evolved psychological functions.

Cartwright's work with people going through divorce is sometimes interpreted as showing that dreams contain solutions, because those who dream of the former spouse "have a better outcome" (1996, p. 185). However, dreaming about a former spouse does not necessarily mean that the dreams contain any solutions to problems arising from the divorce. Instead, it more likely simply "reflects" a concern with the issue. Moreover, Cartwright's study had severe methodological limits; her claims would have to be replicated in new and larger studies before they could be taken seriously as a basis for theorizing. As Cartwright herself concluded:

The study is suggestive. There are many ways in which it could be faulted. There was only one night of dream collection, and some who did not dream of the spouse that night might well be experiencing a great deal of incorporation of the problem of this relationship on other nights. Also there was a long gap between that one night of dreaming and the follow-up interview, during which many new reality factors would have intervened. (Cartwright, 1996, p. 185)

The difficulties of demonstrating problem solving in dreams were shown in a study of 76 college students between ages 19 and 24. To increase relevance and motivation for the task, they were allowed to choose the problem they hoped to resolve (Barrett, 1993). Participants were asked to write out the problem, think about it, and keep a dream journal for a week or until they recalled a dream that seemed to solve the problem. Both the participants and two independent judges rated whether the dreams were (a) on the topic and (b) contained a satisfactory solution.

Only half the participants recalled a dream they felt related to the problem. The dreams usually concerned relationship dilemmas or educational or vocational decisions. Both the dreamer and the two judges agreed that in only two instances the dreams contained the problem and offered a plausible solution. Both dreams seemed to reflect the dreamers' concerns, but they did not contain "solutions." Rather, they dramatized problems, as many dreams do. In the first instance the dreamer is "having major problems with my menstrual cycle and my doctor can't figure out what is wrong." She reported the following dream, with a comment about it at the end:

> My doctor told me I was having a reaction from being on a diet and exercising more than I ever have. In the dream, my doctor gave me medicine to correct this and I would be fine if I took this medicine. In waking life, he did ask about diet and I didn't tell him how much I'm dieting; he's never asked about exercise. I guess I should tell him about diet and exercise, huh? (Barrett, 1993, p. 119)

This dream does seem to reflect her concern about not telling the whole story to her doctor. But the solution to the problem—telling the doctor about her dieting and exercising—is arrived at in waking life by thinking about the dream scene wherein the doctor tells her what is wrong and gives her medicine.

The second dreamer also has a medical problem: "The problem is whether I had taken my medicine. I'm supposed to take just one of these pills a day; it's bad if I take more than one or miss one. I couldn't remember this day if I had taken it and I was really worried." She reported the following dream: "I was drinking water and swallowing pills over and over; it just went on with me drinking and taking pills for a long time" (Barrett, 1993, p. 119). Once again, this dream seems to reflect an emotional preoccupation, but swallowing far more pills than she is supposed to take hardly seems to be a "solution" to the problem. Instead, the dream has that slightly unlikely and dramatic quality—wolfing down all those pills—that makes dreaming distinctive.

In a few cases in Barrett's study, the alleged solution seems to come during waking life in reaction to the dream, as Blagrove (1992, 1996) would predict. This point is best demonstrated by a seemingly metaphoric dream that supposedly indicated the dreamer should go to graduate school in Texas or California, because "the light seems to be further west" than Massachusetts, her home state:

> Problem: I have applied to two clinical psychology programs and two in industrial psychology because I just can't decide which field I want to go into. Dream: A map of the United States. I am in a plane flying over this map. The pilot says we are having engine trouble and need to land and we look for a safe place on the map, indicated by a light. I ask about Massachusetts, which we seem to be over right then, and he says all of Massachusetts is very dangerous. The lights seem to be further west. (Barrett, 1993, p. 118)

The dreamer then reports that she "wakes up and realizes that my two clinical schools are both in Massachusetts, where I have spent my whole life and where my parents live," whereas both of the industrial psychology programs are far away. She thinks the dream is telling her that "getting away is more important than which kind of program I go to" (Barrett, 1993, p. 118). Rather than the dream telling her anything, it is more likely that it is portraying what she has been thinking, because it is likely that the dreamer knew that the industrial programs were both far from home. In addition, the realization of what she should do comes to her from waking reflection on the dream.

Thus, little or no systematic evidence supports the hypothesis that dreams in general have a problem-solving function. The idea therefore is supported with anecdotal testimony concerning solutions to problems that presumably arose within dreams. Barrett (2001) assembled all the past anecdotes and adds several new cases that are based on her own interviews with architects, artists, scientists, and engineers. Some of the most famous anecdotes turned out to be bogus or are only known through secondhand testimony; others seem to have emerged during drowsiness, reverie, or drug-induced states. In one of the most famous examples, the design of an experiment on the transmission of nerve impulses, which led to a Nobel Prize in medicine, the physiologist reports that he woke up and wrote down an idea for the experiment; however, he does not say it came from a dream (Barrett, 2001, p. 91). It is just as likely that it came from the thinking that can go on during sleep and in brief awakenings (Arkin, 1981; Foulkes,

1985). In fact, there are probably more everyday examples of waking up with a new angle on a problem than there are anecdotes about dreams providing a solution to a problem.

In several of the cases in which actual dreams were involved, the discovery was based on a waking interpretation of the dream. For example, the person who invented the process for making gunshot by dropping molten lead into water did so on the basis of a dream in which the raindrops pelting down on him were molten lead. Based on his knowledge that molten lead forms into little balls in water, he interpreted the dream to mean that gunshot could be made in this way (Barrett, 2001, p. 113). In a similar fashion, the idea for how a sewing machine should hold a needle came from waking reflection on a dream in which the native warriors who were surrounding the dreamer had spears with eye-shaped holes near the top. Upon awakening, he decided that the hole in the sewing needle also should be near the top. Notably, the dream and the interpretation of it came during a time when the inventor was working feverishly on his new machine (Barrett, 2001, pp. 113–114).

Barrett also presents cases in which musicians have been inspired to creative efforts by beautiful new music they heard in their dreams. In other examples, writers and poets have used scenes and themes from their dreams as the basis for their waking work. These examples show that dreams can be inspirational and provide the basis for new creative efforts in waking life, but that is not the same thing as solving a problem. As Foulkes (1999) argued, every dream is a novel and creative construction, but that does not mean dreams necessarily have a problem-solving function. Instead, the examples demonstrate waking consciousness making use of dream content.

When all is said and done, then, only occasional anecdotal evidence supports the idea that dreaming itself provides any solutions to problems. This anecdotal evidence is not impressive when it is seen in the context of the small percentage of dreams that are recalled and the even smaller percentage of recalled dreams that might be construed as having a solution to a problem. Dreams sometimes can be useful to waking consciousness as a basis for thinking about problems in a new way, or as a basis for discussing personal problems, as clinical research shows (Fiss, 1991; Greenberg et al., 1992; Hill, 1996). Dreams that have a dramatic emotional impact create a strong subjective sense that they must have an important message. However, it does not follow from usefulness or a waking impression of profundity that dreaming has an adaptive function (Antrobus, 1993).

Do Unrecalled Dreams Have a Function?

Recognizing the problems with theories that attribute a waking function to the few dreams that are recalled, several theorists now claim that dreaming has a function even when dreams are not recalled. Drawing on an analogy with computers, one pair of theorists claims that dreaming clears out useless memories from the day before (Crick & Mitchison, 1983, 1986). Drawing on speculations in evolutionary psychology, others claim that dreams have a social learning (Brereton, 2000) or threat-simulation function (Revonsuo, 2000). Still others attribute psychodynamic functions to unrecalled dreams (Hartmann, 1998; Kramer, 1993).

The idea that dreams help rid the brain of useless recent memories is based on the assumption that the pontine instigators of REM are producing random, meaningless imagery. This claim depends crucially on the contested claim that dreaming is confined to REM, but it is also challenged by three other findings. First, only about half of recalled dreams have even one slight reference to recent events, which is contrary to what the theory would predict (Botman & Crovitz, 1989; Harlow & Roll, 1992). Second, dreams are more coherent and related to waking thoughts than the theory would predict. Third, the findings on the consistency of dream content over years and decades, especially negative dream content, is opposite of what this theory would predict; no evidence supports the idea that repetitive dream content clears out useless memories (Domhoff, 1996; see also chapter 5).

The rehearsal theories put forth by Brereton (2000) and Revonsuo (2000) attempt to build on the evidence for the consolidation of procedural memories during REM (Smith, 1995), but memory consolidation is not the same thing as new learning during sleep through mental rehearsal, for which there is no evidence. Even though some memory consolidation occurs during sleep, it does not follow that dreaming is also occurring (Antrobus, 1993; Flanagan, 2000b).

The rehearsal theories assume that REM and dreaming are one and the same in all mammals, which is a dubious assumption. They use the evidence for memory consolidation during sleep in animal studies to support this assumption, but there is a strong case that no other animals, even other primates, have the conceptual capacities to dream (Foulkes, 1983). The most notable claim for animal dreaming is based on the exploratory and aggressive behaviors displayed by sleeping cats with experimental lesions in the area of the brain stem that inhibits movement during REM (Jouvet, 1999, chapter 4). However, as Foulkes (1983) argued, behavior during sleep does not necessarily indicate dreaming, as seen first of all by the fact that sleepwalking starts in the deepest stages of NREM and usually does not lead to dream reports when awakened. Moreover, the same movements observed during sleep in the cats with experimental lesions also occur periodically when they are awake.

Advocates of animal dreaming sometimes point to an unpublished dissertation in which monkeys were trained to press a bar to avoid waking visual images. After they were trained, they were fitted with contact lenses to eliminate patterned visual stimulation, and then supposedly, and quite unexpectedly, exhibited the bar pressing response during sleep (Vaughan, 1963). However, there are numerous methodological problems with the study. Because the study actually was concerned with the effects of sensory deprivation during the waking state, not sleep, no electrophysiological recordings were made to verify sleep, an extremely seriously problem in that the monkeys seemed to be comatose for the first 27 hours after the lenses were placed over their eyes and later would remain motionless for hours at a time (Foulkes, 1983; Vaughan, 1963, pp. 86, 93, 103). Moreover, the fact that the bar pressing episodes occurred many hours apart and lasted for as long as 5 hours does not fit with the periodicity of REM periods or their usual length. It is a damning commentary that such a seemingly important finding was never published or replicated. It therefore cannot be given any credibility in terms of animal dreaming.

The intriguing idea that only human beings dream is greeted with great surprise and immediate rejection by most dream theorists. They are not impressed with the argument that the lack of cognitive skills for dreaming in young children suggests that less developed animals probably do not dream, and they reject the more direct arguments in the previous paragraphs against the likelihood that either cats or monkeys dream. Instead, they say that Foulkes's evidence with preschool children and his arguments concerning other animals are not foolproof, meanwhile ignoring the fact that their own positive claims about dreaming are far less plausible and far less likely to be supported. Thus, they implicitly seem to recognize that the stakes are great here. If only human beings over age 5 or 6 are able to dream, then evolutionary theories of dream function lose all credibility.

Animal dreaming aside, there are further problems with Revonsuo's version of the rehearsal theory. It stretches the imagination to think that the one-trial system of fear conditioning that has been present in the brain since the evolution of reptiles needs to be primed by dreaming (LeDoux, 1996). The low levels of dreaming in young children and the benign nature of the few dreams they do have do not support Revonsuo's claim that dreams are useful in helping children learn to be vigilant against dangerous animals (Foulkes, 1999). His further claim that trauma may stimulate dreaming in children does not seem plausible in the light of Foulkes's (1982) finding that children with tense home environments did not report more dreams than other children. His vision of the "ancestral environment" as being filled with dangerous predators does not seem credible in the light of primate evidence that fellow members of their own group are the biggest threat.

Revonsuo's theory does not explain the large amount of dream content that does not relate to threat and aggression (Zadra & Donderi, 2000b). He overstates the amount of physical aggression in dreams by downplaying the distinction between physical and nonphysical aggression in the Hall–

Van de Castle coding system. Finally, the theory ignores the fact that nightmarish attack dreams are debilitating for many people, making them less fit for daily life (Levin, 2000; Nielsen & Germain, 2000).

Functionalist Psychodynamic Theories

Building on the general psychodynamic idea that dreaming is an attempt to deal with personal problems, Hartmann (1998) argued that the function of dreams is to help people work through traumatic experiences, whether the dreams are recalled or not. According to his theory, dreams deal with a trauma by putting it in many different mental contexts within the "safe place" of sleep, where psychological "connections" can be made without any personal danger. Studies showing that free associations are more unlikely (i.e., "distant") and imagistic in the waking period shortly after REM than after NREM lend support to this aspect of the theory (Fiss et al., 1966, 1969; Stickgold, Scott, Rittenhouse, & Hobson, 1999).

Although Hartmann's theory does not require that dreams be recalled, the evidence for it rests on alleged changes in the dreams that trauma victims happen to recall. First, Hartmann assumes that the recalled dreams reflect the trauma, often indirectly, through what he calls a *contextualizing metaphor*. These striking images, such as the approach of a tidal wave, epitomize the way in which these dreams are filled with intimations of disaster, misfortunes, violence, and strong negative emotions. Second, he asserts that the posttrauma dreams become less negative over time, suggesting that the trauma is being dealt with by the dream process.

However, the evidence for both of these claims is weak. Although the dream examples Hartmann (1998) presented are filled with negative emotions, his coding system for emotions is unproven, and he offered no normative data to show that the dreams are, in fact, more negative than the dreams of those who have not suffered traumas (see Domhoff, 1999c, for a full critique of Hartmann's method and evidence). For example, if the negative emotions percent in the Hall–Van de Castle norms is taken as a baseline, then it can be expected that 80% of the emotions in any dream sample will be negative. The same figure was reported in three later studies that used dream reports from different eras, the sleep laboratory, and Canada (Hall et al., 1982; Roussy, Raymond, & De Koninck, 2000; Tonay, 1990/1991).

Hartmann (1998) also noted the large amount of aggression and other negative events in the dreams of trauma victims, but he did not provide any systematic studies. If Hall–Van de Castle normative findings are once again taken as a baseline, then 23% of men's dreams and 15% of women's dreams have at least one chase, attack, or murder, and 33% of men's dreams and 36% of women's dreams have at least one misfortune. Even more to the point of Hartmann's studies, which used five recent dreams from each trauma victim, 69% of the men and 54% of the women in the Hall–Van de Castle normative sample had at least one chase, attack, or murder in the five dreams they contributed.

Hartmann's theory crucially hinges on the degree to which the dreams of trauma victims change over time. He asserted (1998) that he found positive changes in several dream series, but he presented no systematic data on declines in particular negative themes or in any content categories that parallel the categories for aggressions, misfortunes, failures, and negative emotions in the Hall–Van de Castle system. He also has not reported any comparisons with possible changes in the dreams of people who have not suffered traumas. The general consistency of dreams over months and decades that has been demonstrated in this book, along with the possibility that the rate of aggression in dreams may decline with age, provides reason to be skeptical about his claims until more systematic findings with an adequate coding system are presented. Such studies might show that the dream content actually stays the same but that the dreamer is less upset in the face of it. This option is not built into Hartmann's theory, but it is suggested by the findings on the Howard subseries in chapter 5. Ideally, future tests of the theory would include dreams from before the traumatic event to provide the best possible baseline.

As do other clinically derived theories of dreaming, Hartmann's theory assumes that the conceptual metaphors so important in waking thought are also operating in dreams. However, as pointed out many times in the course of this book, and as shown at the end of chapter 5, there is still no solid evidence to support this claim. Even if Hartmann were able to answer the empirical objections discussed in the three previous paragraphs, the metaphoric basis of his theory would remain an untested assumption.

In a revision of Freud's theory of dreams as the guardians of sleep, Kramer (1993) developed a theory that takes into account the regularity of dreaming during REM. He argued that the function of dreams is to contain an "emotional surge" that builds up in the course of each REM period, an idea suggesting that the dream process is successful if the person does not wake up and recall the dream. He believes that the larger percentage of REM toward morning is consistent with this idea because the urge to awaken is greater at that point. Kramer presented suggestive evidence from a wide range of his own studies, some only published in abstract form or labeled as pilot studies, to make a case that dreams are "responsive to a number of affective influences" (1993, p. 175).

This theory has several problems. First, it does not account for NREM dreaming and cannot explain why young children and some adults sleep well enough without dreams. Furthermore, the evidence does not consistently suggest the presence of a growing emotional surge during REM. Instead, it suggests a rise in intensity in the middle of the REM period, as indexed by the density of eye movements, followed by a gradual decline. Nor does there seem to be an accumulation of undischarged emotional drive when people are deprived of REM, unlike what might be expected on the basis of Kramer's theory (Greenberg & Pearlman, 1993, 1999).

As one piece of evidence for his theory, Kramer claimed that dream content changes from REM period to REM period throughout the night, particularly in the number of characters, but most studies have found few or no differences (Foulkes, 1966, 1985; Hall, 1966b). According to Kramer's theory, recalling a dream "depends to a degree on a troubled state in the dreamer" (Kramer, 1993, p. 187), but studies of high and low dream recallers do not lend any support to this claim (Blagrove & Akehurst, 2000; Tonay, 1993). One study showed that women recall more dreams when under stress but that men recall fewer dreams (Armitage, 1992). In addition, as Kramer himself says (1993), "Efforts to connect content with variability in autonomic variables have been minimally successful" (p. 145). Moreover, even if dreams are responsive to affective influences, it does not necessarily follow that their function is to contain emotions during sleep.

If the weaknesses of all theories of dream function are combined with the evidence that dreaming is a process that occurs only in human beings and only after age 5 or 6, then it seems highly unlikely that dreams have any adaptive function. They currently seem to be the by-product of two great evolutionary developments, sleep and complex cognitive processes. These minimalist conclusions join with empirical findings presented throughout this book to suggest that cognitive psychology may be the best starting point for developing an adequate model of dreams.

CONCLUSION

As this chapter shows, a large amount of systematic empirical evidence does not fit with the clinical, neuropsychological, and functional theories of dreaming that predominated in the 20th century. This evidence, however, is compatible with an open-ended neurocognitive model. This new model stresses the ways in which a neural network for dreaming can be integrated with findings from developmental studies of dreaming and the content analysis of dream reports.

The model offers hypotheses concerning all the key questions that have been asked about dreaming in the past. It first addresses the issue of the instigation of dreaming by suggesting that this cognitive process occurs in most adult minds when a certain minimal level of neural activation occurs in the context of an occlusion of external stimuli and a relinquishment of self. The model therefore can account for dreaming at sleep onset, in both REM and NREM sleep, and even during relaxed waking states.

By specifying a neural network for dreaming that can develop defects, the neurocognitive model is able to explain the absence of dreaming in some adults, such as those who have suffered brain injuries in specific localities, as well as excesses of dreaming caused by brain injuries or neurochemical imbalances. Although it has a neural grounding, the model also suggests that dreaming is a cognitive achievement that depends on the development of a range of cognitive skills, especially the visuospatial skills that make mental imagery possible. This developmental dimension explains why preschool children rarely report dreams after laboratory awakenings as well as why the dreams they do report are brief and static in nature.

By taking seriously the information on nondreaming in children and adults with brain lesions, the neurocognitive model is able to approach the question of dream function by suggesting that dreaming may have no function. The model raises the possibility that dreaming is a spandrel of the mind, a by-product of the evolution of sleep and consciousness. Although dreams probably have no function, evidence suggests that they have at least some coherence and meaning. Thus, the tendency to conflate function and meaning is not present in the neurocognitive model.

Laboratory awakenings show that most dreams are reasonable simulations of the waking world inhabited by the dreamer. The content analysis of dreams from people of all ages from many different parts of the world suggests that dreams often express conceptions and concerns by at least preadolescence. It is therefore likely that they use many of the same schemata and scripts that are available to waking thought. These parallels with waking thought explain why dreams can be useful in psychotherapy. However, it may be that dreaming is less constrained by present reality in making use of these schemata—which is one reason that dreams can strike people as bizarre.

By stressing the similarities between dreaming and waking cognition, the neurocognitive model opens up the possibility that some of the more puzzling aspects of dream content may be a product of the system of figurative thought that is so pervasive in waking life. The processes of metaphor, metonymy, irony, and conceptual blending may be the germ of truth in Freud's claims about the dream-work. The parallels that dreams have with waking figurative thought can be used to explain why dreams have religious and medicinal uses that were invented by people in different cultures in the course of history.

Despite the possibility that figurative thinking may be present in some dreams, the model does not assume that every aspect of every dream is somehow psychologically meaningful. The extent of meaning is an open question that can only be answered through better and more detailed searches for dream meaning. The degree of coherence and meaningfulness in dreams is an empirical question that must be studied in great detail before any conclusions can be reached. This book shows that psychological information can be extracted from dream reports, a finding that implies that dreams have some meaning, but it also stresses that much dream content is still not understood and may turn out to be the product of freewheeling improvisation of little import.

The neurocognitive model has the virtue of being eminently testable in a variety of ways using the neuroimaging technologies and software programs for content analysis that became available in the 1990s. There is reason to believe that the Hall–Van de Castle coding system may be of value in this effort, especially when applied to long-term dream journals supplied by people who have developmental anomalies, brain injuries, or psychic traumas or who are taking a dream-enhancing or dream-suppressing medication. Rating scales for emotionality–evaluation, rationality–bizarreness, activity, and impression–vividness also can be used. It might even be possible to use the search program and dream archive on Dream-Bank.net to conduct systematic studies of "symbolism" by testing some of the ideas on figurative thinking that have been developed by cognitive linguists and psycholinguists. As stressed in chapter 1, however, metaphorical interpretations of dreams must be seen as the fool's gold of dream theories until systematic evidence for them is produced.

The neurocognitive model is not bogged down by arguments about whether the forebrain dream network always requires stimulation from the REM generator in the pons in order to function. Even if it turns out that this area is always the activating source for the neural network for dreaming, the important point is that the conceptual systems in the forebrain portion of the network produce dreams. Moreover, the theory does not concern itself with the exact nature of the neuromodulation during dreaming. Instead, it starts with the phenomenon of dreaming itself and the dream reports that sometimes eventuate from dreaming, and it then attempts to see how they might relate to the neuropsychological level. It is a theory that puts dreams back into the field of dream research and attempts to relate dreaming to findings in cognitive psychology as well as neurophysiology.

Dreams are much more coherent and meaningful than has been claimed by those who overlook the cognitive dimension of dreaming and instead focus on the neurophysiological and neuropsychological levels. At the same time, dreams also seem to be much less profound than claimed by Freud or

Jung. In light of the systematic dream research used to develop the new model of dreaming and dreams described in this volume, it now seems likely that dreaming is a comprehensible cognitive process with many similarities to waking thought. It remains for future cognitive scientists to test, amend, and expand this neurocognitive model so that the late-night movies in the brain can be incorporated into ambitious theories seeking to explain all aspects of the human mind.

REFERENCES

Abel, B. (1994). *The dream content of menopausal women: An exploratory study.* Unpublished doctoral dissertation, United States International University, San Diego, CA.

Abel, V. (1996). *Cognitive processing styles of creative artists as observed in dream mentation and waking measures.* Unpublished doctoral dissertation, Yeshiva University, New York.

Adolphs, R., & Damasio, A. (1998). The human amygdala in social judgment. *Nature, 393,* 470–474.

Ajilore, O., Stickgold, R., Rittenhouse, C., & Hobson, J. (1995). Nightcap: Laboratory and home-based evaluation of a portable sleep monitor. *Psychophysiology, 32*(1), 92–98.

Allport, G. (1942). *The use of personal documents in psychological science.* New York: Social Science Research Council.

Antrobus, J. (1978). Dreaming as cognition. In A. Arkin, J. Antrobus, & S. Ellman (Eds.), *The mind in sleep: Psychology and psychophysiology* (pp. 569–581). Hillsdale, NJ: Lawrence Erlbaum.

Antrobus, J. (1983). REM and NREM sleep reports: Comparisons of word frequencies by cognitive classes. *Psychophysiology, 20,* 562–568.

Antrobus, J. (1991). Dreaming: Cognitive processes during cortical activation and high afferent thresholds. *Psychological Review, 98,* 96–121.

Antrobus, J. (1993). Dreaming: Could we do without it? In A. Moffitt, M. Kramer, & R. Hoffmann (Eds.), *The functions of dreaming* (pp. 549–558). Albany: State University of New York Press.

Antrobus, J. (2000a). How does the dreaming brain explain the dreaming mind? *Behavioral and Brain Sciences, 23,* 904–907.

Antrobus, J. (2000b). Theories of dreaming. In M. Kryger, T. Roth, & W. Dement (Eds.), *Principles and practices of sleep medicine* (3rd ed., pp. 472–481). Philadelphia: W. B. Saunders.

Antrobus, J., Kondo, T., & Reinsel, R. (1995). Summation of REM and diurnal cortical activation. *Consciousness and Cognition, 4,* 275–299.

Arkin, A. (1981). *Sleep talking: Psychology and psychophysiology.* Hillsdale, NJ: Erlbaum.

Arkin, A., & Antrobus, J. (1991). The effects of external stimuli applied prior to and during sleep on sleep experience. In S. Ellman & J. Antrobus (Ed.), *The mind in sleep: Psychology and psychophysiology* (2nd ed., pp. 265–307). New York: Wiley & Sons.

Armitage, R. (1992). Gender differences and the effect of stress on dream recall: A 30-day diary report. *Dreaming, 2,* 137–142.

Armitage, R., Rochlen, A., Fitch, T., Trivedi, M., & Rush, A. (1995). Dream recall and major depression: A preliminary report. *Dreaming, 5,* 189–198.

Aserinsky, E., & Kleitman, N. (1953). Regularly occurring periods of eye motility, and concomitant phenomena, during sleep. *Science, 118,* 273–274.

Auld, F., Goldenberg, G., & Weiss, J. (1968). Measurement of primary process thinking in dream reports. *Journal of Personality and Social Psychology, 8,* 418–426.

Avila-White, D., Schneider, A., & Domhoff, G. W. (1999). The most recent dreams of 12–13-year-old boys and girls: A methodological contribution to the study of dream content in teenagers. *Dreaming, 9,* 163–171.

Ayella, M. F. (1998). *Insane therapy: Portrait of a psychotherapy cult.* Philadelphia: Temple University Press.

Baekland, F., & Lasky, R. (1968). The morning recall of rapid eye movement period reports given earlier in the night. *Journal of Nervous and Mental Diseases, 147,* 570–579.

Baldwin, A. (1942). Personal structure analysis: A statistical method for investigating the single personality. *Journal of Abnormal and Social Psychology, 37,* 163–183.

Bancaud, J., Brunet-Bourgin, F., Chauvel, P., & Halgren, E. (1994). Anatomical origin of deja vu and vivid "memories" in human temporal lobe epilepsy. *Brain, 117,* 71–90.

Barrett, D. (1992). Just how lucid are lucid dreams? *Dreaming, 2,* 221–228.

Barrett, D. (1993). The "committee of sleep": A study of dream incubation for problem solving. *Dreaming, 3,* 115–122.

Barrett, D. (1996). *Trauma and dreams.* Cambridge, MA: Harvard University Press.

Barrett, D. (2001). *The committee of sleep:* New York: Crown/Random House.

Barrett, D., & Loeffler, M. (1992). Comparison of dream content of depressed vs. nondepressed dreamers. *Psychological Reports, 70,* 403–406.

Beck, A., & Hurvich, M. S. (1959). Psychological correlates of depression: I. Frequency of "masochistic" dream content in a private practice sampling. *Psychosomatic Medicine, 21,* 50–55.

Bednar, J. A. (2000). Internally-generated activity, non-episodic memory, and emotional salience in sleep. *Behavioral and Brain Sciences, 23,* 908–909.

Belicki, K. (1987). Recalling dreams: An examination of daily variation and individual differences. In J. Gackenbach (Ed.), *Sleep and dreams: A sourcebook* (pp. 187–206). New York: Garland.

Bell, A., & Hall, C. (1971). *The personality of a child molester: An analysis of dreams*. Chicago: Aldine.

Berger, R. (1967). When is a dream is a dream is a dream? *Experimental Neurology, 4*(Suppl.), 15–27.

Berger, R. (1969). The sleep and dream cycle. In A. Kales (Ed.), *Sleep: Physiology and Pathology* (pp. 17–32). Philadelphia: Lippincott.

Bernstein, D., & Belicki, C. (1995). Assessing dreams through self-report questionnaires: Relations with past research and personality. *Dreaming, 5*, 13–27.

Berrien, F. (1933). A statistical study of dreams in relation to emotional stability. *Journal of Abnormal and Social Psychology, 28*, 194–197.

Blagrove, M. (1992). Dreams as a reflection of our waking concerns and abilities: A critique of the problem-solving paradigm in dream research. *Dreaming, 2*, 205–220.

Blagrove, M. (1996). Problems with the cognitive psychological modeling of dreaming. *Journal of Mind and Behavior, 17*, 99–134.

Blagrove, M., & Akehurst, L. (2000). Personality and dream recall frequency: Further negative findings. *Dreaming, 10*, 139–148.

Block, H. (1999, June). *The ex-husband dreams in a long dream journal*. Paper presented at the annual meeting of the Association for the Study of Dreams, Santa Cruz, CA.

Bonato, R. A., Moffitt, A., Hoffmann, R., & Cuddy, M. A. (1991). Bizarreness in dreams and nightmares. *Dreaming, 1*(1), 53–61.

Boselli, M., Parrino, L., Smerieri, A., & Terzano, M. (1998). Effect of age on EEG arousal in normal sleep. *Sleep, 21*, 351–357.

Bosinelli, M., & Cicogna, P. C. (2000). REM and NREM mentation: Nielsen's model once again supports the supremacy of REM. *Behavioral and Brain Sciences, 23*, 913–914.

Boss, M. (1958). *The analysis of dreams*. New York: Philosophical Library.

Boss, M. (1977). *I dreamt last night*. New York: Gardner Press.

Botman, H., & Crovitz, H. (1989). Dream reports and autobiographical memory. *Imagination, Cognition and Personality, 9*, 213–214.

Bowen, M., & Dunn, S. (1999, June). *Findings from a long dream journal*. Paper presented at the annual meeting of the Association for the Study of Dreams, Santa Cruz, CA.

Bradley, L., Hollifield, M., & Foulkes, D. (1992). Reflection during REM dreaming. *Dreaming, 2*, 161–166.

Braun, A., Balkin, T., Wesensten, N., Carson, R., Varga, M., Baldwin, P., et al. (1997). Regional cerebral blood flow throughout the sleep-wake cycle: An (H2O)-O-15 PET study. *Brain, 120*, 1173–1197.

Braun, A., Balkin, T., Wesensten, N., Gwadry, F., Carson, R., Varga, M., et al. (1998). Dissociated pattern of activity in visual cortices and their projections during human rapid eye movement sleep. *Science, 279,* 91–95.

Brenneis, C. (1975). Developmental aspects of aging in women: A comparative study of dreams. *Archives of General Psychiatry, 32,* 429–434.

Brereton, D. (2000). Dreaming, adaptation, and consciousness: The social mapping hypothesis. *Ethos, 28,* 379–409.

Buckley, J. (1970). *The dreams of young adults.* Unpublished doctoral dissertation, Wayne State University, Detroit, MI.

Bulkeley, K. (1999). *Visions of the night: Dreams, religion, and psychology.* Albany: State University of New York Press.

Bulkeley, K. (Ed.). (2001). *Dreams: A reader on the religious, cultural, and psychological dimensions of dreaming.* New York: Palgrave.

Bulkeley, K., Dunn, S., & Domhoff, G. W. (2001). *Creating categories for the study of impactful and memorable dreams.* Unpublished manuscript, Santa Clara University.

Bursik, K. (1998). Moving beyond gender differences: Gender role comparisons of manifest dream content. *Sex Roles, 38,* 203–214.

Busink, R., & Kuiken, D. (1996). Identifying types of impactful dreams: A replication. *Dreaming, 6,* 97–119.

Butler, S., & Watson, R. (1985). Individual differences in memory for dreams: The role of cognitive skills. *Perceptual and Motor Skills, 53,* 841–864.

Calkins, M. (1893). Statistics of dreams. *American Journal of Psychology, 5,* 311–343.

Cartwright, D. (1953). Analysis of qualitative material. In L. Festinger & D. Katz (Eds.), *Research methods in the behavioral sciences* (pp. 421–470). New York: Holt, Rinehart, and Winston.

Cartwright, R. (1992). Masochism in dreaming and its relation to depression. *Dreaming, 2,* 79–84.

Cartwright, R. (1996). Dreams and adaptation to divorce. In D. Barrett (Ed.), *Trauma and dreams* (pp. 179–185). Cambridge, MA: Harvard University Press.

Cartwright, R., & Romanek, I. (1978). Repetitive dreams of normal subjects. *Sleep Research, 7,* 174.

Cavallero, C., & Foulkes, D. (1993). *Dreaming as cognition.* New York: Harvester Wheatsheaf.

Ceci, S. J., Bruck, M., & Battin, D. B. (2000). The suggestibility of children's testimony. In D. F. Bjorklund (Ed.), *False-memory creation in children and adults: Theory, research, and implications* (pp. 169–201). Mahwah, NJ: Lawrence Erlbaum Associates.

Chapman, P., & Underwood, G. (2000). Mental states during dreaming and daydreaming: Some methodological loopholes. *Behavioral and Brain Sciences, 23,* 917–918.

Chugani, H. (1999). Metabolic imaging: A window on brain development and plasticity. *Neuroscientist, 5,* 29–40.

Cicogna, P., Natale, V., Occhionero, M., & Bosinelli, M. (1998). A comparison of mental activity during sleep onset and morning awakening. *Sleep, 21*, 462–470.

Cipolli, C. (2000). Iterative processing of information during sleep may improve consolidation. *Behavioral and Brain Sciences, 23*, 919.

Cipolli, C., & Poli, D. (1992). Story structure in verbal reports of mental sleep experience after awakening in REM sleep. *Sleep, 15*, 133–142.

Clark, J., Trinder, J., Kramer, M., Roth, T., & Day, N. (1972). An approach to the content analysis of dream scales. In M. Chase, W. Stern, & P. Walter (Eds.), *Sleep research* (Vol. 1, pp. 118–119). Los Angeles: Brain Research Institute, University of California.

Cohen, D. (1979). *Sleep and dreaming.* New York: Pergamon Press.

Cohen, D., & Wolfe, G. (1973). Dream recall and repression: Evidence for an alternative hypothesis. *Journal of Consulting and Clinical Psychology, 41*, 349–355.

Cohen, J. (1977). *Statistical power for the behavioral sciences.* New York: Academic Press.

Cohen, J. (1990). Things I have learned (so far). *American Psychologist, 45*, 1304–1312.

Cohen, J. (1994). The earth is round (*p* < .05). *American Psychologist, 49*, 997–1003.

Conduit, R., Crewther, S. G., & Coleman, G. (2000). Shedding old assumptions and consolidating what we know: Toward an attention-based model of dreaming. *Behavioral and Brain Sciences, 23*, 924–928.

Cory, T. L., Ormiston, D. W., Simmel, E., & Dainoff, M. (1975). Predicting the frequency of dream recall. *Journal of Abnormal Psychology, 84*, 261–266.

Cote, L., Lortie-Lussier, M., Roy, M., & DeKoninck, J. (1996). The dreams of women throughout adulthood. *Dreaming, 6*, 187–199.

Crick, F., & Mitchison, G. (1983). The function of dream sleep. *Nature, 304*, 111–114.

Crick, F., & Mitchison, G. (1986). REM sleep and neural nets. *Journal of Mind and Behavior, 7*, 229–250.

Dallett, J. (1973). Theories of dream function. *Psychological Bulletin, 79*, 408–416.

Damasio, A. (1999). *The feeling of what happens.* New York: Harcourt Brace & Company.

Damasio, A., Graff-Radford, N., Eslinger, P., Damasio, H., & Kassell, N. (1985). Amnesia following basal forebrain lesions. *Archives of Neurology, 42*, 263–271.

de Rivera, J., & Sarbin, T. (Eds.). (1998). *Believed-in imagings: The narrative construction of reality.* Washington, DC: American Psychological Association.

Dement, W. (1955). Dream recall and eye movements during sleep in schizophrenics and normals. *Journal of Nervous and Mental Diseases, 122*, 263–269.

Dement, W., Kahn, E., & Roffwarg, H. P. (1965). The influence of the laboratory situation on the dreams of the experimental subject. *Journal of Nervous and Mental Disease, 140*, 119–131.

Dement, W., & Kleitman, N. (1957a). Cyclic variations in EEG during sleep and their relation to eye movements, body motility, and dreaming. *Electroencephalography and Clinical Neurophysiology, 9,* 673–690.

Dement, W., & Kleitman, N. (1957b). The relation of eye movements during sleep to dream activity: An objective method for the study of dreaming. *Journal of Experimental Psychology, 53,* 339–346.

Dement, W., & Wolpert, E. (1958a). Relationships in the manifest content of dreams occurring in the same night. *Journal of Nervous and Mental Disease, 126,* 568–578.

Dement, W., & Wolpert, E. (1958b). The relation of eye movement, body motility, and external stimuli to dream content. *Journal of Experimental Psychology, 44,* 543–555.

Domhoff, G. W. (1969). Home dreams and laboratory dreams: Home dreams are better. In M. Kramer (Ed.), *Dream psychology and the new biology of dreaming* (pp. 119–217). Springfield, IL: C. C. Thomas.

Domhoff, G. W. (1993a). *Personal dream histories: Their theoretical and practical relevance.* Unpublished manuscript, University of California, Santa Cruz.

Domhoff, G. W. (1993b). The repetition of dreams and dream elements: A possible clue to a function of dreams. In A. Moffitt, M. Kramer, & R. Hoffmann (Eds.), *The functions of dreams* (pp. 293–320). Albany: State University of New York Press.

Domhoff, G. W. (1996). *Finding meaning in dreams: A quantitative approach.* New York: Plenum Publishing.

Domhoff, G. W. (1999a). Drawing theoretical implications from descriptive empirical findings on dream content. *Dreaming, 9,* 201–210.

Domhoff, G. W. (1999b). New directions in the study of dream content using the Hall and Van de Castle coding system. *Dreaming, 9,* 115–137.

Domhoff, G. W. (1999c, June). *Using Hall/Van De Castle dream content analysis to test new theories: An example using a theory proposed by Ernest Hartmann.* Paper presented at the annual meeting of the Association for the Study of Dreams, Santa Cruz, CA.

Domhoff, G. W., & Gerson, A. (1967). Replication and critique of three studies on personality correlates of dream recall. *Journal of Consulting Psychology, 31,* 431.

Domhoff, G. W., & Kamiya, J. (1964a). Problems in dream content study with objective indicators: I. A comparison of home and laboratory dream reports. *Archives of General Psychiatry, 11,* 519–524.

Domhoff, G. W., & Kamiya, J. (1964b). Problems in dream content study with objective indicators: III. Changes in dream content throughout the night. *Archives of General Psychiatry, 11,* 529–532.

Domhoff, G. W., & Schneider, A. (1998). New rationales and methods for quantitative dream research outside the laboratory. *Sleep, 21,* 398–404.

Domhoff, G. W., & Schneider, A. (1999). Much ado about very little: The small effect sizes when home and laboratory collected dreams are compared. *Dreaming, 9,* 139–151.

Doricchi, F., & Violani, C. (2000). Mesolimbic dopamine and the neuropsychology of dreaming: Some caution and reconsiderations. *Behavioral and Brain Sciences, 23,* 930–931.

Downing, J., & Marmorstein, R. (1973). *Dreams and nightmares: A book of Gestalt therapy sessions.* New York: Harper & Row.

Dudley, L., & Fungaroli, J. (1987). The dreams of students in a women's college: Are they different? *ASD Newsletter, 4,* 6–7.

Dudley, L., & Swank, M. (1990). A comparison of the dreams of college women in 1950 and 1990. *ASD Newsletter, 7,* 3.

Dunlap, W., Cortina, J., Vaslow, J., & Burke, M. (1996). Meta-analysis of experiments with matched groups or repeated measures designs. *Psychological Methods, 1*(2), 170–177.

Dunn, S. (2000). *Dreams of Derek: A Hall/Van de Castle coding and analysis.* Unpublished manuscript, University of California, Santa Cruz.

Ekman, P. (1992a). An argument for basic emotions. *Cognition and Emotion, 6*(3–4), 169–200.

Ekman, P. (1992b). Are there basic emotions? *Psychological Review, 99,* 550–553.

Ellis, H. (1928). The synthesis of dreams: A study of a series of one hundred dreams. In H. Ellis (Ed.), *Studies in the psychology of sex* (Vol. 7, pp. 237–346). Philadelphia: F. A. Davis Company.

Farley, F. H., Schmuller, J., & Fischbach, T. J. (1971). Dream recall and individual differences. *Perceptual and Motor Skills, 33,* 379–384.

Fauconnier, G. (1997). *Mappings in thought and language.* New York: Cambridge University Press.

Feinberg, I. (2000). REM sleep: Desperately seeking isomorphism. *Behavioral and Brain Sciences, 23,* 931–934.

Ferguson, G. A. (1981). *Statistical analysis in psychology and education.* New York: McGraw-Hill.

Fisher, C. (1954). Dreams and perception: The role of preconscious and primary modes of perception in dream formation. *Journal of the American Psychoanalytic Association, 2,* 389–445.

Fisher, S., & Greenberg, R. (1977). *The scientific credibility of Freud's theories and therapy.* New York: Basic Books.

Fisher, S., & Greenberg, R. (1996). *Freud scientifically appraised.* New York: John Wiley.

Fiss, H. (1983). Toward a clinically relevant experimental psychology of dreaming. *Hillside Journal of Clinical Psychiatry, 5,* 147–159.

Fiss, H. (1986). An empirical foundation for a self-psychology of dreaming. *Journal of Mind and Behavior, 7*(2–3), 161–191.

Fiss, H. (1991). Experimental strategies for the study of the function of dreaming. In J. Antrobus & S. Ellman (Eds.), *The mind in sleep: Psychology and psychophysiology* (2nd ed., pp. 308–326). New York: John Wiley & Sons.

Fiss, H. (1993). The "royal road" to the unconscious revisited: A signal detection model of dream function. In A. Moffitt, M. Kramer, & R. Hoffmann (Eds.), *The functions of dreaming* (pp. 381–418). Albany: State University of New York Press.

Fiss, H., Ellman, S. J., & Klein, G. S. (1969). Waking fantasies following interrupted and completed REM periods. *Archives of General Psychiatry, 21,* 230–239.

Fiss, H., Klein, G. S., & Bokert, E. (1966). Waking fantasies following interruption of two types of sleep. *Archives of General Psychiatry, 14,* 543–551.

Fitch, T., & Armitage, R. (1989). Variations in cognitive style among high and low frequency dream recallers. *Personality and Individual Differences, 10,* 869–875.

Flanagan, O. (1995). Deconstructing dreams: The spandrels of sleep. *Journal of Philosophy, 92,* 5–27.

Flanagan, O. (2000a). Dreaming is not an adaptation. *Behavioral and Brain Sciences, 23,* 936–939.

Flanagan, O. (2000b). *Dreaming souls: Sleep, dreams, and the evolution of the conscious mind.* New York: Oxford University Press.

Fosse, R., Stickgold, R., & Hobson, J. (2001). Brain–mind states: Reciprocal variation in thoughts and hallucinations. *Psychological Science, 12,* 30–36.

Foulkes, D. (1962). Dream reports from different states of sleep. *Journal of Abnormal and Social Psychology, 65,* 14–25.

Foulkes, D. (1966). *The psychology of sleep.* New York: Charles Scribner's Sons.

Foulkes, D. (1967). Dreams of the male child: Four case studies. *Journal of Child Psychology and Psychiatry, 8,* 81–98.

Foulkes, D. (1978). *A grammar of dreams.* New York: Basic Books.

Foulkes, D. (1979). Home and laboratory dreams: Four empirical studies and a conceptual reevaluation. *Sleep, 2,* 233–251.

Foulkes, D. (1982). *Children's dreams.* New York: Wiley.

Foulkes, D. (1983). Cognitive processes during sleep: Evolutionary aspects. In A. Mayes (Ed.), *Sleep mechanisms and functions in humans and animals: An evolutionary perspective* (pp. 313–337). Wokington, England: Van Nostrand Reinhold.

Foulkes, D. (1985). *Dreaming: A cognitive–psychological analysis.* Hillsdale, NJ: Lawrence Erlbaum.

Foulkes, D. (1990a). Dreaming and consciousness. *European Journal of Cognitive Psychology, 2,* 39–55.

Foulkes, D. (1990b). Reflective consciousness and dreaming. *Contemporary Psychology, 35,* 120–122.

Foulkes, D. (1993). Data constraints on theorizing about dream function. In A. Moffitt, M. Kramer, & R. Hoffmann (Eds.), *The functions of dreaming* (pp. 11–20). Albany: State University of New York Press.

Foulkes, D. (1996a). Dream research: 1953–1993. *Sleep, 19*, 609–624.

Foulkes, D. (1996b). Misrepresentation of sleep-laboratory dream research with children. *Perceptual and Motor Skills, 83*, 205–206.

Foulkes, D. (1999). *Children's dreaming and the development of consciousness.* Cambridge, MA: Harvard University Press.

Foulkes, D., & Fleisher, S. (1975). Mental activity in relaxed wakefulness. *Journal of Abnormal Psychology, 84*, 66–75.

Foulkes, D., Hollifield, M., Sullivan, B., Bradley, L., & Terry, R. (1990). REM dreaming and cognitive skills at ages 5–8: A cross-sectional study. *International Journal of Behavioral Development, 13*, 447–465.

Foulkes, D., Larson, J., Swanson, E., & Rardin, M. (1969). Two studies of childhood dreaming. *American Journal of Orthopsychiatry, 39*, 627–643.

Foulkes, D., Meier, B., Strauch, I., Kerr, N., Bradley, L., & Hollifield, M. (1993). Linguistic phenomena and language selection in the REM dreams of German-English bilinguals. *International Journal of Psychology, 28*(6), 871–891.

Foulkes, D., Pivik, R., Steadman, H., Spear, P., & Symonds, J. (1967). Dreams of the male child: An EEG study. *Journal of Abnormal Psychology, 72*, 457–467.

Foulkes, D., & Rechtschaffen, A. (1964). Presleep determinants of dream content: Effects of two films. *Perceptual and Motor Skills, 19*, 983–1005.

Foulkes, D., & Schmidt, M. (1983). Temporal sequence and unit comparison composition in dream reports from different stages of sleep. *Sleep, 6*, 265–280.

Foulkes, D., & Scott, E. (1973). An above-zero baseline for the incidence of momentarily hallucinatory mentation. *Sleep Research, 2*, 108.

Foulkes, D., & Shepherd, J. (1971). *Manual for the scoring system for children's dreams* [Mimeograph]. Laramie: University of Wyoming.

Foulkes, D., Sullivan, B., Kerr, N., & Brown, L. (1988). Appropriateness of dream feelings to dreamed situations. *Cognition and Emotion, 2*, 29–39.

Foulkes, D., & Vogel, G. (1965). Mental activity at sleep onset. *Journal of Abnormal Psychology, 70*, 231–243.

Frank, J. (1946). Clinical survey and results of 200 cases of prefrontal leucotomy. *Journal of Mental Sciences, 92*, 497–508.

Frank, J. (1950). Some aspects of lobotomy (prefrontal leucotomy) under psychoanalytic scrutiny. *Psychiatry, 13*, 35–42.

Franklin, R. D., Allison, D. B., & Gorman, B. S. (1997). *Design and analysis of single-case research.* Mahwah, NJ: Lawrence Erlbaum Associates.

Freud, S. (1900). *The interpretation of dreams* (J. Crick, Trans.). London: Oxford University Press.

Freud, S. (1912/1961). Totem and taboo. In J. Strachey (Ed. & Trans.), *The standard edition of the complete psychological works of Sigmund Freud* (Vol. 13, pp. 1–161). London: Hogarth Press. (Original work published 1912)

Freud, S. (1920/1961). *Beyond the pleasure principle.* In J. Strachey (Ed. & Trans.), *The standard edition of the complete psychology works of Sigmund Freud* (Vol. 18, pp. 7–64). London: Hogarth Press. (Original work published 1920)

Freud, S. (1933/1961). New introductory lectures on psychoanalysis. In J. Strachey (Ed. & Trans.), *The standard edition of the complete psychological works of Sigmund Freud* (Vol. 22, pp. 7–30). London: Hogarth Press. (Original work published in 1933)

Fromm, E. (1949). The nature of dreams. *Scientific American, 181*(5), 44–47.

Fromm, E. (1951). *The forgotten language.* New York: Grove Press.

Fudin, R. (1999). Subliminal psychodynamic activation: Methodological problems and questions in Silverman's experiments. *Perceptual and Motor Skills, 89,* 235–244.

Gackenbach, J. (1988). The psychological content of lucid dreams. In J. Gackenbach & S. LaBerge (Eds.), *Conscious mind, sleeping brain: Perspectives on lucid dreaming* (pp. 181–200). New York: Plenum.

Gackenbach, J., & Bosveld, J. (1989). *Control your dreams.* New York: Harper & Row.

Giambra, L., Jung, R., & Grodsky, A. (1996). Age changes in dream recall in adulthood. *Dreaming, 6,* 17–31.

Gibbs, R. (1994). *The poetics of mind: Figurative thought, language, and understanding.* New York: Cambridge University Press.

Gibbs, R. (1999). Speaking and thinking with metonymy. In K. Panther & G. Radden (Eds.), *Metonymy in language and thought* (pp. 61–75). Philadelphia: John Benjamins.

Gironell, A., Calzada, M., Sagales, T., & Barraquer-Bordas, L. (1995). Absence of REM sleep and altered non-REM sleep caused by a haematoma in the pontine tegmentum. *Journal of Neurology, Neurosurgery, and Psychiatry, 59,* 195–196.

Goodenough, D. (1991). Dream recall: History and current status of the field. In S. Ellman & J. Antrobus (Eds.), *The mind in sleep: Psychology and psychophysiology* (2nd ed., pp. 143–171). New York: John Wiley & Sons.

Gottesmann, C. (1999). Neurophysiological support of consciousness during waking and sleep. *Progress in Neurobiology, 59,* 469–508.

Gottesmann, C. (2000). Each distinct type of mental state is supported by specific brain functions. *Behavioral and Brain Sciences, 23,* 941–943.

Gottschalk, L., & Gleser, G. (1969). *The measurement of psychological states through the content analysis of verbal behavior.* Berkeley: University of California Press.

Grady, J. (1999). A typology of motivation for conceptual metaphor: Correlation vs. resemblance. In R. Gibbs & G. Steen (Eds.), *Metaphor in cognitive linguistics* (pp. 79–100). Philadelphia: John Benjamins.

Grady, J., Oakley, T., & Coulson, S. (1999). Blending and metaphor. In R. Gibbs & G. Steen (Eds.), *Metaphor in cognitive linguistics* (pp. 101–124). Philadelphia: John Benjamins.

Greenberg, R., Katz, H., Schwartz, W., & Pearlman, C. (1992). A research based reconsideration of the psychoanalytic theory of dreaming. *Journal of the American Psychoanalytic Association, 40,* 531–550.

Greenberg, R., & Pearlman, C. (1993). An integrated approach to dream theory: Contributions from sleep research and clinical practice. In A. Moffitt, M. Kramer, & R. Hoffmann (Eds.), *The functions of dreaming* (pp. 363–380). Albany: State University of New York Press.

Greenberg, R., & Pearlman, C. (1999). The interpretation of dreams: A classic revisited. *Psychoanalytic Dialogues, 9,* 749–765.

Greenwald, A. G. (1992). New look 3: Unconscious cognition reclaimed. *American Psychologist, 47,* 766–779.

Greenwald, A. G., Draine, S. C., & Abrams, R. L. (1996). Three cognitive markers of unconscious semantic activation. *Science, 273,* 1699–1702.

Gregor, T. (1981). A content analysis of Mehinaku dreams. *Ethos, 9,* 353–390.

Griffith, R., Miyago, O., & Tago, A. (1958). The universality of typical dreams: Japanese vs. Americans. *American Anthropologist, 60,* 1173–1179.

Hall, C. (1947). Diagnosing personality by the analysis of dreams. *Journal of Abnormal and Social Psychology, 42,* 68–79.

Hall, C. (1951). What people dream about. *Scientific American, 184,* 60–63.

Hall, C. (1953a). A cognitive theory of dream symbols. *Journal of General Psychology, 48,* 169–186.

Hall, C. (1953b). A cognitive theory of dreams. *Journal of General Psychology, 49,* 273–282.

Hall, C. (1953c). *The meaning of dreams.* New York: McGraw-Hill.

Hall, C. (1956). Current trends in research on dreams. In D. Brower & L. Abt (Eds.), *Progress in clinical psychology* (Vol. 2, pp. 239–257). New York: Grune and Stratton.

Hall, C. (1966a). A comparison of the dreams of four groups of hospitalized mental patients with each other and with a normal population. *Journal of Nervous and Mental Diseases, 143,* 135–139.

Hall, C. (1966b). Studies of dreams collected in the laboratory and at home. *Institute of Dream Research Monograph Series* (No. 1). Santa Cruz, CA: Institute of Dream Research.

Hall, C. (1967). Caveat lector. *Psychoanalytic Review, 54,* 655–661.

Hall, C. (1969a). Content analysis of dreams: Categories, units, and norms. In G. Gerbner (Ed.), *The analysis of communication content* (pp. 147–158). New York: Wiley.

Hall, C. (1969b). Normative dream content studies. In M. Kramer (Ed.), *Dream psychology and the new biology of dreaming* (pp. 175–184). Springfield, IL: Charles C. Thomas.

Hall, C. (1984). A ubiquitous sex difference in dreams, revisited. *Journal of Personality and Social Psychology, 46,* 1109–1117.

Hall, C., & Domhoff, G.W. (1963a). A ubiquitous sex difference in dreams. *Journal of Abnormal and Social Psychology, 66,* 278–280.

Hall, C., & Domhoff, G. W. (1963b). Aggression in dreams. *International Journal of Social Psychiatry, 9,* 259–267.

Hall, C., & Domhoff, G. W. (1964). Friendliness in dreams. *Journal of Social Psychology, 62,* 309–314.

Hall, C., Domhoff, G. W., Blick, K., & Weesner, K. (1982). The dreams of college men and women in 1950 and 1980: A comparison of dream contents and sex differences. *Sleep, 5,* 188–194.

Hall, C., & Lind, R. (1970). *Dreams, life and literature: A study of Franz Kafka.* Chapel Hill: University of North Carolina Press.

Hall, C., & Nordby, V. (1972). *The individual and his dreams.* New York: New American Library.

Hall, C., & Van de Castle, R. (1966). *The content analysis of dreams.* New York: Appleton-Century-Crofts.

Harlow, J., & Roll, S. (1992). Frequency of day residue in dreams of young adults. *Perceptual and Motor Skills, 74,* 832–834.

Hartmann, E. (1968). The day residue: Time distribution of waking events. *Psychophysiology, 5,* 222.

Hartmann, E. (1984). *The nightmare.* New York: Basic Books.

Hartmann, E. (1998). *Dreams and nightmares.* New York: Plenum.

Hartmann, E. (2000). The waking-to-dreaming continuum and the effects of emotion. *Behavioral and Brain Sciences, 23,* 947–950.

Hartmann, E., Elkin, R., & Garg, M. (1991). Personality and dreaming: The dreams of people with very thick or very thin boundaries. *Dreaming, 1,* 311–324.

Hartmann, E., Rosen, R., & Rand, W. (1998). Personality and dreaming: Boundary structure and dream content. *Dreaming, 8,* 31–39.

Hartmann, E., Russ, D., Oldfield, M., Falke, R., & Skoff, B. (1980). Dream content: Effects of l-DOPA. *Sleep Research, 9,* 153.

Hauri, P. (1975). Categorization of sleep mental activity for psychophysiological studies. In G. Lairy & P. Salzarulo (Eds.), *The experimental study of sleep: Methodological problems* (pp. 271–281). New York: Elsevier Scientific Publishing.

Heiss, W., Pawlik, G., Herholz, K., Wagner, R., & Wienhard, K. (1985). Regional cerebral glucose metabolism in man during wakefulness, sleep, and dreaming. *Brain Research, 327,* 362–366.

Herman, J., Ellman, S., & Roffwarg, H. (1978). The problem of NREM dream recall reexamined. In A. Arkin, J. Antrobus, & S. Ellman (Eds.), *The mind in sleep: Psychology and psychophysiology* (pp. 59–62). Hillsdale, NJ: Erlbaum.

Heynick, F., & deJong, M. (1985). Dreams elicited by the telephone: A comparative content analysis. In W. Koella, E. Ruther, & H. Schulz (Eds.), *Sleep '84* (pp. 341–343). New York: Verlage.

Hill, C. E. (1996). *Working with dreams in psychotherapy.* New York: Guilford Press.

Hill, C. E., Kelley, F. A., Davis, T. L., Crook, R. E., Maldonado, L. E., Turkson, M. A., et al. (2001). Predictors of outcome of dream interpretation sessions: Volunteer client characteristics, dream characteristics, and type of interpretation. *Dreaming, 11*(2), 53–72.

Hiscock, M., & Cohen, D. (1973). Visual imagery and dream recall. *Journal of Research in Personality, 72*, 179–188.

Hobson, J. (1988). *The dreaming brain.* New York: Basic Books.

Hobson, J. (2000). The ghost of Sigmund Freud haunts Mark Solms's dream theory. *Behavioral and Brain Sciences, 23*, 951–952.

Hobson, J., Hoffman, S., Helfand, R., & Kostner, D. (1987). Dream bizarreness and the activation–synthesis hypothesis. *Human Neurobiology, 6*, 157–164.

Hobson, J., & McCarley, R. (1977). The brain as a dream state generator: An activation–synthesis hypothesis of the dream process. *American Journal of Psychiatry, 134*, 1335–1348.

Hobson, J., McCarley, R., & Wyzinski, P. (1975). Sleep cycle oscillation: Reciprocal discharge by two brainstem neuronal groups. *Science, 189*, 55–58.

Hobson, J., Pace-Schott, E. F., & Stickgold, R. (2000a). Dream science 2000: A response to commentaries on dreaming and the brain. *Behavioral and Brain Sciences, 23*, 1019–1034.

Hobson, J., Pace-Schott, E. F., & Stickgold, R. (2000b). Dreaming and the brain: Toward a cognitive neuroscience of conscious states. *Behavioral and Brain Sciences, 23*, 793–842.

Hobson, J., Stickgold, R., & Pace-Schott, E. F. (1998). The neuropsychology of REM sleep dreaming. *NeuroReport, 9*, R1–R14.

Holland, D., & Kipnis, A. (1994). Metaphors for embarrassment and stories of exposure: The not-so-egocentric self in American culture. *Ethos, 22*, 316–342.

Howard, M. (1978). *Manifest dream content of adolescents.* Unpublished doctoral dissertation, Iowa State University, Ames.

Howe, J. B., & Blick, K. (1983). Emotional content of dreams recalled by elderly women. *Perceptual and Motor Skills, 56*, 31–34.

Howe, M. (2000). *The fate of early memories.* Washington, DC: American Psychological Association.

Hunt, H. (1989). *The multiplicity of dreams: Memory, imagination, and consciousness.* New Haven, CT: Yale University Press.

Hunt, H. (2000). New multiplicities of dreaming and REMing. *Behavioral and Brain Sciences, 23*, 953–955.

Hunt, H., Ogilvie, R., Belicki, K., Belicki, D., & Atalick, E. (1982). Forms of dreaming. *Perceptual and Motor Skills, 54*, 559–633.

Hunt, H., Ruzycki-Hunt, K., Pariak, D., & Belicki, K. (1993). The relationship between dream bizarreness and imagination: Artifact or essence? *Dreaming, 3*, 179–199.

Hunter, J. (1997). Needed: A ban on the significance test. *Psychological Science, 8*, 3–7.

Hurovitz, C., Dunn, S., Domhoff, G. W., & Fiss, H. (1999). The dreams of blind men and women: A replication and extension of previous findings. *Dreaming, 9,* 183–193.

Janowsky, J., & Carper, R. (1996). Is there a neural basis for cognitive transitions in school-age children? In A. Sameroff & M. Haith (Eds.), *The five to seven year shift* (pp. 33–60). Chicago: University of Chicago Press.

Jouvet, M. (1999). *The paradox of sleep: The story of dreaming.* Cambridge, MA: MIT Press.

Jung, C. (1963). *Memories, dreams, reflections.* New York: Pantheon.

Jung, C. (1974). *Dreams.* Princeton, NJ: Princeton University Press.

Jus, A., Jus, K., Villeneuve, A., Pires, A., Lachance, R., Fortier, J., et al. (1973). Studies on dream recall in chronic schizophrenic patients after prefrontal lobotomy. *Biological Psychiatry, 6,* 275–293.

Kamiya, J. (1961). Behavioral, subjective, and physiological aspects of drowsiness and sleep. In D. W. Fiske & S. R. Maddi (Eds.), *Functions of varied experience* (pp. 145–174). Homewood, IL: Dorsey.

Kane, C. M., Mellen, R. R., Patten, P., & Samano, I. (1993). Differences in the manifest dream content of Mexican, Mexican American, and Anglo American college women: A research note. *Hispanic Journal of Behavioral Sciences, 15,* 134–139.

Kerr, N., & Foulkes, D. (1981). Right hemispheric mediation of dream visualization: A case study. *Cortex, 17,* 603–610.

Kerr, N., Foulkes, D., & Jurkovic, G. J. (1978). Reported absence of visual dream imagery in a normally sighted subject with Turner's syndrome. *Journal of Mental Imagery, 2,* 247–264.

Ketchum, J., Sidell, F., Crowell, E., Aghajanian, G., & Hayes, A. (1973). Atropine, scopolamine, and ditran: Comparative pharmacology and antagonists in man. *Psychopharmacologia, 28,* 121–145.

Kirschner, N. (1999). Medication and dreams: Changes in dream content after drug treatment. *Dreaming, 9,* 195–200.

Klinger, E., & Cox, W. (1987/1988). Dimensions of thought flow in everyday life. *Imagination, Cognition, and Personality, 7,* 105–128.

Knudson, R. M., & Minier, S. (1999). The on-going significance of significant dreams: The case of the bodiless head. *Dreaming, 9,* 235–245.

Krakow, B., Kellner, R., Pathak, D., & Lambert, L. (1995). Imagery rehearsal treatment for chronic nightmares. *Behaviour Research and Therapy, 33,* 837–843.

Kramer, M. (1993). The selective mood regulatory function of dreaming: An update and revision. In A. Moffitt, M. Kramer, & R. Hoffmann (Eds.), *The functions of dreams* (pp. 139–195). Albany: State University of New York Press.

Kramer, M. (1999, June). *A review of dreaming by psychiatric patients: An update.* Paper presented at the annual meeting of the Association for the Study of Dreams, Santa Cruz, CA.

Kramer, M. (2000a). Dreaming has content and meaning not just form. *Behavioral and Brain Sciences, 23,* 959–961.

Kramer, M. (2000b). Dreams and psychopathology. In M. Kryger, T. Roth, & W. Dement (Eds.), *Principles and practices of sleep medicine* (3rd ed., pp. 511–519). Philadelphia: W. B. Saunders.

Kramer, M., Kinney, L., & Scharf, M. (1983). Sex differences in dreams. *Psychiatric Journal of the University of Ottawa, 8,* 1–4.

Kramer, M., & Roth, T. (1973). Comparison of dream content in laboratory dream reports of schizophrenic and depressive patient groups. *Comprehensive Psychiatry, 14,* 325–329.

Kramer, M., & Roth, T. (1979). Dreams in psychopathology. In B. Wolman (Ed.), *Handbook of dreams* (pp. 361–367). New York: Van Nostrand Reinhold.

Kramer, M., Roth, T., & Trinder, J. (1975). Dreams and dementia: A laboratory exploration of dream recall and dream content in chronic brain syndrome patients. *International Journal of Aging and Human Development, 6,* 169–178.

Kramer, M., Schoen, L., & Kinney, L. (1987). Nightmares in Vietnam veterans. *Journal of the American Academy of Psychoanalysis, 15,* 67–81.

Krohn, A., & Mayman, M. (1974). Object relations in dreams and projective tests. *Bulletin of the Menninger Clinic, 38,* 445–466.

Kuiken, D., & Sikora, S. (1993). The impact of dreams on waking thoughts and feelings. In A. Moffitt, M. Kramer, & R. Hoffmann (Eds.), *The functions of dreaming* (pp. 419–476). Albany: State University of New York Press.

LaBerge, S. (1985). *Lucid dreaming.* Los Angeles: J. P. Tarcher.

LaBerge, S., Nagel, L., Dement, W., & Zarcone, V. (1981). Lucid dreaming verified by volitional communication during REM sleep. *Perceptual and Motor Skills, 52,* 727–732.

Lakoff, G. (1987). *Women, fire, and dangerous things.* Chicago: University of Chicago Press.

Lakoff, G. (1993a). How metaphor structures dreams. *Dreaming, 3,* 77–98.

Lakoff, G. (1993b). The contemporary theory of metaphor. In A. Ortony (Ed.), *Metaphor and thought* (2nd ed., pp. 202–251). New York: Cambridge University Press.

Lakoff, G. (1997). How unconscious metaphorical thought shapes dreams. In D. Stein (Ed.), *Cognitive science and the unconscious* (pp. 89–120). Washington, DC: American Psychiatric Press.

Lakoff, G., & Johnson, M. (1999). *Philosophy in the flesh.* New York: Basic Books.

Lakoff, G., & Turner, M. (1989). *More than cool reason.* Chicago: University of Chicago Press.

Latta, C. (1998). The manifest dream content of premenarcheal and postmenarcheal girls. *Dissertation Abstracts International, 59*(6), 3064B.

Lavie, P. (1984). Localized pontine lesion: Nearly total absence of REM sleep. *Neurology, 34,* 118–120.

Lavie, P. (1990). Penile erections in a patient with nearly total absence of REM: A follow-up study. *Sleep, 13,* 276–278.

Leach, C. (1979). *Introduction to statistics.* New York: Wiley.

LeDoux, J. (1996). *The emotional brain.* New York: Simon & Schuster.

Levin, R. (2000). Nightmares: Friend or foe? *Behavioral and Brain Sciences, 23,* 965.

Lilienfeld, S., Wood, J., & Garb, H. (2000). The scientific status of projective techniques. *Psychological Science in the Public Interest, 1*(2), 27–66.

Lindorff, D. (1995). One thousand dreams: The spiritual awakening of Wolfgang Pauli. *Journal of Analytical Psychology, 40,* 555–569.

Livingston, G., & Levin, R. (1991). The effects of dream length on the relationship between primary process in dreams and creativity. *Dreaming, 1,* 301–309.

Llinas, R., & Pare, D. (1991). Of dreaming and wakefulness. *Neuroscience, 44,* 521–535.

Loftus, E., Joslyn, S., & Polage, D. (1998). Repression: A mistaken impression? *Development and Psychopathology, 10,* 781–792.

Loftus, E., & Ketcham, K. (1994). *The myth of repressed memory.* New York: St. Martin's Press.

Loftus, E., & Polage, D. (1999). Repressed memories: When are they real? How are they false? *Psychiatric Clinics of North America, 22,* 61–70.

Lortie-Lussier, M., Cote, L., & Vachon, J. (2000). The consistency and continuity hypotheses revisited through the dreams of women at two periods of their lives. *Dreaming, 10,* 67–76.

Lortie-Lussier, M., Schwab, C., & de Koninck, J. (1985). Working mothers versus homemakers: Do dreams reflect the changing roles of women? *Sex Roles, 12,* 1009–1021.

Lortie-Lussier, M., Simond, S., Rinfret, N., & De Koninck, J. (1992). Beyond sex differences: Family and occupational roles' impact on women's and men's dreams. *Sex Roles, 26,* 79–96.

Luria, A. (1973). *The working brain: An introduction to neuropsychology.* New York: Penguin.

Maharaj, N. (1997). *An investigation into the content and structure of schizophrenic dreams.* Unpublished doctoral dissertation, Leiden University, Leiden, The Netherlands.

Mahowald, M., & Schenck, C. (2000). REM sleep parasomnias. In M. Kryger, T. Roth, & W. Dement (Eds.), *Principles and practices of sleep medicine* (3rd ed., pp. 724–741). Philadelphia: W. B. Saunders.

Mamelak, A. N., & Hobson, J. (1989). Dream bizarreness as the cognitive correlate of altered neuronal behavior in REM sleep. *Journal of Cognitive Neuroscience, 1,* 201–222.

Maquet, P. (2000). Functional neuroimaging of normal human sleep by positron emission tomography. *Journal of Sleep Research, 9,* 207–231.

Maquet, P., Peters, J. M., Aerts, J., Delfiore, G., Dequerldre, C., Luxen, A., et al. (1996). Functional neuroanatomy of human rapid-eye-movement sleep and dreaming. *Nature, 383,* 163–166.

Markman, A. B. (1999). *Knowledge representation.* Mahwah, NJ: Erlbaum.

Marquardt, C. J. G., Bonato, R. A., & Hoffmann, R. (1996). An empirical investigation into the day-residue and dream-lag effects. *Dreaming, 6,* 57–65.

Martinelli, R. (1983). Dream recall, imaginal processes, and short-term memory: A pilot study. *Perceptual and Motor Skills, 57,* 718.

Mathur, R., & Douglas, N. (1995). Frequency of EEG arousals from nocturnal sleep in normal subjects. *Sleep, 18,* 330–333.

Matlock, T. (1988, August). *The metaphorical extension of "see."* Paper presented at the proceedings of the Western Conference on Linguistics, Berkeley, CA.

Matlock, T., & Sweetser, E. (1989). *Semantic change of perception verbs to evidentials and mental state verbs.* Unpublished manuscript, University of California, Santa Cruz.

Mattoon, M. (1978). *Applied dream analysis: A Jungian approach.* New York: Wiley & Sons.

Mazziotta, J. C. E., Toga, A. W. E., & Frackowiak, R. S. J. E. (Eds.). (2000). *Brain mapping: The disorders.* San Diego, CA: Academic Press.

Mazzoni, G., & Loftus, E. (1998). Dreaming, believing, and remembering. In J. de Rivera & T. Sarbin (Eds.), *Believed-in imaginings: The narrative construction of reality* (pp. 145–156). Washington, DC: American Psychological Association.

Mazzoni, G., Loftus, E., Seitz, A., & Lynn, S. (1999). Changing beliefs and memories through dream interpretation. *Applied Cognitive Psychology, 13,* 125–144.

McCarley, R., & Hobson, J. (1975). Discharge patterns of cat pontine brain stem neurons during desynchronized sleep. *Journal of Neurophysiology, 38,* 751–766.

Meehl, P. (1997). The problem is epistemology, not statistics: Replace significance tests by confidence intervals and quantify accuracy of risky numerical predictions. In L. Harlow, S. Muliak, & J. Steiger (Eds.), *What if there were no significance tests?* (pp. 392–425). Mahwah, NJ: Erlbaum Associates.

Meier, B. (1993). Speech and thinking in dreams. In C. Cavallero & D. Foulkes (Eds.), *Dreaming as cognition* (pp. 58–76). New York: Harvester Wheatsheaf.

Meier, C. (Ed.). (1992). *Wolgang Pauli und C. G. Jung: Ein Briefwechsel 1932–1958* [Letters between Pauli and Jung, 1932–1958]. Berlin: Springer.

Meier, C., Ruef, H., Zeigler, A., & Hall, C. (1968). Forgetting of dreams in the laboratory. *Perceptual and Motor Skills, 26,* 551–557.

Merritt, J., Stickgold, R., Pace-Schott, E. F., Williams, J., & Hobson, J. (1994). Emotion profiles in the dreams of men and women. *Consciousness and Cognition, 3,* 46–60.

Micceri, T. (1989). The unicorn, the normal curve, and other improbable creatures. *Psychological Bulletin, 105,* 156–166.

Mooney, C., & Duval, R. (1993). *Bootstrapping: A nonparametric approach to statistical inference.* Newbury Park, CA: Sage Publications.

Morrison, A. R., & Sanford, L. D. (2000). Critical brain characteristics to consider in developing dream and memory theories. *Behavioral and Brain Sciences, 23*, 977.

Murphy, G., & Lassaline, M. (1997). Hierarchical structure in concepts and the basic level of categorization. In K. Lamberts & D. Shanks (Eds.), *Knowledge, concepts, and categories* (pp. 93–131). Cambridge, MA: MIT Press.

Murri, L., Massetani, R., Siciliano, G., & Arena, R. (1985). Dream recall after sleep interruption in brain-injured patients. *Sleep, 8*, 356–362.

Nanna, M., & Sawilowsky, S. (1998). Analysis of Likert scale data in disability and medical rehabilitation research. *Psychological Methods, 3*, 55–67.

Neher, A. (1996). Jung's theory of archetypes: A critique. *Journal of Humanistic Psychology, 36*, 61–91.

Nielsen, T., & Powell, R. (1992). The day-residue and dream-lag effect. *Dreaming, 2*, 67–77.

Nielsen, T., Zadra, A., Germain, A., & Montplaisir, J. (1999). The typical dreams of sleep patients: Consistent profile with 284 new cases. *Sleep, 22*, S177.

Nielsen, T. (2000a). A review of mentation in REM and NREM sleep: "Covert" REM sleep as a possible reconciliation of two opposing models. *Behavioral and Brain Sciences, 23*, 851–866.

Nielsen, T. (2000b). Covert REM sleep effects on REM mentation: Further methodological considerations and supporting evidence. *Behavioral and Brain Sciences, 23*, 1040–1057.

Nielsen, T., & Germain, A. (2000). Post-traumatic nightmares as a dysfunctional state. *Behavioral and Brain Sciences, 23*, 978–979.

Nishigawa, N., Brubaker, L., & Domhoff, G. W. (2001). *The dreams of Japanese women: A replication and extension.* Unpublished manuscript, University of California, Santa Cruz.

Nofzinger, E., Berman, S., Fasiczka, A., Miewald, J. M., Meltzer, C. C., Price, J. C., et al. (2001). Effects of bupropion SR on anterior paralimbic function during waking and REM sleep in depression: Preliminary findings using (18F)-FDG PET. *Psychiatry Research, 106*, 95–111.

Nofzinger, E., Mintun, M., Wiseman, M., Kupfer, D., & Moore, R. (1997). Forebrain activation in REM sleep: An FDG PET study. *Brain Research, 770*, 192–201.

Nofzinger, E., Nichols, T. E., Meltzer, C. C., Price, J., Steppe, D. A., Miewald, J. M., et al. (1999). Changes in forebrain function from waking to REM sleep in depression: Preliminary analyses of (18F)-FDG PET studies. *Psychiatry Research, 91*, 59–78.

Nomura, M. (1996). The ubiquity of the fluid metaphor in Japanese: A case study. *Poetica, 46*, 41–75.

Noreen, E. (1989). *Computer intensive methods for testing hypotheses: An introduction.* New York: John Wiley & Sons.

Ofshe, R., & Watters, E. (1994). *Making monsters: False memories, psychotherapy, and sexual hysteria.* New York: Charles Scribner's Sons.

Ogilvie, R. (1982). Lucid dreaming and alpha activity: A preliminary report. *Perceptual and Motor Skills, 55*(3, Pt. 1), 795–808.

Ogilvie, R., Hunt, H., Sawicki, C., & Samahalskyi, J. (1982). Psychological correlates of spontaneous middle ear muscle activity during sleep. *Sleep, 5,* 11–27.

Ogilvie, R., Takeuchi, T., & Murphy, T. (2000). Expanding Nielsen's covert REM model, questioning Solms's approach to dreaming and REM sleep, and reinterpreting the Vertes and Eastman view of REM sleep and memory. *Behavioral and Brain Sciences, 23,* 981–983.

O'Nell, C., & O'Nell, N. (1977). A cross-cultural comparison of aggression in dreams: Zapotecs and Americans. *International Journal of Social Psychiatry, 125,* 35–41.

Osgood, C. (1959). The representation model and relevant research methods. In I. de Sola Pool (Ed.), *Trends in content analysis* (pp. 54–78). Urbana: University of Illinois Press.

Osgood, C., May, W., & Miron, M. (1975). *Cross-cultural universals of affective meaning.* Urbana: University of Illinois Press.

Pace-Schott, E. F. (2000). Nielsen's concept of covert REM sleep is a path toward a more realistic view of sleep psychophysiology. *Behavioral and Brain Sciences, 23,* 983–984.

Paolino, A. F. (1964). Dreams: Sex differences in aggressive content. *Journal of Projective Techniques and Personality Assessment, 28,* 219–226.

Paus, T., Zijdenbos, A., Worsely, K., Collins, D., Blumenthal, J., Giedd, J., et al. (1999). Structural maturation of neural pathways in children and adolescents: In vivo study. *Science, 283,* 1908–1911.

Pennebaker, J. W., & Graybeal, A. (2001). Patterns of natural language use: Disclosure, personality, and social integration. *Current Directions in Psychological Science, 10,* 90–93.

Pennebaker, J. W., & Keough, K. A. (1999). Revealing, organizing, and reorganizing the self in response to stress and emotion. In R. Contrada & R. Ashmore (Eds.), *Self, social identity, and physical health: Interdisciplinary explorations.* (pp. 101–121). New York: Oxford University Press.

Pennebaker, J. W., & Seagal, J. D. (1999). Forming a story: The health benefits of narrative. *Journal of Clinical Psychology, 55,* 1243–1254.

Perry, E., & Piggott, M. (2000). Neurotransmitter mechanisms of dreaming: Implication of modulatory systems based on dream intensity. *Behavioral and Brain Sciences, 23,* 990–992.

Perry, E., Walker, M., Grace, J., & Perry, R. (1999). Acetylcholine in mind: A neurotransmitter correlate of consciousness? *Trends in Neurosciences, 22,* 273–280.

Pivik, R. T. (1986). Sleep: Physiology and psychophysiology. In M. Coles, E. Donchin, & S. Porges (Eds.), *Psychophysiology: Systems, processes and applications* (pp. 378–406). New York: Guilford Press.

Pivik, R. T. (2000). Psychophysiology of dreams. In M. Kryger, T. Roth, & W. Dement (Eds.), *Principles and practices of sleep medicine* (3rd ed., pp. 491–501). Philadelphia: W. B. Saunders.

Popp, C., Luborsky, L., & Crits-Christoph, P. (1992). The parallel of the CCRT from therapy narratives with the CCRT from dreams. In L. Luborsky & P. Crits-Christoph (Eds.), *Understanding transference* (pp. 158–172). New York: Basic Books.

Rechtschaffen, A. (1978). The single-mindedness and isolation of dreams. *Sleep, 1,* 97–109.

Rechtschaffen, A. (1997). Postscript, 1995: The single-mindedness and isolation of dreams. In M. Myslobodsky (Ed.), *The mythomanias: The nature of deception and self-deception* (pp. 219–223). Mahwah, NJ: Lawrence Erlbaum Associates.

Reichers, M., Kramer, M., & Trinder, J. (1970). A replication of the Hall–Van de Castle character scale norms. *Psychophysiology, 7,* 238.

Reinsel, R., Antrobus, J., & Wollman, M. (1992). Bizarreness in dreams and waking fantasy. In J. Antrobus & M. Bertini (Eds.), *The neuropsychology of sleep and dreaming* (pp. 157–184). Hillsdale, NJ: Erlbaum.

Reinsel, R., Wollman, M., & Antrobus, J. (1986). Effects of environmental context and cortical activation on thought. *Journal of Mind and Behavior, 7,* 259–275.

Reis, W. (1959). A comparison of the interpretation of dream series with and without free associations. In M. F. DeMartino (Ed.), *Dreams and personality dynamics* (pp. 211–225). Springfield, IL: Charles C. Thomas.

Resnick, J., Stickgold, R., Rittenhouse, C., & Hobson, J. (1994). Self-representation and bizarreness in children's dream reports collected in the home setting. *Consciousness and Cognition, 3,* 30–45.

Revonsuo, A. (2000). The reinterpretation of dreams: An evolutionary hypothesis of the function of dreaming. *Behavioral and Brain Sciences, 23,* 877–901.

Revonsuo, A., & Salmivalli, C. (1995). A content analysis of bizarre elements in dreams. *Dreaming, 5,* 169–187.

Reynolds, H. (1984). *Analysis of nominal data.* Newbury Park, CA: Sage Publications.

Rittenhouse, C., Stickgold, R., & Hobson, J. (1994). Constraint on the transformation of characters, objects, and settings in dream reports. *Consciousness and Cognition, 3,* 100–113.

Rivkin, M. (2000). Developmental neuroimaging of children using magnetic resonance techniques. *Mental Retardation and Developmental Disabilities Research Reviews, 6,* 68–80.

Roberts, C. W. (1997). *Text analysis for the social sciences: Methods for drawing statistical inferences from texts and transcripts.* Mahwah, NJ: Erlbaum.

Robertson, L. (1998). Visuospatial attention and parietal function: Their role in object perception. In R. Parasuraman (Ed.), *The attentive brain* (pp. 257–278). Cambridge, MA: MIT Press.

Rogoff, B. (1990). *Apprenticeship in thinking: Cognitive development in social context.* New York: Oxford University Press.

Rosenthal, R., Rosnow, R. L., & Rubin, D. B. (2000). *Contrasts and effect sizes in behavioral research: A correlational approach.* New York: Cambridge University Press.

Rosenthal, R., & Rubin, D. B. (1982). A simple general purpose display of magnitude of experimental effect. *Journal of Educational Psychology, 74,* 166–169.

Rosnow, R. L., & Rosenthal, R. (1997). *People studying people: Artifacts and ethics in behavioral research.* New York: W. H. Freeman.

Roth, T., Kramer, M., & Salis, P. (1979). Drugs, REM sleep, and dreams. In B. Wolman (Ed.), *Handbook of dreams* (pp. 203–225). New York: Van Norstrand Reinhold.

Roussy, F. (2000). Testing the notion of continuity between waking experience and REM dream content. *Dissertation Abstracts International, 61*(2), 1106B.

Roussy, F., Brunette, M., Mercier, P., Gonthier, I., Grenier, J., Sirois-Berliss, M., et al. (2000). Daily events and dream content: Unsuccessful matching attempts. *Dreaming, 10,* 77–83.

Roussy, F., Raymond, I., & De Koninck, J. (2000). Affect in REM dreams: Exploration of a time-of-night effect. *Sleep, 23,* A174–A175.

Rubenstein, K., & Krippner, S. (1991). Gender differences and geographical differences in content from dreams elicited by a television announcement. *International Journal of Psychosomatics, 38,* 40–44.

Salin-Pascual, R., Gerashchenko, D., & Shiromani, P. J. (2000). Some myths are slow to die. *Behavioral and Brain Sciences, 23,* 999–1000.

Saline, S. (1999). The most recent dreams of children ages 8–11. *Dreaming, 9,* 173–181.

Sauvageau, A., Nielsen, T., & Montplaisir, J. (1998). Effects of somatosensory stimulation on dream content in gymnasts and control participants: Evidence of vestibulomotor adaptation in REM sleep. *Dreaming, 8,* 125–134.

Sawilowsky, S. S., & Blair, R. C. (1992). A more realistic look at the robustness and Type II error properties of the t test to departures from population normality. *Psychological Bulletin, 111,* 352–360.

Scarr, S. (1997). Rules of evidence: A larger context for the statistical debate. *Psychological Science, 8,* 16–17.

Schmidt, F. (1996). Statistical significance testing and cumulative knowledge in psychology: Implications for training of researchers. *Psychological Methods, 1,* 115–129.

Schneider, A., & Domhoff, G. W. (1995, updated 2002). *The quantitative study of dreams.* Retrieved July 29, 2002, from http://www.dreamresearch.net/

Schneider, A., & Domhoff, G. W. (1999, updated 2002). *DreamBank.* Retrieved July 29, 2002, from http://www.dreambank.net/

Schredl, M. (2000). Dream research: Integration of physiological and psychological models. *Behavioral and Brain Sciences, 23,* 1001–1003.

Schredl, M., & Montasser, A. (1996). Dream recall: State or trait variable? Part I: Model, theories, methodology and trait factors. *Imagination, Cognition and Personality, 16*, 181–210.

Schredl, M., & Montasser, A. (1997). Dream recall: State or trait variable? Part II: State factors, investigations and final conclusions. *Imagination, Cognition and Personality, 16*, 239–261.

Shapiro, D., Wu, J., Hong, C., Buchsbaum, M., Gottschalk, L., Thompson, V., Hillyard, D., et al. (1995). Exploring the relationship between having control and losing control to functional neuroanatomy during the sleeping state. *Psychologia, 38*, 133–145.

Shaver, P., Schwarz, J., Kirson, D., & O'Connor, D. (1987). Emotion knowledge: Further explorations of prototype approach. *Journal of Personality and Social Psychology, 52*, 1061–1086.

Sheppard, E. (1963). Systematic dream studies: Clinical judgment and objective measurements of ego strength. *Comprehensive Psychiatry, 4*, 263–270.

Sheppard, E. (1969). Dream content analysis. In M. Kramer (Ed.), *Dream psychology and the new biology of dreaming* (pp. 225–254). Springfield, IL: Charles C. Thomas.

Shevrin, H. (1986). Subliminal perception and dreaming. *Journal of Mind and Behavior, 7*(2–3), 379–395.

Shevrin, H. (1996). *Conscious and unconscious processes: Psychodynamic, cognitive, and neurophysiological convergences.* New York: Guilford Press.

Shevrin, H., & Eiser, A. (2000). Continued vitality of the Freudian theory of dreaming. *Behavioral and Brain Sciences, 23*, 1004–1006.

Shevrin, H., & Fisher, C. (1967). Changes in the effects of a waking subliminal stimulus as a function of dreaming and nondreaming sleep. *Journal of Abnormal Psychology, 72*, 362–368.

Siegel, S., & Castellan, N. J. (1988). *Nonparametric statistics for the behavioral sciences* (2nd ed.). New York: McGraw-Hill.

Slipp, S. (2000). Subliminal stimulation research and its implications for psychoanalytic theory and treatment. *Journal of the American Academy of Psychoanalysis, 28*, 305–320.

Smith, C. (1995). Sleep states and memory processes. *Behavioural Brain Research, 69*(1–2), 137–145.

Smith, C. (2000). Content analysis and narrative analysis. In H. Reis & C. Judd (Eds.), *Handbook of research methods in social and personality psychology* (pp. 313–335). New York: Cambridge University Press.

Smith, M., & Hall, C. (1964). An investigation of regression in a long dream series. *Journal of Gerontology, 19*, 66–71.

Snyder, F. (1970). The phenomenology of dreaming. In L. Madow & L. Snow (Eds.), *The psychodynamic implications of the physiological studies on dreams* (pp. 124–151). Springfield, IL: C.C. Thomas.

Solms, M. (1997). *The neuropsychology of dreams: A clinico-anatomical study*. Mahwah, NJ: Lawrence Erlbaum.

Solms, M. (2000). Dreaming and REM sleep are controlled by different brain mechanisms. *Behavioral and Brain Sciences, 23*, 843–850.

States, B. (1987). *The rhetoric of dreams*. Ithaca, NY: Cornell University Press.

Stekel, W. (1911). *Die sprache des traumes* [The language of dreams]. Wiesbaden, Germany: J. F. Bergmann.

Steriade, M. (2000). Brain electrical activity and sensory processing during waking and sleep states. In M. Kryger, T. Roth, & W. Dement (Eds.), *Principles and practices of sleep medicine* (3rd ed., pp. 93–111). Philadelphia: W. B. Saunders.

Stewart, L., Ellison, A., Walsh, V., & Cowey, A. (2001). The role of transcranial magnetic stimulation (TMS) in studies of vision, attention and cognition. *Acta Psychologica, 107*(1–3), 275–291.

Stickel, E. (1956). *Dream frequency and personality variables*. Unpublished doctoral dissertation, Case Western Reserve University, Cleveland, OH.

Stickgold, R., Pace-Schott, E. F., & Hobson, J. (1994). A new paradigm for dream research: Mentation reports following spontaneous arousal from REM and NREM sleep recorded in a home setting. *Consciousness and Cognition: An International Journal, 3*, 16–29.

Stickgold, R., Scott, L., Rittenhouse, C., & Hobson, J. (1999). Sleep-induced changes in associative memory. *Journal of Cognitive Neuroscience, 11*, 182–193.

Strauch, I. (1969, August). *Psychological aspects of dream recall*. Paper presented at the 19th International Congress of Psychology, London.

Strauch, I. (1996, June). *Self-representation in REM dreams and waking fantasies at ages 9–11 and 11–13: A longitudinal study*. Paper presented at the annual meeting of the Association for the Study of Dreams, Berkeley, CA.

Strauch, I., & Lederbogen, S. (1999). The home dreams and waking fantasies of boys and girls ages 9–15. *Dreaming, 9*, 153–161.

Strauch, I., & Meier, B. (1996). *In search of dreams: Results of experimental dream research*. Albany: State University of New York Press.

Sweetser, E. (1990). *From etymology to pragmatics*. New York: Cambridge University Press.

Takeuchi, T., Ogilvie, R., Ferrelli, A. V., Murphy, T. I., & Belicki, K. (2001). The Dream Property Scale: An exploratory English version. *Consciousness and Cognition: An International Journal, 10*, 341–355.

Tedlock, B. (1991). The new anthropology of dreaming. *Dreaming, 1*, 161–178.

Thatcher, R. (Ed.). (1996). *Developmental neuroimaging*. San Diego, CA: Academic Press.

Thompson, B. (1999a). If statistical significance tests are broken/misused, what practices should supplement or replace them? *Theory and Psychology, 9*, 165–181.

Thompson, B. (1999b). Statistical significance tests, effect size reporting and the vain pursuit of pseudo-objectivity. *Theory and Psychology, 9*, 191–196.

Thompson, B. (1999c). Why "encouraging" effect size reporting is not working: The etiology of researcher resistance to changing practices. *Journal of Psychology, 133,* 133–140.

Thompson, N. (2000). Evolutionary psychology can ill afford adaptionist and mentalist credulity. *Behavioral and Brain Sciences, 23,* 1013–1014.

Tonay, V. (1990/1991). California women and their dreams: A historical and subcultural comparison of dream content. *Imagination, Cognition, and Personality, 10,* 83–97.

Tonay, V. (1993). Personality correlates of dream recall: Who remembers? *Dreaming, 3,* 1–8.

Torda, C. (1969). Dreams of subjects with loss of memory for recent events. *Psychophysiology, 6,* 358–365.

Trinder, J., & Kramer, M. (1971). Dream recall. *American Journal of Psychiatry, 128,* 296–301.

Trosman, H., Rechtschaffen, A., Offenkrantz, W., & Wolpert, E. (1960). Studies in the psychophysiology of dreams. IV: Relations among dreams in sequence. *Archives of General Psychiatry, 3,* 602–607.

Trupin, E. (1976). Correlates of ego-level and agency-communion in stage REM dreams of 11–13 year old children. *Journal of Child Psychology and Child Psychiatry, 17,* 169–180.

Tyson, P. D., Ogilvie, R., & Hunt, H. (1984). Lucid, prelucid, and nonlucid dreams related to the amount of EEG alpha activity during REM sleep. *Psychophysiology, 21,* 442–451.

Urbina, S. P. (1981). Methodological issues in the quantitative analysis of dream content. *Journal of Personality Assessment, 45,* 71–78.

Van de Castle, R. (1969). Problems in applying methodology of content analysis. In M. Kramer (Ed.), *Dream psychology and the new biology of dreaming* (pp. 185–197). Springfield, IL: Charles C. Thomas.

Van de Castle, R. (1983). Animal figures in fantasies and dreams. In A. Katcher & A. Beck (Eds.), *New perspectives on our lives with companion animals* (pp. 148–173). Philadelphia: University of Pennsylvania Press.

Van der Kolk, B., Blitz, R., Burr, W., Sherry, S., & Hartmann, E. (1984). Nightmares and trauma: A comparison of nightmares after combat with lifelong nightmares in veterans. *American Journal of Psychiatry, 141*(2), 187–190.

Van Rompay, T. (2000). *Emma's dreams.* Undergraduate senior thesis, Department of Psychology, Leiden University, Leiden, The Netherlands.

Vaughan, C. (1963). *The development and use of an operant technique to provide evidence for visual imagery in the rhesus monkey under sensory deprivation.* Unpublished doctoral dissertation, University of Pittsburgh, Pittsburgh, PA.

Verdone, P. (1965). Temporal reference of manifest dream content. *Perceptual and Motor Skills, 20,* 1253–1268.

Vogel, G. (1991). Sleep-onset mentation. In S. Ellman & J. Antrobus (Eds.), *The mind in sleep: Psychology and psychophysiology* (2nd ed., pp. 125–136). New York: Wiley & Sons.

Vogel, G. (2000). Critique of current dream theories. *Behavioral and Brain Sciences, 23,* 1014–1016.

Vogel, G., Barrowclough, B., & Giesler, D. (1972). Limited discriminability of REM and sleep onset reports and its psychiatric implications. *Archives of General Psychiatry, 26,* 449–455.

von Meyenn, K. (Ed.). (1993). *W. Pauli: Scientific correspondence with Bohr, Einstein, Heisenberg 1940–1949.* (Vol. 3). Berlin: Springer.

Ward, C., Beck, A., & Rascoe, E. (1961). Typical dreams: Incidence among psychiatric patients. *Archives of General Psychiatry, 5,* 606–615.

Webb, E., Campbell, D., Schwartz, R., Sechrest, L., & Grove, J. (1981). *Nonreactive measures in the social sciences* (2nd ed.). Chicago: Rand McNally.

Weed, S., & Hallam, F. (1896). A study of dream-consciousness. *American Journal of Psychology, 7,* 405–411.

Weinstein, L., Schwartz, D., & Arkin, A. (1991). Qualitative aspects of sleep mentation. In S. Ellman & J. Antrobus (Eds.), *The mind in sleep: Psychology and psychophysiology* (pp. 172–213). New York: John Wiley & Sons.

Weisz, R., & Foulkes, D. (1970). Home and laboratory dreams collected under uniform sampling conditions. *Psychophysiology, 6,* 588–596.

Welsh, M., Pennington, B., & Groisser, D. (1993). A normative-developmental study of executive function: A window on prefrontal function in children. *Developmental Neuropsychology, 7,* 131–149.

Whalen, P. (1998). Fear, vigilance, and ambiguity: Initial neuroimaging studies of the human amygdala. *Current Directions in Psychological Science, 7,* 177–188.

Whitman, R., Kramer, M., & Baldridge, B. (1963). Which dream does the patient tell? *Archives of General Psychiatry, 8,* 277–282.

Whitman, R., Pierce, C., Maas, J., & Baldridge, B. (1961). Drugs and dreams. II. Imipramine and prochlorperazine. *Comprehensive Psychiatry, 2,* 219–226.

Whitman, R., Pierce, C., Maas, J., & Baldridge, B. (1962). The dreams of the experimental subject. *Journal of Nervous and Mental Disease, 134,* 431–439.

Whitty, C., & Lewin, W. (1957). Vivid day-dreaming: An unusual form of confusion following anterior cingulectomy. *Brain, 80,* 72–76.

Wichlinski, L. J. (2000). The pharmacology of threatening dreams. *Behavioral and Brain Sciences, 23,* 1016–1017.

Winegar, R. K., & Levin, R. (1997). Sex differences in the object representations in the dreams of adolescents. *Sex Roles, 36,* 503–516.

Winget, C., & Kramer, M. (1979). *Dimensions of dreams.* Gainesville: University of Florida Press.

Wood, J. S. D., & Domino, G. (1989). Do creative people have more bizarre dreams? A reconsideration. *Imagination, Cognition, and Personality, 9,* 3–16.

Woolley, J. (1995). The fictional mind: Young children's understanding of imagination, pretense, and dreams. *Developmental Review, 15,* 172–211.

Yamanaka, T., Morita, Y., & Matsumoto, J. (1982). Analysis of the dream contents in college students by REM-awakening technique. *Folia Psychiatrica et Neurologica Japonica, 36,* 33–52.

Yu, N. (1999). *The contemporary theory of metaphor: The Chinese perspective.* Philadelphia: John Brightmans.

Zabriskie, B. (1995). Jung and Pauli: A subtle symmetry. *Journal of Analytical Psychology, 40,* 531–553.

Zadra, A. (1996). Recurrent dreams: Their relation to life events. In D. Barrett (Ed.), *Trauma and dreams* (pp. 231–247). Cambridge, MA: Harvard University Press.

Zadra, A., & Donderi, D. C. (2000a). Nightmares and bad dreams: Their prevalence and relationship to well-being. *Journal of Abnormal Psychology, 109,* 273–281.

Zadra, A., & Donderi, D. C. (2000b). Threat perceptions and avoidance in recurrent dreams. *Behavioral and Brain Sciences, 23,* 1017–1018.

Zadra, A., Nielsen, T., & Donderi, D. C. (1998). Prevalence of auditory, olfactory and gustatory experiences in home dreams. *Perceptual and Motor Skills, 87*(3, Pt 1), 819–826.

Zepelin, H. (1972, June). *Comparison of dreams recalled in the laboratory and at home.* Paper presented at the annual meeting of the Association for the Psychophysiological Study of Sleep, Chicago.

Zepelin, H. (1980). Age differences in dreams: I. Men's dreams and thematic apperceptive fantasy. *International Journal of Aging and Human Development, 12,* 171–186.

Zepelin, H. (1981). Age differences in dreams: II. Distortion and other variables. *International Journal of Aging and Human Development, 13,* 37–41.

Zimmerman, W. (1970). Sleep mentation and auditory awakening thresholds. *Psychophysiology, 6,* 540–549.

INDEX

age and gender differences in, 21, 22

cognitive structure dreaming, 22

content *vs.* adult content, 21–22

participation in dreams, 22

recall in, 21, 22, 23

visuospatial skills and, 22

developmental dimension of dreaming in, 20

dreams as shared fantasies in, 23, 24

frontal-lobe executive functions in longitudinal study, 20–21

Cholinergic pathway

in dream generation, 16

Cholinergic system

in neuromodulation during REM hallucinatory imagery and, 150

Cognitive processes

development of dreaming and, 4, 5

Cohen, D., 52

Collective unconscious, 144

Compensatory function of dreams, 145

Conceptual system

of dreamer, 32, 33

experiential categories in, 30–31

interaction of neural structures and environmental stimuli in, 30–31

sensorimotor, 31

spatial relations, 31

expression in dreams, 32

figurative concepts in, 33

Condensation

in dream-work, 137

Confusion

production of, 72

Consciousness

development of, 37

Consistency

of adult content, 3

in content, 27, 28

vs. change in reaction to content, 166

Contempt

in anger category of Hall–Van de Castle system, 70

Content analysis. *See also* DreamBank.net

DreamBank.net for, 98–102

Hall–Van de Castle system of. *See also* Hall–Van de Castle system of content analysis

Content and waking cognition

conceptual system in, 30–31

Contingency analysis

of Hall–Van de Castle coding categories, 76–77

Continuity

in Barb Sanders, 126

between content and waking thought, 26

in Emma series, 105

in Lucille, 110

vs. Jung's compensatory function, 145–146

Continuity principle, 26–27

connection of dreaming and waking cognition and, 30

Cortical network for spatial representation

in dreaming, 12–13

Culture

and content, 26

Disgust

in anger category of Hall–Van de Castle system, 70

Displacement

in dream-work, 137

Dopaminergic system

in dream generation, 16

in dreaming, 141

Dorsolateral prefrontal cortex

in dreaming, 12

DreamBank.net

consistency in dreams and, 101–102

in content analysis

comparison with normative group, 98, 99

definition of categories in, 98, 99

dreams of blind persons, 101

frequency counts, 98, 99

generation of percentages, 98, 99

scales independent of Hall–Van de Castle system, 100–101

sensory references coding scale in, 100–101

dream series available on, 97

elements with common words or phrases, 97–98

Emma series study, 103–105

facilitation of Hall–Van de Castle content analysis, 96–98

conceptual systems in forebrain and, 169

content in, 25–30

and waking cognition, 30–37

dream function and nondreaming in children and adults with brain lesions, 168

dreaming as cognitive process and, 169–170

dreaming cognition in, 18–25

integration with developmental studies and content analysis, 167

lucid dreaming and, 17–18

neural network in, 9–17

similarities between dreaming and waking cognition in, 168

testability of, 169

Neuroimaging studies

REM and NREM stages in, 10

Neuropsychological information

Solms study of dreaming and focal brain lesions, 10–15

Nightcap

sleep monitor, 49

Nightmares

brain sites in, 11, 14

with epilepsy, 15, 28

new endings for, 37

in posttraumatic stress disorder, 27, 28

Nominal categories

conversion to percentages and ratios, 63

in Hall–Van de Castle coding system, 61, 63

Nominal scales

reliability of, 61

vs. rating scales, 61

Ordinal scales, 58

Ordinary dreams, 79

Parietal lobe

content and, 30

in dreaming, 24

visuospatial skills and, 24

Parietal regions

in symbolic and spatial mechanisms, 13

Participation

in children, 22, 37

index of sense of self, 37

Pauli, Wolfgang

dream journals of and Jung's analysis, 49

Percentage indicators

in comparison of REM and NREM reports, 63

Positron emission tomography (PET), 9

of lucid dreaming, 18

Problem-solving theory

in Cartwright study of divorce, 159, 160

recaller and nonrecallers and, 158–159

refutation of, 158–159

solution in waking reflection on dream, 161, 162

in study of college students, 160–161

Psychotherapy

dream reports in

demand characteristics of therapeutic relationship in, 51

dream journals in, 51–52

focus on problems vs. dreams, 51

most recent dream method in, 51

metaphoric interpretations of dreams in, 37

Randomization strategies

approximate, 87–88

bootstrapping, 87–88

utility of, 85

Rating scales

applications of, 58–59

for content analysis, 58–69

for dimensions of dream salience, 59

for emotionality dimension, 59

in relation of dreaming to neurophysiology of sleep, 60

Recall

in children, 21, 22, 23

dream duration and, 42

recency and duration in, 42

Recallers

cognitive variables in, 52

comparison with nonrecallers, 52

interest in dreams and, 52–53

personality variables in, 52

ABOUT THE AUTHOR

G. William Domhoff received his BA at Duke University, his MA at Kent State University, and his PhD at the University of Miami—all in psychology. He has taught at the University of California, Santa Cruz, since 1965, where he is now a research professor. He is the author of *The Mystique of Dreams* (1985) and *Finding Meaning in Dreams* (1996) as well as numerous journal articles on dream content.